Conservatives Versus Wildcats

Conservatives Versus Wildcats

A Sociology of Financial Conflict

Simone Polillo

Stanford University Press

Stanford, California

Stanford University Press
Stanford, California

Printed in the United States of America on acid-free, archival-quality paper

Library of Congress Cataloging-in-Publication Data

Polillo, Simone, author.
  Conservatives versus wildcats : a sociology of financial conflict / Simone Polillo.
    pages cm.
  Includes bibliographical references and index.
  ISBN 978-0-8047-8509-9 (cloth : alk. paper)
  1. Banks and banking—Social aspects—Case studies. 2. Credit—Social
aspects—Case studies. 3. Finance—Social aspects—Case studies. 4. Banks and
banking—Social aspects—United States—History—19th century. 5. Banks and
banking—Social aspects—Italy—History—19th century. I. Title.

HG1601.P65 2013
306.3—dc23

2012033970

Typeset at Stanford University Press in 11/13.5 Adobe Garamond

Contents

Prologue

IN THE WAKE OF the ongoing financial crisis, academic and public opinion on the nature of finance has changed dramatically. Prior to the crisis, financial markets seemingly embodied all that was rational about capitalism. Finance was widely hailed as the most efficient and dynamic sector in the U.S., even the world, economy; financial innovators were praised for their talent and courage in spotting new opportunities for investment and generating new wealth; and increased access to financial services, especially in the market for mortgages, seemed to point the way toward a new capitalist utopia: the "ownership society," where wealth and financial security would finally be within reach of most. It was widely argued that freeing up markets, deregulating banks and financial transactions, and giving financial firms and their managers new incentives (and adequate remuneration) to innovate would unleash the full potential of rational capitalism.

When the financial crisis hit in 2007, only to explode on a larger scale in 2008, it injured society's trust in this ideology. Greenspan had complained about the irrational exuberance of financial markets as early as 1996. But in 2007 and 2008, for the first time in more than half a century, politicians and their economic advisers came face to face with the danger of this mindset on a large scale. Suddenly, they came to see finance as driven by speculative behavior, and the current crisis as a pathological outcome of this underlying foundation. Arguments about the irrationality of finance finally found serious intellectual footing in new theories emphasizing the emotional, even the temperamental, aspects of economic behavior in general, and financial behavior in particular. Rather than depicting rationality, finance unleashes "animal spirits." Rather than a solution to inefficient allocation of resources, finance, especially unregulated finance, came to be understood as an integral part of our woes.

It would be difficult to exaggerate the magnitude of these changes in intellectual climate and public opinion. And yet, it would be deeply problematic to ignore what has *not* changed in the wake of the crisis. A major element of continuity in economic approaches to finance—an element that has proved to be remarkably resistant to change—is the tendency to take an individualistic approach—to argue that the individual rational actor (and his/her potential shortcomings) is the bedrock of economic processes. One of the problems that immediately results from accepting the individual as the basic unit of analysis is that economic approaches are then relegated to psychological explanations. Was this or that analyst rational or irrational in his or her financial behavior? This becomes the root question in order to explain why financial processes can unfold so smoothly for so long, to then be so quickly, and spectacularly, disrupted.

But when we look back in history from the distant future, we will not count this crisis as one of individual rationality. We will see it, I believe, as a crisis of collective behavior. This requires that we shift attention from individuals to *organized financial groups*. In this light, we can see that finance is about conflict, centered around turf wars and ideologies that play out on a quiet, buttoned-up battlefield such as Wall Street. And finance becomes stable only so long as warring factions of bankers and financiers lay down their arms and embrace *collective* arrangements that curtail their freedom to innovate. Understanding finance, in other words, means understanding in detail how these factions organize themselves and maneuver in order to gain control—until a systemic equilibrium is reached, only in time to be broken by a new battle. Revealing this storyline, its actors, and its influence is the main goal of this book. As we proceed, history will illustrate this perspective—reflecting this most recent crisis as the twenty-first-century version of an ongoing financial pattern, shining a distinctly different light on our current circumstances.

Conservatives Versus Wildcats

Introduction

JUST AS IT IS DIFFICULT TO JUDGE the quality of a used car on the spot, it is difficult to judge the truthfulness of a promise to pay off a mortgage at the time that a loan is made to a borrower: in both cases, sellers/creditors and buyers/borrowers will have incentive to exaggerate the quality of their offer, and only time will reveal whether, and the extent to which, they are lying or dealing honestly. These scenarios spotlight three key facts: information is scarce, valuable, and subject to manipulation. These truths color all kinds of economic transactions, but they are particularly challenging when the accuracy of information can be assessed only after a transaction is completed—as is the case when credit is involved. To further complicate matters, information, however accurate and pertinent at the time of collection, may be irrelevant for future dealings. Credit and finance are particularly vulnerable on this account; borrowers may default because of conditions completely outside their control; financial assets may lose value because other assets, however remotely connected to them, lose value. And, the possibilities go on . . . .

Recognizing the scarcity and unreliability of information gives rise to our understanding of money, credit, and banking, whereby the central problems faced by financial providers are those of matching the demand for, and supply of, financing—of coordinating flows of financial resources and thus of decreasing opportunities for malfeasance while managing the potential effects of uncertainty. In this view, financial providers who specialize in assessing the credibility of a borrower's promises and who successfully hedge against future uncertainty allocate their resources better than do those who ignore problems associated with these gray areas. Success is measured in terms of how these providers alleviate potential asymmetries in information between people with viable business plans but no capital, and people with capital but no intent to invest it actively. By the same token, the value of credit and financial instruments is a reflection of the value of some underlying asset; the longer the duration of a financial relationship, the higher the risk. But financial instruments make this risk more manageable and, within the limits of probability, more predictable. In short, banks and other providers of financial services use different kinds of financial tools to match the credit needs of their customers. The art of banking, and more generally of finance, is the art of developing ways to make this match as effectively as possible, which leads to financial markets that run smoothly and efficiently.

However plausible this account of finance may seem, judging money, credit, and banks in terms of how financial actors approximate their views of markets, means adopting the "categories of practice" (to use a term that Brubaker and Cooper [2000] elaborate from Pierre Bourdieu) that financial actors use—the justifications that they themselves employ to rationalize and legitimize their behavior. This is particularly the case when it comes to economic theories, which, in spite of a long tradition of empirical work in economic history, tend to focus on free, competitive, and frictionless markets at the expense of appreciating the social nature of each and the importance of money in particular (Smithin 1994, 2000; Davidson 2002: 78). As a result, it is a trademark of economic approaches that credit and finance are judged in terms of how they approximate, or differ from, idealized markets, as opposed to being valued on their own terms. This is also the case for behavioral approaches to finance, which tend to emphasize flaws in the individual rationality of economic actors to explain why finance does not live up to the ideal of efficiency. Sociological theories, by contrast, are quick to accept a division of intellectual labor whereby the character of money, banking, and credit is considered too "economic," and thus by definition outside the scope of sociological analysis (Collins 1979a). But the outcome is the same: sociologists, quite paradoxically, tend to idealize money and markets and, with few notable exceptions, pay little attention to financial processes.

Now that money, credit, and banking are at the center of several intellectual efforts, aimed at rethinking the nature of the capitalist process, in literatures as disparate as the comparative analysis of capitalist systems

(Hall and Soskice 2001); the economic history of financial systems (Allen and Gale 2000; Verdier 2003); the sociology of banking (Stearns and Allan 1996; Carruthers 2005, 2011); and the sociology of money (Ingham 2004), the legacy of inattention to the social foundations of money, credit, and banking is especially troubling. This book is an attempt to interrogate some of the fundamental premises that underlie these conversations.

Coordination in finance, I submit, is indeed a problem—but it is not a problem of devising efficient solutions that ensure optimal collective outcomes, as information-based approaches imply. It is rather a problem of organizing powerful coalitions in "the financial field" to monopolize the appropriation of collective benefits. The financial field is an arena of conflict, where competing financial elites organize in order to prevail, not to facilitate external economic processes. The contours of this conflict can be delineated only if one (1) understands the centrality of conflict to capitalism in general; and (2) spells out what shape this conflict takes, what conflict entails for the financial field, and how "categories of practices" (fungible money, banks as institutions of intermediation, creditworthiness as an objective trait, and so forth) are mobilized in this struggle. In this introduction, I argue that a sociology of financial instruments constitutes the foundation on which to construct a more general sociology of finance. Attention to financial instruments allows us to understand the centrality of conflict in capitalism generally, and finance in particular. I will also discuss the relationship between democracy and financial conflict, introducing the empirical material on which this book will be based.

From Money to Financial Instruments

Discussions of finance tend to take an idealized view of money: they argue, specifically, that the purpose of finance is to make qualitatively different assets commensurable, both with other assets and with comparable assets over time. Financial instruments are the medium in which this process of evaluation takes place: they assign assets a quantitative value, and devise rules that recalibrate it over time (Bryan and Rafferty 2007). Exchanges mediated by financial instruments constitute *forward markets* where "the buyer and seller enter into a contractual agreement today for payment and delivery at specific dates in the future" (Davidson 2002: 71). The problem with financial contracts is that they often lead to systematic mispricings—such as financial bubbles—in which the financial assessment of the value of an asset turns out to be plain wrong, or off the predicted value in ways large enough to make payment of the liability impossible (Minsky 1986; see Zuckerman 2012 for a review). The effectiveness of financial instruments is thus judged in terms of how well they reflect intrinsic value.

But, for the moment, let us bracket off the issue of what the financial instrument represents—or of how well it represents value—and let us concentrate on what holders of financial instruments can do with them. The properties of financial instruments can be captured by two general dimensions, which I will call *exclusivity* and *financial control*:

1. *Exclusivity:* This is the degree to which possession of the instrument is restricted. As a result, the circuit in which the instrument is issued, owned, and exchanged can be more or less exclusive. That is, membership in the circuit may be restricted to few elite players or, at the other extreme, open to all. Hedge funds and exclusive cards are two examples.

2. *Financial Control:* This is the degree to which the holder of the instrument has control over its value. On one end, when control is highest, the holder can shape markets for the instrument so as to increase (or decrease) its value. On the other end, when control is lowest, the holder of the instrument cannot affect the price of the instrument. For instance, the holder of food stamps has little control over their value; the manager of a hedge fund, by contrast, has, to the extent that she is successful in her portfolio strategies, tight control over its value.

Let us discuss this latter example, the hedge fund, at greater length. A hedge fund is an unregulated investment vehicle that is high both in exclusivity and in financial control. The first claim is easy to defend: a hedge fund manages the wealth of carefully selected, extremely rich individuals; in order to take advantage of the U.S. tax code, the assets each investor puts at the fund's disposal have to exceed $5 million (Fung and Hsieh 1999). Normally, the fund is privately controlled: it takes the legal status of a limited partnership; it often locks the funds of its investors in for a given period of time—formally to avoid liquidity mismatches and thus gain the ability to concentrate on long-term investments (Das 2005), but symbolically to create the conditions for the development of a long-term bond between managers and investors.

How do hedge funds achieve financial control? For one, the assets in which hedge funds invest are traded in financial markets, of course, but

TABLE O.I
Two Dimensions of Financial Conflict

	Degree of Financial Control	
	(More)	(Less)
Exclusivity		
(More)	Hedge Funds	Exclusive Credit Cards
(Less)	Relationship Banking	Mortgage-Backed Securities

the ownership of the fund itself is usually not (although funds of funds are possible too). The managers of the fund have *discretionary control* over their investment strategies, though they are subject to the informal pressure that investors put on them, and to rules regulating when the funds invested must be released (Lewis 2010). What give hedge fund managers financial control are alliances with academic theorists and other financial providers, and access to financial technologies through which they get to shape markets (MacKenzie and Millo 2003). Their financial control also depends on carefully managing impressions, and first and foremost, orchestrating social experiences of financial control for one's investors. This, most importantly, includes a claim to membership in a "smart money" elite (Mallaby 2010). These experiences, to be sure, are validated only to the extent that the fund earns its investors high rates of return; but, arguably, it is precisely because managers of the fund have access to information that others ignore (a practice that often spills into insider trading), that their fund thrives. The fact that their financial control can only be temporary tells us something about the social process whereby hedge funds succeed: once the investment strategies of a successful hedge fund are copied by a multiplicity of actors, the hedge fund loses its competitive edge and may ultimately collapse (MacKenzie 2003). A hedge fund can best be thought of as a contemporary illustration of Weber's "closed status group": the exclusivity of its membership and the idiosyncrasy of its practices are key ingredients to its continued success.

Now compare the exclusivity and financial control of a hedge fund to those of a financial instrument, such as a credit line issued to a selected clientele. An exclusive credit card has restricted membership—the most exclusive ones are, in fact, by invitation only (Moyer 2007). In exchange for a hefty fee, an exclusive credit card grants the holder several perks, usually related to travel assistance and entertainment. The exclusive credit card, however, gives the holder no control over exchanges in financial markets. In fact, it is often celebrities who are invited to apply: their desirable social characteristics (reputation, fame, public exposure) are ideal ingredients for the creation of a prestigious circuit. By the same token, possession of an exclusive credit card is less prestigious than investing in a hedge fund, because situations in which the possession of an exclusive card commands prestige are, in essence, consumption experiences. Such experiences are crucial to the constitution of status groups sharing a similar lifestyle, as Weber recognized, but only outside of financial markets, in which they command no prestige. A credit card is thus high in exclusivity but low in control.

A mortgage-backed security is an example of an instrument that is low in both exclusivity and financial control. In some unexpected ways, the MBS has features similar to those of a credit card, to the extent that it affords little control in financial markets to its possessor, let alone its originator. The security conveys some degree of control over a consumption experience, associated with the purchase of a house that it facilitates. But, much like credit card debt, a mortgage-backed security is exchanged as a commodity in financial markets, and so the originator of the security quickly loses any control over it. Of course, a mortgage-backed security is less exclusive than an elite credit card, although (much like a credit card) a mortgage is given a rating that determines how favorable its terms will be to the debtor (Rajan et al. 2008).

Finally, consider an ongoing credit relationship between a bank and a customer. It is discriminating to the extent that it depends on whether the customer meets the criteria of creditworthiness set by the bank, often buttressed by collateral (Boot 2000). But because of informational asymmetries—the fact, in particular, that a borrower will always know more about her financial situation than will a banker—relationship banking affords more opportunities of financial control to the borrower than an impersonal credit relationship would. The banker and the customer become committed to each other over time, developing a relationship that may then go on to facilitate the customer in securing more resources on more advantageous terms in financial markets as well (Diamond 1984; Calomiris 1995). So even though relationship banking can be less exclusive than selective, elite financial relations such as the possession of an exclusive credit card (depending, of course, on the prestige of the bank itself [Podolny 1993]), it is an important marker of the financial status of the borrower:

the relationship is supposed to continue over time, allowing banks to act as monitors and guarantors of the financial situation of the borrower, and allowing the borrower in turn to benefit from the prestige of being associated with the bank.

These distinctions among financial instruments on the two dimensions of exclusivity and financial control bring into relief two counterintuitive points. First, the *prestige* of a financial instrument often increases as the instrument loses its connection to underlying, physical assets—in clear contrast to "real" economic analysis which would have us believe that the most desirable assets are those that are valued closely to their "intrinsic" value defined by a material good. Thus, investing in a hedge fund is more prestigious than possessing an exclusive credit card or issuing a mortgage-backed security, let alone getting a mortgage, because a hedge fund gives the investor access to prestigious networks of financial interaction in ways that "lesser" financial instruments do not. Similarly, relationship banking is more prestigious than a one-time financial transaction because it may open up opportunities for further financial transactions, whereas a one-time debt only finances an expenditure. Moving on to the second point, the prestige of having access to instruments that are denied to others, what one might call the prestige of exclusion, allows financial elites to make long-term alliances with each other. But these alliances, depending on the exclusivity of the relationship, produce mutual obligations and mutual commitments that extend into the future, locking different elites to each other. Networks of favors and informal relations take the place of market-based exchanges denominated in prices; confidence in the perpetuation of those relationships builds up. As in Randall Collins's theory of interaction rituals, financial instruments serve as symbolic currencies loaded with the solidarity and the social honor of membership that allow individuals to forge "interaction ritual chains" with those who are like them (Collins 2004). Much like the men of early-twentieth-century America analyzed by Viviana Zelizer (1994), who earmarked a significant proportion of their earnings to spend it on rituals of sociability with other men (such as drinking together), financial elites earmark the most prestigious financial instruments to "spend" them in financial interactions with other financial elites, in the activity of trading that allows them to be at the center of vibrant financial markets (Collins 2000).

The two dimensions that define financial instruments are therefore obviously interrelated. Exclusivity and financial control feed off each other, as one way to increase the prestige of a given financial instrument by restricting its possession to only those who possess desirable social characteristics. At one extreme, only members of the circuit become entitled to the holding of the instrument, either by law or through informal means. Thus we learn from Lamoreaux's economic history of antebellum New England (1994) that entrepreneurs and bankers there tended to belong to the same kinship networks, supporting each other's endeavors and sharing each other's gains and losses. A weaker form of exclusivity is obtained by restricting the financial instrument to certain uses, while banning others. We learn, for example, from Abolafia's analysis (1996) of the rise and fall of junk bonds: when Michael Milken started borrowing money with below–investment grade stocks as collateral (leveraged buyouts), he was considered a successful, if idiosyncratic, financier. But when he began using leveraged buyouts to acquire control over established corporations, Milken quickly became a pariah and was eventually defeated through a coordinated effort of established financial elites and regulators.

At the other end of the continuum, possession of the instrument is permitted to outsiders as well, regardless of their social identity. One can tell such a story about any financial instrument that we have over time come to take for granted, such as, for instance, deposit banking or credit cards—financial services that have grown in leaps and bounds over the past fifty years (Guseva and Rona-Tas 2001; Guseva 2008).

The distinction between exclusivity of ownership and degree of financial control, in short, serves to emphasize an aspect of financial instruments that makes them inextricably related to experiences of power and prestige in the context of identifiable, concrete financial communities, rather than to experiences of command over material consumption. Financial instruments, that is, belong to the politics of status groups.[1] This means that financial instruments are instruments of conflict.

Capitalist Conflict

I take it to be one of the main lessons of Marx, Weber, and Schumpeter that capitalism is, by its very nature, a dynamic system; stability can only be temporary and can be ensured only through *organizational* means, which in turn generate conflict. Marx (especially 1921, 1909) emphasized that capitalism is characterized by a sequence of booms and busts, that it thus alternates between periods of prosperity and periods of deprivation, each caused by contradictory dynamics internal to capitalist development (class struggle), and each having tremendous implications for the distribution of economic and political power. But Marx did not have a theory of money and credit that recognized its autonomous properties and dynamics (Ingham 1984, 1996; Nitzan 1998). So he had little to say about the political aspects of finance. Weber, by contrast, argued that capitalism is based on a complex and fragile balance of power between the political authorities that uphold the law and protect private property, and the capitalist interests that accumulate wealth and power, with alliances between and within those groups giving further dynamism to the system (Weber 1978, 1981). The secret of capitalist dynamism is that it institutionalizes conflict, opening certain markets to competition, and forcing their incumbents to react to the challenge (see, esp., Collins 1980). Yet Weber's theory of money remained underdeveloped.[2] Finally, Schumpeter (1911, 1939, 1962) put the "gale of creative destruction," the relentless process of innovation, at the very foundation of economic development, highlighting the fact that the economic winners of one wave of innovation then struggle to protect their position through economic and social barriers—from patents to industrial espionage; but the innovative process inevitably makes those barriers obsolete over time. Schumpeter, however, like Weber, did not develop a full-fledged theory of money and banking, one that would match his theory of entrepreneurship (Schumpeter 1991; Swedberg 2003).

Marx's focus on the expansion and concentration of the capitalist system; Weber's focus on the political foundations of economic action; and Schumpeter's focus on the political struggle between innovators and the old guard all point to the porosity, instability, and temporary nature of economic boundaries; they also highlight the centrality of conflict to the capitalist economy. But, with the notable exception of Schumpeter, classical theorists did not provide a sustained analysis of the agents and organizations most directly involved in the construction and transgression of economic boundaries.

Schumpeter came close. He most explicitly recognized the centrality of the banking system to capitalism, and proposed the beginnings of a theory of the conflicts that take place within it. But he also held fast to an idealized view of the capitalist process in which bankers played only a functional role—as long as they were properly professionalized into acting as objective allocators of resources and in which financial speculation was nothing but an aberration, brought about by actors with no appropriate training in matters financial or with explicitly subversive purposes in mind. Schumpeter did not recognize that, because bankers play an organizational role within capitalism, struggles among bankers cannot result solely from professional or moral failings on the part of individual bankers.

Conflict is a team sport and success depends on mobilization, which is only possible to the extent that team members solve the dilemmas inherent to collective action.[3] Collective action is predicated on, among other things, a common identity through which members of the collectivity develop solidarity with one another—an identity that gives members of the collectivity the criteria by which to judge the actions of others so that members can mobilize to exclude others (see, esp., Tilly 1998; Collins 2000; Zelizer and Tilly 2006). A new sociological consensus is emerging: in order to understand how capitalist economies work, one must first understand the processes and mechanisms whereby groups organize themselves into collective actors with the power to monopolize certain resources and exclude others from exploiting the same opportunities (H. C. White 1981, 1992, 2002). These insights must be incorporated in our theories of finance.[4]

This book develops a conflict-centered perspective in the context of finance to contribute to this emergent discussion. It focuses on how bankers commit to and inhabit common identities as a collective; how bankers control the form, direction, and use of credit through those identities; and finally, how bankers use these identities to exclude other actors from engaging in financial activities. Since bankers, unlike other economic actors, specialize in niche aspects of financial activity, their role in the capitalist process is unique. To be sure, any economic group that benefits from the collective appropriation of a resource will be faced with the challenge of creating commitments to a shared identity, so as to forestall self-interested behavior that might undermine the cohesion of the group. But bankers, I will argue, are specialists in the activity of producing collective financial identities, and linking those to financial instruments, which they then police by restricting their circulation. As each aspect of financial activity generates conformity, so too does it produce resistance and opposition. Bankers are always faced with the pressure to conform to their shared identities; therefore, they are also always faced with the option to rail against existing understandings about how credit should be used and to disregard the call to enforce existing exclusions. Bankers are, in short, highly vulnerable to formidable collective action dilemmas, and an understanding of banking is not possible without an analysis of the challenges aimed at altering the financial status quo, and of the mechanisms that attenuate such challenges.

In the chapters to come, I develop a parsimonious theoretical continuum that will surely strike some readers as simplistic, but I think that it holds great promise in characterizing the nuanced aspects of banking conflict: on one end is the ideal type of conservative bankers; on the other, the ideal type of what I will call "wildcats." Such a distinction between conservative and wildcat bankers refers to the different logics that drive the allocation, exchange, and use of credit—a distinction first, but only partially, developed by Schumpeter (esp. 1911: 116). The *exclusionary* logic embraced by conservative bankers assigns money in specific forms to clients that these bankers deem reputable—for instance, through revolving lines of credit, or unsecured loans based on the client's credentials, rather than the client's collateral. The *inclusionary* logic embraced by wildcat bankers, by contrast, gives more prestigious kinds of money to less prestigious clients—for instance, by opening access to stock market financing to firms with low credit ratings or inventing instruments that rely on new and widely available forms of collateral, such as long-term employment or home mortgages.

Importantly, this basic opposition between these two ways of doing business translate into two opposite moral claims about capitalism. Wildcats contest the financial elitism of conservative bankers; in turn, they propose a vision of financial democracy. Conservative bankers reject the speculations of the wildcats as irresponsible: only their own (in their eyes) better strategy ensures financial stability. The predominance of either moral claim, I add, serves not only to justify capitalism (Boltanski and Thévenot 2006). These assertions also make possible the appropriation of resources on which the power of financial elites, especially dominant and entrenched ones, depends; alternatively, they justify full-scale attacks on the foundations of the financial status quo. So bankers' claims that they submit to time-honored traditions in their allocation of credit, to standards of prudence in their assessment of the creditworthiness of their customers, and to strict and objective criteria in their distribution of financial resources have all served as much to create professional cohesion and unity of intent among bankers as to regulate transactions with outsiders. Sound banking, in short, is the collective identity that dominant financial elites develop so as to reproduce their cohesion and bolster their collective power. But depending on the balance of power within banking, as well as in the political system in which banking takes place, claims to sound banking are vulnerable to accusations that they are too strict, traditional, and conservative; too prudent and austere; too restrictive and backward-looking. Since a weakening of the collective commitment to sound banking on the part of conservative bankers, as Schumpeter recognized, would eventually mark their demise, conservative bankers will fight such challenges. Finance, then, is about organized conflict, and the ideologies that are mobilized in the context of conflict are weapons that banking factions mobilize to preserve, or change, the financial status quo.

A number of myths cloud our understanding of finance, as a result of which conservative and wildcat banking have been conceptualized not as conflictual strategies within the financial field but as responses to temporary shocks or disequilibria. The most important of the myths are these: (1) money is fungible and neutral, (2) banks are intermediary institutions, and (3) creditworthiness is an objective assessment. Embracing these myths leads to an understanding of finance wherein financial markets are fully capable of overcoming any challenge, if given sufficient time, and financial inclusion and stability can both be achieved. This book paints a more realistic, historically rooted image of financial action in which the political aspects of money and credit are central: the tradeoffs among these aspects of the system are not only an integral part of the inner dynamic of capitalism but also two structural positions within finance that challenging actors can occupy in the struggle for dominance. Exclusion and stability on the one hand, inclusion and change on the other, are our key ingredients. For this reason, the myths of money as fungible, banks as intermediaries, and creditworthiness as objective should never be our analytical categories. At best, they are *ideological aspects* of the collective identity of sound banking that financial elites have mobilized to justify and then naturalize their strategies. When used as analytical categories, the myths hide the political nature of finance and the sources from which financial incumbents draw power and authority.

When we view the financial field as conflictual, we see that stability is a fragile and temporary political accomplishment, leading to new questions about how changes in the larger structure of political opportunities affect the balance of power within finance. In fact, the collective identities that are organized and mobilized against one another within the financial field—with sound banking as the ideology that commits bankers to exclusion and stability, and wildcat banking as the ideology that commits them to inclusion and innovation—may clash with the ideologies of political movements outside finance, thus creating the possibility of larger conflicts, as well as the space for potential alliances. Allow me to single out one important structural source of political conflict to illustrate this point: the opposition between the *exclusionary* strategy of conservative bankers and the *inclusive* logic of democratic regimes.

Financial Conflict and Democracy

Important analyses have praised the alleged compatibility of and positive link between capitalism and democratic regimes (classically, North and Weingast 1989; see also Acemoglu and Robinson 2011). In this new-institutionalist perspective, free markets and free institutions go together because of the ability of democratic states to make promises that are credible. When political control is democratic, commitment to contractual obligations is more likely to be protected and guaranteed, and so free markets can thrive.[5]

The problem with this view, of course, as with any view that equates democracy and capitalist markets, is that capitalism as it actually exists is not reducible to free markets, a point clearly recognized by both Weber and Schumpeter; finance in particular is a realm not of intermediation and efficient allocation of resources, but of an organized push and pull to control the shape, direction, and intensity of financial flows. Financial actors actively resist the encroachment of competition on the niches they monopolize, so they experience free capitalist markets as threats to their power, and resist them accordingly, rather than accepting them as normal processes to which they must adapt. But this also means that demands for freer markets are not demands for more accountable systems that better guarantee private property, as the neoinstitutionalists would say. Rather, they are attacks against entrenched positions, aimed at corroding those old networks and at creating the space for new systems with a different architecture of exclusion. To analyze the effects of democracy on capitalism thus means to account for the social processes that threaten the boundaries that incumbents erect in order to protect their market position.

For analytical purposes, democratic regimes should provide a context in which conflicts between conservative and wildcat bankers can be more clearly observed. In authoritarian settings, bankers will not see challenge from outsiders once they gain political privileges. But in democratic systems, elected political officials are often attentive to demands for financial inclusion: they may even find it strategically convenient to encourage financial speculation, using credit as a way to win political favors from the constituencies that stand to benefit from it. In this way democratic regimes can be difficult environments for conservative bankers, as they provide wildcat bankers with the means (such as public debt), the space, and the legitimacy to spread the use of credit to new constituencies.

It can be expected that conservative bankers will not passively succumb to these wildcat challenges. Historically, ideas about the inherently technical and nonpolitical nature of money and creditworthiness, and the importance of professional autonomy from political power in the banking business, arose precisely to limit democratic challenges to banking authority (Ingham 1984 classically shows this for the British case). But in democracies, such arguments tend to be insufficient. How, then, will conservative bankers attempt to maintain authority in regimes in which the right to set boundaries around credit can be contested?

The Empirical Cases and Their Theoretical Relevance

How conservative bankers bolster their authority to draw exclusive boundaries around the allocation of credit is an empirical question at the core of our exploration. One possible analytical strategy to characterize the internal dynamics of finance, and tease out how external processes affect them, would be to select several country-level case studies, with sufficient variation in their degree of democratization. Guiding questions for such a strategy would be: is banking more (or less) conservative in democratic or authoritarian settings? Are wildcat speculators more (or less) prevalent in democracies or dictatorships? Is the banking system as a whole more (or less) autonomous from politics in democracies or in authoritarian regimes? Several works in comparative-historical sociology follow this Millsian approach (Skocpol and Somers 1980; Mahoney and Rueschemeyer 2003).

In the context of this study, however, such an approach would not be entirely satisfactory because of the inevitable loss of depth it would entail. My intention, in fact, is not to show that macropolitical variables, such as democratization, affect national financial dynamics, a proposition for which large literatures already exist (see, for instance, Sylla, Tilly, and Tortella 1999). Rather, the aim is to investigate *how* financial status groups organize in democratic settings to preserve, or change, the distribution of financial advantages; what kinds of claims incumbents make in order to counter wildcat challenges; and what effects such conflicts have on the power and autonomy of the financial field as a whole. To borrow an explanation from Michael Wievorka (Ragin and Becker 1992: 160), I look for cases that offer the "opportunity for relating facts and concepts, reality and hypotheses," cases that "draw [their] unity not from the theoretical tools used to analyze [them], but from the way [they] take shape, namely as social or historical fact[s] combining all sorts of elements into a set comprising social roles, an institution, [etc.]"

I have selected two cases—the United States (ca. 1800–1913) and Italy (ca. 1860–1913) that afford such an opportunity in a particularly useful fashion. While there is no striking, macrosocial similarity between the two cases, in both countries, during this period, the openness of democratic regimes increased, affecting the local organization of finance in dramatic ways. In both countries the local level had been the arena in which financial status groups had consolidated their power, but increased democratic openness led to powerful demands for financial expansion. In the U.S. case, these demands also originated at the local level where financial power resided; in the Italian case, by contrast, these calls for expansion came from above. Therefore, these two instances allow us to view top-down and bottom-up shifts side by side.

More specifically, *decentralized political authority*—the limited capacity of the federal government in the United States, and the corresponding strength of subnational authorities (in particular, state governments)—set the stage for change. As political movements emerged to challenge the privileges of elites, wildcats began threatening sound bankers at the local level, where they could rally state governments around projects for liberalization in the name of financial democracy. Initially (in the antebellum period), conservative bankers fought to maintain a privileged relationship with state legislatures, but they lost that battle to the Jacksonians in what came to be known as Andrew Jackson's "war on banks," which prepared the ground for the passing of general incorporation laws. After these liberalizing laws were passed, legislative approval was no longer needed to open a bank. So, in the postbellum period, bankers abandoned the strategy of seeking formal political privileges, cultivating instead an image of banking and finance as autonomous from politics. Ostensibly nonpolitical criteria for the allocation of credit became the battleground on which financial conflict occurred, as conservative bankers sought to regain control by couching sound banking in ideological terms (a myth of creditworthiness) emphasizing middle-class values of reputation, honesty, and moral probity (B. H. Mann 2002; Olegario 2006). In contrast with the well-developed local administrations of the United States, local political authorities in Italy had little capacity (Sabetti 2000; Ziblatt 2006). After a chaotic process of unification, the central state stepped in and forced conservative bankers to deal with a new, powerful actor. The state's own openness to new social forces invested in financial expansion called existing boundaries of the allocation of credit into question. Unlike U.S. bankers who, in the face of strong sectional opposition to centralized authority, capitalized on their allegedly nonpolitical role, Italian bankers embraced this politicization of credit by subordinating themselves to the project of state-building. Some banking factions, in conflict with their more powerful counterparts, pushed this identification further, and began arguing that the fate of banking was connected to the fate of the nation. In the wake of their success, creditworthiness came to be understood in terms of one's loyalty to the nation; through a national myth of creditworthiness, bankers would draw the boundary between those deserving of credit, and those who should be denied access, along nationalist terms.

At the minimum, then, this book questions the existence of any "elective affinity" between open financial markets and democratic regimes, for it treats the former as causes of instability to which conservative bankers respond by drawing on the political resources that democratic regimes make available to them. The shape of their strategy, in turn, is affected by the level from which wildcats launch their attack on sound banking: local challenges will be dealt with differently than challenges coming from above. To put it slightly differently, my comparative design exploits variation in the two cases, between the levels that Diana Vaughan terms "interactional" and "contextual" (Ragin and Becker 1992: 179). "Interactional" dynamics characterize how groups coalesce around identities; "contextual" dynamics refer to the means they have at their disposal to reproduce those identities. U.S. conservative bankers, I submit, were not subject to the same kind of "contextual" constraints on their "interactional" activities that Italian conservative bankers, in the face of a centralized state, were forced to deal with. Analysts who understand credit to work best when it is regulated by free market forces, rather than political considerations, would consider the Italian case an aberration and would celebrate the U.S. case as a better exemplar of proper relations between the economy, credit markets, and politics. As I discuss in the conclusion, the aim of the study is to demonstrate how finance is dependent on the creation of boundaries: conservative and wildcat bankers fight about where such boundaries should be drawn, with wildcats often couching their demands in terms of inclusion, and with the political system in which finance takes place giving those boundaries more specific contents.

My intention is not to judge the appropriateness of those boundaries. But, by looking at how different levels of the social and political structure affected the cohesion of financial elites in Italy and the United States, I am able to specify a more dynamic link between democracy and finance than previous theories have, as well as foreground the effect of financial conflict on the formation of financial systems.

Plan of the Book

In the first chapter, I lay the foundations for the project by delineating in more detail the myths of money, credit, and creditworthiness. The purpose of the discussion is to show that the three are always contested, with certain bankers striving to reinforce the boundaries drawn around each phenomenon, while other bankers strive to transgress those boundaries. The nature of finance in the capitalist process is that of organized conflict between inclusion and exclusion, in which the myths of fungible money, of banks as institutions of intermediation, and of creditworthiness as objective assessment are mobilized as ideological instruments for dominance.

Building on the distinction between money as a means of personal enrichment and money as a token of membership in an economic community, a distinction proposed by Simmel, the second chapter argues that bankers mediate the tension between private uses of money and the collective identities sustained by money using specific financial instruments. Bankers, however, can use both conservative and wildcat strategies to manage and exploit this tension: they can emphasize the need to keep access to and trade of the instrument restricted to certain uses and not others; or they can emphasize the need to keep money fungible and generalized, thus transgressing the boundaries that the economic community builds around the circulation of the instrument. The chapter argues that, once a status quo is established within the financial field, financial activities originating outside of it, in particular the financial activities of the state, must also be mediated so that the status quo will be reproduced. The chapter maps out the complex relationship between conservative bankers and political elites that allows the former to consolidate and reproduce the principles of sound banking through which they dominate the financial field. The chapter also hypothesizes that democratic regimes are particularly prone to wildcat challenges, because of their tendency to issue debt to finance political projects over which conservative bankers have no control, and to politicize the boundaries built around credit by making the collective identities whose management the conservative bankers strive to monopolize open to political contestation.

The second chapter concludes the theoretical part of the book, and the remaining four chapters are dedicated to the empirical analyses of the two cases, Italy and the United States. The questions that run through these chapters include: what shape do the myths of fungible money, banking as intermediation, and creditworthiness as objective assessment take in different social and political contexts? How are the myths mobilized to justify inclusions and exclusions? Where are the boundaries drawn between those worthy and those unworthy of credit?

In Chapter Three, I begin by discussing the myth of creditworthiness in the nineteenth-century United States. Creditworthiness was thought to be a character trait of individual borrowers—a conceptualization that characterized the British credit system as well and that has since become accepted as self-evident. Why would a borrower that did not display honesty, capacity for hard work, and a solid and reliable reputation be entrusted with money? I argue, however, that this is too narrow a basis for our understanding of the organization of the financial field. Rather, we must begin with the realization that the use of reputation as an indicator of creditworthiness originated in mercantile networks, where concerns about the ability of borrowers to pay were particularly pressing. But the financial field included actors whose business did not entail lending to individuals—actors who, for instance, engaged in developmental projects controlled by state legislatures and who specialized in corporate restructuring and consolidation (Sklar 1987; Fligstein 1990). Justification of the business of banking as the activity of assessing reputations remained, nonetheless, widespread: embedded in what contemporary economists call the "real bills" doctrine, we see the link between reputation and credit as the rallying point for a powerful reform movement that was eventually determinant in the passing of the Federal Reserve Act (Wiebe 1962; Livingston 1986; Broz 1997).

This focus on reputation as the precondition of credit, I argue, became widespread in the context of the prolonged power struggle that, throughout the nineteenth century, characterized U.S. finance. The power to issue money and credit was intensely contested in the antebellum United States; this was particularly the case in the Northern states, where banks were chartered and taxed by state legislatures, and where their relationship with political power was visible and open for contestation. In the South, by contrast, where local politics was not democratic because of the institution of slavery, banks were not taxed, and as a consequence, their privileged relationship with political elites was not open to contestation. As a result, the South had fewer banks, fewer banknotes in circulation, and fewer wildcats. The chapter argues that Northern conservative bankers appropriated the myth of creditworthiness as a character trait of individual borrowers to commit both other bankers and their borrowers to *depoliticized* collective identities, and so neutralize the challenge to sound banking posed by wildcat bankers in the name of financial democracy.

In the Jacksonian period, wildcat bankers succeeded in weakening their conservative counterparts, as they subjected the financial field to general incorporation laws, severing the political link between banks and state legislatures. This momentary win is the subject of Chapter Four. We will see that the National Banking Laws of the Civil War simply applied similarly liberal banking principles at the federal level, thus reinforcing the wildcat dynamic. Yet, because of the continued conflict over the nature of money, and the continued conflict over the power of banks, throughout the postbellum period, conservative bankers once again invested in the myth of creditworthiness to legitimize their credit practices. In the decentralized, (relatively) democratic political context of the postbellum United States, the conservative narrative about concerns with reputation became of crucial importance to maintaining control over the creation and distribution of financial resources among elites.

Chapter Five discusses how the weak capacity of local governments, coupled with the centralizing thrust of the state, affected the development of banking in the Italian case. Unlike U.S. conflicts, which were based on reputation and creditworthiness, I argue that Italian banking conflicts referred primarily to the relationship between centralized political power and credit. Conservative bankers, because they could not rely on strong local governments that would protect their privileges and status, vied instead to gain the support of central political elites. Since Italian political elites viewed the spread of credit as a project of political and social development, and they entrusted the credit system with the diffusion of new collective identities binding citizens to the state, wildcat bankers had an in: they could attack conservative bankers on the basis initially of regional identity, and then of nationalism. The chapter reviews the early debates among political and financial elites in which this defense was first articulated.

Chapter Six focuses on the later part of this debate, between 1890—when wildcat challenges to conservative banking at the local level led to a widespread financial crisis—and World War I. By that time, a central bank was firmly in control of the finances of the state and engaged in a struggle with the "universal banks" of the North, until they were linked to the development of the heavy industrial sector but increasingly viewed as agents of international finance. The chapter shows how the myth of creditworthiness became anchored to nationalism. Given that the U.S. articulation is the one that gained more legitimacy in the contemporary literature, so that creditworthiness is now mostly understood as the trait of the individual borrower, the chapter deals with the question as to whether there is something inherently specific to the Italian political environment of the time that makes the myth of creditworthiness as a display of national loyalty a matter of limited historical and sociological interest. But I submit that the Italian case is in fact more useful than the U.S. case in delineating the contours of creditworthiness precisely because it highlights the collective basis upon which it is articulated. The goal of the chapter is to show that, within the political context in which the Italian banking system was embedded, the myth of creditworthiness as the display of nationalist loyalty served to build a common language of communication for bankers—and that while the content of those discussions is historically specific, its nature is not. Even contemporary articulations of creditworthiness as a trait of individual character are ways of committing bankers to common understandings of money and credit so as to stabilize broader conflicts.

We conclude with Chapter Seven, which briefly returns to the ways that my theory of finance as organized conflict relates to approaches that emphasize scarce information as the reason for the existence of banks. The chapter discusses how the theory extends Schumpeter's insights on the relationship between bankers and entrepreneurs. It summarizes my findings from the comparison between the United States and Italy, emphasizing the role of the politics of the budget and of political culture. It concludes by sharpening my typology of wildcat and conservative bankers, and discussing how it helps us understand more contemporary financial events, such as the arguably risky rise of financial innovation over the past thirty years.

1

Money, Banks, and Creditworthiness
Three Myths?

THREE FUNDAMENTAL ASSUMPTIONS characterize scholarly understandings of money, banks, and creditworthiness, and in what follows I will, perhaps a bit irreverently, refer to them as *myths*. The first myth depicts money as a neutral means of accounting for value—as a *fungible* instrument that serves to establish commensurability among qualitatively different commodities. The second myth depicts banks as institutions of intermediation; it sees them as responsible for the allocation and distribution of scarce financial resources (capital), so that banks intermediate between savers and spenders. Finally, the myth of creditworthiness as objective assessment understands the criteria by which borrowers are granted credit to be a function of the traits of the borrower: the better these criteria capture such underlying traits, the better the odds that the financial obligation will be met in the future.

Understanding the nature of these myths, I claim, is essential for understanding the conflictual nature of finance. There are three reasons: (1) money can reflect both a logic of inclusion and one of exclusion; it is both fungible and incommensurable. (2) Banks do not move resources, but create financial claims whose circulation they strive to restrict to certain circuits. (3) The criteria whereby creditworthiness is adjudicated serve not to capture some objective trait in the borrower, but to create collective identities to which both bankers and their clients must commit. By committing, they can continue exploiting opportunities and restricting access to advantages to their own status group. Therefore, money, credit, and creditworthiness are always contested, with certain bankers striving to reinforce the boundaries drawn around each phenomenon, while other bankers strive to transgress those boundaries. The myths of fungible money, of banks as institutions of intermediation, and of creditworthiness as objective assessment, are categories of practice rather than analytical categories; they emerge in the course of financial struggle to abet the political projects of conflicting banking groups. This makes conflict central to the nature of finance in the capitalist process, and recurrent claims to inclusion and exclusion intrinsic to financial exchange. This chapter investigates the nature of each myth in some depth.

The Myth of Fungible Money

A new sociological literature, emerging over the past twenty years, explores whether money is a set of financial and monetary instruments that are only potentially commensurable with one another, or an abstract system of accounting for value that generates equivalences and commensurability through the quantification of value. Here I will claim that the first claim is more accurate than the second. Money takes specific forms, which then signal something about their possessor to other financial players: they signal membership in financial communities variably characterized by exclusivity and control. As a consequence, specifically, the possessors of specific financial instruments gain access to particular financial experiences, as well as to common identities that commit them to collective enterprises. In order to understand the importance of this claim we must begin by questioning the fungible status of money.

What I call the myth of fungible money derives from a large, mostly polemical literature, dating back to the writings of Karl Marx and Georg Simmel, that identifies in money the power of transcending any and all social boundaries that individuals may erect to contain its spread—and the spread of commercialization and cold calculation that money brings with it. *Non olet*, money does not smell (1921: 124), as Marx put it, referring to Roman emperor Vespasian's quip upon imposing a tax on public lavatories: for Marx, money is a "universal equivalent," deriving its power precisely from its detachment from commodities, rather than from its origins, no matter how undignified they might be.

Simmel joins Marx in thinking of money as anonymous and depersonalized. But he pushes the idea of the transformative power of money in a different direction from Marx, to argue that money is freedom, a freedom that entails a high cost: "[M]odern man is free, free because he can sell everything, and free because he can buy everything . . . . [T]hrough money, man is no longer enslaved in things, so on the other hand is the content of his Ego, motivation and determination so much identical with concrete possessions that the constant selling and exchanging of them—even the mere fact that they are saleable—often means a selling and uprooting of personal values" (Simmel 1990: 404).

With money comes modernity (Poggi 1993), and in particular, detachment from more traditional sources of authority and identity. A similar theme is later also developed by anthropologists witnessing the transition to market economies in non-Western societies, where, with the advent of colonialism and capitalism, "special monies" were allegedly being replaced by generalized monies (Bohannan 1959). The idea that money is "special" conveys how the different kinds of monetary tokens that pre-existed the market economy circulated in restricted spheres of exchange—characterized by specific obligations and loyalties, and never by a market logic of free exchange. The advent of modern money, by virtue of its neutrality to values and social attachments, is understood as a break in those circuits, signaling the beginning of an era of generalized, market-based exchange (Polanyi 1944; Parry and Bloch 1989).

Marx and Simmel, and later economic anthropologists, in short, make fundamental contributions to a tradition of thinking of money as a "cold cash nexus" that dehumanizes social relations, deprives them of content and emotion, and subjects them to an alienating form of rationality (see, for example, Berman 1983). Thus neither Marx nor Simmel, nor any of their followers, consider the possibility that the actual forms taken by money, and the ways that these forms are used, may be wholly dependent on the relations through which these monetary media are assigned to particular kinds of people, circulating in certain networks and not others. To be sure, because of its ability to break pre-existing social bonds and solidarities, money is understood as presenting new challenges, but also opening new possibilities—new challenges insofar as it increases anomie and alienation (about which Durkheim as well as Marx were most concerned), new possibilities insofar as it opens the space for new forms of individual freedom (as Simmel emphasized). Yet what money makes possible, in the Marx-Simmel framework, is a world eventually devoid of human relations.

The Relational Analysis of Money

With the emergence of new ethnographic studies of money—such as Viviana Zelizer's work (1994) on the attempts of the early-twentieth-century U.S. government to create a homogeneous monetary system—sociologists begin to understand that, counter to the predictions of Marx and Simmel, money continues being segregated and "earmarked" in modern contexts as well. To put it differently, the special monies of so-called primitive societies never disappear, so the all-pervasive commensurability of modern money turns out to be an exaggeration. As social relations become more differentiated, in fact, money becomes more differentiated too.

Zelizer (ibid.), for instance, shows that even in a case of widespread consensus over the unit of account (for example, the dollar), such as the United States in the nineteenth century, people struggled to understand whether the money earned by women was the same as the money earned by men; whether money earned illegally was the same as money earned through legal means; whether money exchanged as a gift was the same as money earned as a compensation for a service, and so on. Moreover, where money's previous, specialized purposes were questioned, individuals engaged in frantic efforts to create new distinctions congruent with the social relations at hand. U.S. families thus engaged in heated arguments about whether the newly elevated and more emancipated status of women required a reworking of the elaborate and humiliating system through which "doles" had hitherto been administered by male breadwinners. And with the entry of more women into the formal labor market, how to classify women's wages (Were they "pin-money"? For what purposes could they be used?) became a source of conflict and debate. In short, where Marx and Simmel would have seen homogeneity, equivalence, fungibility, and fetishism, Zelizer finds nuance and differentiation. Because different social groups will invariably invest money with local meaning, the uses of money will be restricted to acceptable goals, its alleged fungibility broken into multiple, nontransferable currencies. Money, concludes Zelizer, should be understood as ultimately nonfungible. In this perspective, inspired most directly by the principles of *relational analysis,* money becomes a short-hand for the multiplicity of currencies whose circulation is limited to some networks, and impossible in others.

Zelizer's path-breaking study of how money acquires meaning, based on diffuse but mundane monetary practices such as tipping or gift-giving, soon develops into a more structural account of how "circuits of commerce" come about—full-fledged networks defined by strong boundaries against outsiders, shared understandings about how commercial transactions interpenetrate other social exchanges that take place within the network, and common media of exchange that tend to lose value or become altogether unacceptable outside the boundaries of the network (Zelizer 2001, 2005a; Zelizer and Tilly 2006; see also Collins 1995, 2000). Paradigmatic cases are migrant remittance networks, known for their inventiveness in coordinating large sums of payments through cross-national borders, often with specifically devised currencies and units of account, as well as shared understandings of what remittances should be spent on (Zelizer and Tilly 2006). Another example is the proliferation of local currency schemes with their elaborate systems of allocation and accounting (Zelizer 2005b). In this view, money in general, and not just in its uses, is defined by its unfungibility. Different forms of money, to the extent that they circulate in different "circuits," are linked to different social experiences and thus are not commensurable.

Because this literature focuses primarily on the uses of money by marginalized groups, however, it conflates several issues: interpretation and agency in the face of structural constraints, for instance; or the maintenance of social relations in the face of commercialization. This literature debunks the "myth of fungible money" only with respect to actors who are interstitial to the official economy, and primarily only with respect to uses of official moneys. So its impact on an understanding of moneys other than those circulating outside the mainstream banking system has been muted. This leaves open an important analytical space that a second theory of money, more in line with the concerns of the classical theorists, but also more aggressive toward neoclassical economics than relational analysis is, has begun to occupy. And to this second theory of money the very logic behind relational analysis seems suspicious.

This second theory of money, neochartalism, points to the rise of the modern state, and the rationalization of the economy and more generally of social life it made possible, as the processes that must be understood in order to analyze money. The theme of the rise of the modern state was developed in sociology by Weber and his followers, but it was heterodox economists working in the post-Keynesian tradition (Wray 1990, 1999; Wray and Bell 2004; Wray and Forstater 2009; Lavoie 2006; see also Minsky 1986; B. J. Moore 1988), and allied social scientists, most notably

Geoffrey Ingham (see esp. 2004), who specified how money fits in this narrative. To this literature, broadly labeled neochartalism, after Georg Knapp's terminology (Knapp 1924), we now turn.

Neochartalism

From the point of view of neochartalism, of the many functions fulfilled by money, that of serving as a *unit of account* is the most important. Economists since Adam Smith (1976: esp. 309) tell a stylized story about the origins of money as a common medium that individual participants to market exchange agree upon out of convenience (Menger 1892; Jones 1976: 309; Schumpeter 1994): they thus privilege the means-of-exchange and store-of-value functions of money. But neochartalists reject this story, and the emphasis on circulation and storage of value it implies, both on historical and logical grounds (see, esp., Innes 1913 for a classical statement; and Smithin 2000 for a recent synthesis). Money is a collective process, they argue, backed by an authority that establishes a system of accounting for value that all those who are subject to the authority then have to accept. The logic of this argument is that, much as we measure distance with reference to an abstract system (such as the metric system), and we do not expect it to vary depending on the specific ruler we use to measure it, we should define money by virtue of its abstract nature as a measure of value, not in terms of the actual forms it takes (Innes 1913).[1] The "primary concept of a Theory of Money" is money of account, to quote Keynes (1930: 1).

The emphasis on money as money-of-account naturally leads to questions about the authority that underlies it. In fact, if money arose out of simple convenience, that would imply that private agents agreed to a common standard of accounting for value: but why would they not privilege whatever good they were most endowed with instead (Ingham 1996)? Simmel provides a useful answer, one that neochartalists emphasize over the more cultural understandings of money as a leveler of social distinctions that I discussed briefly above. Simmel argues that money is "a bill of exchange from which the name of the drawee is lacking, or alternatively, which is guaranteed rather than accepted." Crucially, money is dependent on a "third factor [that] is introduced between the two parties [to an exchange]: the community as a whole, which provides real value corresponding to money." Money becomes "a relationship with the economic community that accepts the money"; money is thus "minted by its highest representative. This is the core truth in the theory that money is only a claim upon society" (Simmel 1990: 177).

Simmel, then, by pointing to the nature of money as a "claim upon society" in units of account set by its "highest representative," effectively introduces the role of a collective authority, rather than the spontaneous coordination of private actors, in the production of money. And he suggests none other than the modern state as the strongest expression of monetary authority. But the nature of that authority is more specific than what Simmel had in mind. It is, according to neochartalists, fiscal. This has important implications for a theory of money.

In this tax-centered view of monetary processes, the nature of modern money is "chartalist," to use Knapp's term (1924): it is a token claim to value whose unit of account and acceptability is enforced by the state through fiscal policy. What matters to money is that it is denominated in the monetary units prescribed by the state, or, as Keynes has it: "[M]oney-of-account is the *description* or *title* and the money is the *thing* which answers that description. . . . [The state] claims the right to declare *what thing* corresponds to the name" (1930: 4).[2] In modern capitalism, whatever currency the state will ask its citizens to pay taxes in, that currency will become money.

The neochartalist perspective as a consequence puts much emphasis on the fiscal origins of money, and the coercive aspects of revenue extraction. To be sure, the acceptance of legal tender can be enforced by the state's legal system—but it is ultimately the state's fiscal capacity that grounds the monetary system (a point clearly articulated by Knapp). Moreover, because the money issued by the state acquires liquidity within the political boundaries of the state, it also serves as a "reserve" for the private issue of monetary and nonmonetary instruments (Wray 1999). The money of the state thus becomes the most desirable and safest in a hierarchy of money because it is the currency that is most acceptable and most liquid (Bell 2001). The concentration of political authority in the hands of the state has historically led to the rise and institutionalization of national currencies as the dominant form of monetary exchange and, most important, of accounting for value (Ingham 1999, 2001, 2004, 2006).

In sum, to the extent that the state develops sufficient control and authority over its territory, and can impose taxes on its citizens, it determines in what unit of account prices will be denominated. The state "monetizes" social life through taxation, because through taxes it imposes an abstract system of accounting for value that private actors then come to rely upon for their private transactions as well. In this theoretical tradition, as a result, the specific characteristic of money is singled out in its serving as an abstract unit of account. Analysts thereby also privilege Simmel's criterion that for something to act as money, it must turn qualitative distinctions into quantitative ones. "By being the equivalent to all the manifold things in one and the same way, money becomes the most frightful leveller. Money, with all its colorlessness and indifference, becomes the common denominator of all values; irreparably it hollows out the core of things, their individuality, their specific value, and their incomparability. All things float with equal specific gravity in the constantly moving stream of money" (Simmel 1950: 414).

The New Monetary Controversies

As we just saw, since the publication of Zelizer's historical ethnography of the social meanings of money, sociologist Geoffrey Ingham's work on its political economy (1994), and the revival of the state-centered theory of money by heterodox economists (Wray 1990; B. J. Moore 1988), the study of money is on much firmer theoretical foundations. This new literature on money successfully transcends disciplinary distinctions and, more important, proposes a convincing historical and sociological account of the rise and workings of modern money. Yet the two main processes highlighted by the literature point in two different directions, so the potential for a more general theory remains untapped.

To reiterate: the first process is the rationalization of social and economic life brought about by the emergence of the modern state. The more reliable and durable the authority that guarantees money, in the neochartalist tradition that best exemplifies this line of theory, the more stable the money itself: hence, the centrality of the modern state to the monetary and financial system. The second process highlighted by the new literature of money is the differentiation of social and economic life brought about by the pervasiveness and resilience of social rituals: with modern capitalism, money may have spread into spheres of social life that, over long periods of human history, were sheltered from the market (Bohannan 1959); but individuals have negotiated this increasing commercialization by personalizing money itself (Zelizer 2001, 2005a, 2005b; Zelizer and Tilly 2006). Analysts of this second process see the individuals' ability to resist the kind of rationality intrinsic to money as the main aspect that makes it sociologically relevant. The development of more formalized kinds of money, then, is not understood to imply that social relations, once commercialized, will lose their meanings and context: money always comes to be invested with local significance in and of itself. This framework I have labeled the relational theory of money.

The chasm between the two camps, neochartalism and relational analysis, as a result, seems impossible to bridge. Where neochartalism sees the authority and power of the state, relational sociologists see the influence of bottom-up transactions; where neochartalists see taxes, relational sociologists see the importance of unofficial and informal circuits. Finally, where neochartalists emphasize the commensurability brought about by money, relational sociologists emphasize how social differences persist in the face of money.

Yet these disagreements are only on the surface about the fungibility money. Both neochartalists and relational analysts emphasize that social and political processes underlie the ability of money to function as a more or less *homogenizing* currency. Neither theory begins with the assumption that money has some intrinsic power to it to which the authority of the state or the relational processes of the circuits that use it are external. The disagreement between the two theories is about which level of analysis is most appropriate for an understanding of money.

As is often the case, one way out of this conundrum is the identification of an empirical problem common to both theories, a resolution of which points in a new direction. And in this particular case, the empirical problem should not involve the level of analysis privileged by either theory—it should in fact allow us to assess whether and how different levels of analysis interpenetrate in the production of a given phenomenon—namely, money.

One such problem is the stratification of financial instruments. The myth of fungible money, that is, loses its face-value persuasiveness once we realize that its main assumption about money—that money is homogenous—is violated as a matter of everyday practice in financial markets, where money is exchanged in the form of financial instruments. And attention to financial markets, furthermore, allows us to introduce both the characters that manage the complexity of money—the bankers—and the strategies they employ to do so, in particular the mobilization of the myth of banks as institutions of intermediation and the attendant myth of creditworthiness as objective assessment.

Financial Instruments as Markers of Exclusivity

Status groups, famously argued Weber, benefit from the systematic and exclusive appropriation of opportunities and resources, which they monopolize and redistribute among members of the group at the expense of outsiders. A status group is thus defined by a common orientation to and exploitation of an economic opportunity. Economists call it a monopolistic group to point to its control over a market. But the status group also has a common lifestyle and collective identity that marks members of the status group off from outsiders. Common lifestyle and exploitation of an economic opportunity, in fact, are not separate or mutually exclusive aspects of membership in a status group. Neither is common lifestyle simply a hedonistic pursuit. The lifestyle serves to create a boundary between members and outsiders, and also commits members of the group to a common identity (Barnes 1992). The boundary that defines membership in the group, importantly, is arbitrary (Weber 1978: 341–42), but is also consequential. The boundary commits members of a group to a distinctive lifestyle and a common, collective identity.

Commitment to a lifestyle serves to solve the tension that inevitably exists between the collective interests of a status group, and the individual interests of its members—the dilemma of collective action (Olson 1965). Members of a status group benefit individually from the appropriation of a resource based on the collective power of the group. So it is in their interest to transcend the collective requirements the group imposes on the mode of appropriation and push instead for individual appropriation. At an extreme, individual members may even push for the right to sell the means of appropriation of the resource on open markets—trading with individuals with whom they don't share membership in the status group, with insiders and outsiders alike. This bodes disaster for the status group. Open markets erode the source of the status group's privileged position; they open access to the very market opportunities status groups thrive on by closing them off to outsiders.

But if members of the status group value not merely the private, economic benefits deriving from the appropriation of the resource but also the social benefits they draw from membership in the status group—if the lifestyle and the forms of sociability they afford members of the status group are valued on their own terms, that is—members are now faced by a different kind of calculation. Appropriating advantages and opportunities *at the expense of* the group is no longer possible without suffering social consequences, consequences that can be very serious depending on how exclusive membership in the status group is. Social ostracism must now be weighed against personal enrichment.

Money contributes fundamentally to the lifestyle of the status group in at least two ways. First, and most obviously, money makes possible access to resources, and thus to consumption experiences, with which members of the status group can enforce the boundary against outsiders. Sociologists have appropriated the term "economic capital" to describe this function of money.

Money, however, is more than a means of personal enrichment and accumulation—even though, of course, it encourages both: it is also a token of membership in prestigious communities of investors in and of itself, because it comes in differentiated forms whose possession is stratified. The empirical reality of money is that it is exchanged in the form of financial instruments—stocks, bonds, junk bonds, credit default swaps, mortgages, commercial paper, and the like—with each instrument designed to be held by particular actors or organizations, and to be traded, often through the intermediation of yet other actors or organizations, in particular kinds of markets. In the two cases of the nineteenth-century United States and Italy, which I discuss at length below, having a relationship with a bank at all constituted a badge of elite status, signaling the debtor's membership in a larger financial community that enhanced his social status.

This view implies that the value of money cannot be assessed independently of its empirical differentiation, because specialized, elite actors—financial elites—use different classes of instruments for different purposes, which makes the question of value a structural one. We cannot answer this question without explicit reference to the practices by which financiers assign value. The value of an instrument, rather, depends on the prestige of the instrument itself, and this prestige is a product of the social processes through which financial elites consolidate and reproduce their power. Financial instruments are the glue that binds financial elites together. The differentiation of money serves to mark off social boundaries.

In the next chapter, I will argue that the tension between exclusivity and inclusion lies at the heart of money. Bankers must solve this tension for money to be stable. They must act as gatekeepers of "status groups," investing the possessors of particular "currencies" with the prestige of membership in the status group, and excluding others from such benefits. How central money is to the reproduction of status inequalities has always been clear to political movements invested in opening up economic opportunities to new social constituencies, as was the case with Andrew Jackson's populist attack against the system of government-authorized charters that regulated banking in the Northern states of the United States up until the mid-1800s. Bankers must be careful when dealing with individuals they consider speculators: under the right conditions, speculators can recast the austerity and conservatism of bankers in a very different light—as expressions of opportunity hoarding and discrimination.

Fungible money, in summary, turns out to be a mythical construct because financial instruments are differentiated, and because their differentiation depends on very real social distinctions. They work more like *devices* through which financial elites reproduce a common culture and life-style—in other words, membership in Weberian status groups—than like neutral means that facilitate real transactions. Sociability in the context of a prestigious group, because it facilitates both coordination and commitment to common objectives and a common identity (Barnes 1992; Tilly 1998), has very real consequences, to be sure. But the important point is that financial instruments are defined by the financial access and control they afford their holders; they respond to the logic of prestige and exclusion that characterizes high-status financial networks.

It is crucial in this respect to identify the social sources of the distinctions drawn by financial actors as they assign different financial instruments to different constituencies. In order to do so, we must confront two interrelated and mutually reinforcing myths: the myth of banking as intermediation, and the myth of objective creditworthiness. That is, without an understanding of the struggles that characterize the banking system, a theory of the unfungibility of money can be applied only to limited, relatively mundane or altogether unofficial monetary transactions. And without an understanding of the processes whereby judgments on the creditworthiness of debtors are made, financial relations can appear only as derivative of more fundamental *real* processes, rather than as central to the reproduction of economic conflict under capitalism.

The Myth of Banks as Institutions of Intermediation

What I call the myth of banks as institutions of intermediation is the idea that banks are neutral institutions whose spread produces a more efficient allocation of resources, because they connect savers to borrowers.

Given the assumption of fungible money that characterized classical socio-logical thought, sociologists paid relatively little attention to banks—with some notable but also rare exceptions (Carruthers 2011)[3]—thus leaving the field to political economists who, in turn, treated banks as essentially secondary to more fundamental processes of resource accumulation. Because of great variation in financial systems, a large literature focused, and disagreed, on what system is more economically efficient (Calomiris 1995; Fohlin 2007) at the expense of engaging directly with what bankers actually do.[4] Important exceptions exist within the economic camp too (Guinnane 2002), but in the main economists and scholars in political economy more generally tend to espouse a traditional view that bankers are specialists in *intermediation* (Diamond 1984; Allen and Gale 2000).[5]

A growing number of non-neoclassical economists, associated with the neochartalist tradition I discussed above, have taken issue with this intermediation-based view to emphasize instead that bankers incessantly create money through the lending process (Schumpeter 1911; Minsky 1986; B. J. Moore 1988), because money, as Ingham perceptively argues, is always a social relation of credit and debt (Ingham 1996). Money in technical terms is an ex nihilo accounting operation: it is a simultaneous act of crediting the account of the client (creating a liability for the bank) and crediting the bank for the amount of the loan (creating an asset for the bank), with some quantity of money set aside for prudential purposes (Innes 1914). Banks and only banks do this (something we return to in the next chapter). This point is very important to a more general theory of banking because it frees us from the assumption that bankers move piles of money, so to speak.

To illustrate this through a simple example, consider the following. By the principles of double-entry bookkeeping, a loan from a bank is noth-ing but an increase in the borrower's deposit with the bank in the amount of the loan itself, and thus an increase in the bank's assets, matched by an equivalent increase in the bank's liabilities, also by the amount of the loan. The fact that the bank has a reserve of money at hand (in its vaults) ready to be loaned, and the notion that a loan simply transfers money from savers to borrowers, are utterly fictional. Banks lend several times the amount they have in their deposits; and as Wray puts it, "[No] officer ever checks the bank's reserve position before approving a loan" (1999: 107). To be sure, bankers accumulate or borrow from other bankers safe and liquid assets—such as "base" or "reserve" money—that allow them to meet exceptional demand for cash, and in most systems are required to do so by law (contemporary Canada is a notable exception). Yet banks profit by *minimizing* their holdings of this reserve money that, by virtue of its safety, yields little to no interest—and this was recognized long ago (Bagehot 1920: 232). In nineteenth-century Italy, as was the case in several other nations where the gold standard was intermittently upheld, banks issued money upon authorization by the government, with the limits on the amount of banknotes in circulation only loosely connected to the amount of gold reserves they held. And with the advent of universal banks, commercial institutions that collected deposits and simultaneously dealt in industrial securities (Gerschenkron 1962; Verdier 2003), the very fact that deposits appeared to be financing stock market operations created vitriolic debates about the speculative nature of banking, a characterization resisted by bankers, as we shall see, who invoked their superior ability to direct resources into productive uses, and not the strength of their balance sheets, as a guarantee of the soundness of their operations.

Bankers, in short, are not constrained by existing stocks of money, capital, or deposits: they specialize in the creation of money. If they create money, attention must be paid to the criteria they employ in doing so, because the value of their loans will depend on how that money is employed in the future; and more important, on the capacity of bankers to guarantee that part of that future income flow will go into their coffers, rather than being pocketed (or reinvested) by their borrowers.[6]

This opens us two potential lines of inquiry. The first is an investigation of the conditions under which bankers cooperate with each other to realize value for their investment in the future. The political economy literature has long recognized that rival factions of bankers struggle with one another by attaching themselves to groups that have different economic interests, and that the outcome of those alliances affects the stability of the financial system and thus of money (De Cecco 1974, 1986; Arrighi 1994; Aglietta and Breton 2001). Industrialists usually demand cheap, flexible, and long-term credit instruments, while bankers tend to impose on them high-interest, strict, and short-term credit; it is, then, more speculative bankers that often come to the aid of industrialists, and do so by devising instruments with which they can break the hold mainstream bankers have on industrial financing (Ingham 1984; Davis and Mizruchi 1999; Verdier 2003). Which side prevails has important implications for the structure of the financial system: it determines, for instance, whether stock markets or large banks will be central; and it determines the degree of state involvement in the organization of credit (Zysman 1983).

At the international level, as Giovanni Arrighi (1994) has shown, building on Fernand Braudel's seminal work, world-capitalism witnesses cyclical shifts in the composition of the capitalist class: there is a cycle of material production, when money is invested in productive activities, such as trade or industry; and a cycle of financial expansion, when money is pulled out of production and invested in financial instruments themselves, as well as in other arenas that promote cultural distinction, such as the arts. At a certain point in this process, the only strategy that affords capitalists increasing returns becomes that of pulling money away from production altogether, recycling the profits that still flow from it into activities that are removed from production, such as financial exchange. By Arrighi's account, about half the history of world-capitalism cannot be understood in terms of linkages between production and finance, because in cycles of financial expansion, finance refocuses on itself to find outlets for its investments. Capitalism, in the long duree, is just as likely to be concentrated on financial exchange as it is on material production.

We can take this one step further. Because bankers always focus on financial outcomes, it is the dynamic of how bankers relate to each other that drives whether the banking system will compete with outside actors for the provision of credit (in what Arrighi calls financialization); or will remain in control of the credit process. Financialization, that is, may result when bankers are no longer able to monopolize the credit creation process because the producers they finance have established their own ways of financing themselves. To put it differently, it is the power that bankers exercise over other (potential) financial agents that determines how financial investments are managed and where financial flows are directed. The next chapter develops this argument at greater length.

For now, suffice it to say that the myth of neutral banking, in sum, turns out to be a myth because financial conflict appears to be the defining aspect of banking activities. If bankers do not depend directly on outside resources for the reproduction of their power, because their ability to accumulate resources is a result of their cohesion; and if status is a fundamental aspect of their cohesion because it backs the collective processes of appropriation—then a focus on the struggles among bankers should take priority over one on the alliances they make with outsiders. As Verdier (2003) has argued, we should move from a focus on the demand for credit to a focus on its supply—which, I might add, is endogenously created by the banking system (a step Verdier does not take).

The immediate objection to this argument is that there is a world out there the judgment of which gives bankers the ability to lend appropriately. This is the second line of inquiry opened up by the debunking of the myth of banks as institutions of intermediation. To this myth of creditworthiness we now turn.

The Myth of Creditworthiness

What I call the "myth of creditworthiness" is the idea that creditworthiness is a neutral and objective system, through which creditors assess whether borrowers can pay back the loans they owe. The myth is not so much in the specification of the problem—namely, that future uncertainty forces lenders to devise robust strategies to minimize losses and maximize gains. Rather, it is in the implication drawn from the problem, one that reduces creditworthiness to a search of objective, neutral means of assessing it. I touched upon some of the issues that relate to this problem in my discussion, above, of the myth of banks as institutions of intermediation. To reiterate the argument briefly, if the struggle among providers of credit, and the means by which that struggle is avoided or at least controlled, are both so central to money, concerns with efficiency can only be secondary to concerns with power. If money acquires value to the extent that it circulates in the form of instruments that only certain kinds of actors can hold and exchange, control over such circuits is crucial.

The idea that concerns with efficiency, especially in situations characterized by high uncertainty, are less crucial than concerns with legitimacy, is, of course, a classical theme in the neoinstitutional literature in sociology (Roy 1997; Fligstein 1990; DiMaggio and Powell 1983). But in the case of creditworthiness, an engagement with the critical literature on credit allocation practices reveals another dimension to the problem. Because of the injustices, discrimination, and predatory practices that often characterize lending, particularly when it concerns marginalized individual borrowers, the critical literature emphasizes that access to credit can be a source of inequality of its own. This literature tends to assume that there is one efficient, effective, objective way of allocating credit, and that deviations from it derive from noneconomic considerations.

It is undeniable that stigmatized identities (be they based on race,

gender, or religion) affect the likelihood of a client's getting credit independently of her objective ability to pay back the loan (for example, sufficient
income). (For contermporary analyses of mortgage markets, see Overby
1994; Swire 1995; Calder 1999; Gabriel and Rosenthal 2005.) In an earlier era
of banking, such as the eighteenth century in the United States, or the
seventeenth century in Britain (Carruthers 1996), partisan affiliation was
as crucial to the provision of credit. Yet current economic analyses limit
their focus on the utilitarian and pragmatic aspects of credit discrimination, and so write about discriminatory practices (without necessarily
including in their discussion discrimination on the basis of ascribed attributes) as (dysfunctional) responses to market failures (as in the concept
of "statistical discrimination," Bielby and Baron [1986]), which in the case
of credit refer specifically to the presence of informational asymmetries
(Stiglitz 2011). Or they compartmentalize the problem by attributing discrimination exclusively to nonmarket forces (for example, preferences),
adding that the institutional setting makes those forces more or less relevant to any given decision (see, for example, Kyriacou 2005). Blanchflower,
Levine, and Zimmerman (2003: 930) are typical in this respect: "Discrimination occurs whenever the terms of a transaction are affected by personal
characteristics of the participants that are not relevant to the transaction.
In credit markets, discrimination on the basis of race and/or gender exist
if loan approval rates or interest rates charged differ across groups with
equal ability to repay."

Economists, then, tend to reduce discrimination to instances where
"personal characteristics" impinge upon what should be "neutral" and
"objective" transactions. The focus is self-consciously on the individual
and his/her attributes. Collective processes of appropriation of resources
and opportunities are by definition left out of the analysis.

This cannot be said about a second, relational approach to discrimination that finds in Tilly (1998) its most sophisticated statement. Here the
very boundary between *economic* (information-based) and *noneconomic*
(prejudice-based) discrimination dissolves because the nature and dynamics of the economic process itself are conceptualized differently. Instead of
putting individuals at the center of the model, and considering advantages
(or disadvantages) accruing to individuals on the basis of some ascribed
category as an aberration, Tilly argues that economic benefits are always
distributed on the basis of group membership. And because his focus is on
the sources of durable inequality, Tilly also argues that the main mecha-

nism whereby discrimination is reproduced is organizational adoption of bounded categories (for example, male/female, white/nonwhite, Christian/non-Christian) as the grounds on which to parse out the benefits of membership in the organization.

Tilly does not extend his approach to durable inequality to the context of credit markets. A difficulty immediately resulting from such an attempt would be that the boundaries that credit institutions draw around the instruments they produce are likely to be more endogenous to the credit field itself than are the boundaries drawn by organizations when, say, they decide whom to employ. That is to say, boundaries based on categorical identities become less salient the further one moves toward the core of financial markets, where identity takes more localized meanings. For instance, the corporate raiders who precipitated the 1980s U.S. merger movement, though outsiders to the WASP financial elite of Wall Street by virtue of their ethnicity (some, for instance, were Jewish) or geographic provenance (some were Southerners), consolidated their reputation as deviant innovators because of the practices they carried out, and particularly because of an alliance with Michael Milken that crystallized through the use of "junk bonds" for hostile takeovers (Stearns and Allan 1996). They were subsequently expelled from the financial elite on such a basis. A focus on durable inequalities in the context of struggles for credit, then, may be somewhat limited when it comes to explaining processes that are removed from the public eye, and thus do not carry the same costs and benefits as the more visible discriminatory practices that nonfinancial actors and organizations engage in.[7] As we shall see, the connection between outside categories, and the categories through which access to credit was regulated, was much tighter in the nineteenth century, when debates about banking were often, simultaneously, debates about how to organize the polity.

Nevertheless, the relational approach to inequality helps us illuminate important aspects of finance. If credit is disbursed in the form of differentiated financial instruments as a result of conflicts between contrasting strategies, inequality is built into the very nature of capitalist money and is necessarily a constitutive aspect of financial markets, not an aberration. From this necessarily follows that the criteria by which credit is assigned are *political:* whether loans, stocks and bonds, and the whole gamut of financial instruments are granted to particular groups depends on the balance of power that obtains within financial markets, not on some intrinsic reliability or creditworthiness of their clients. In the nineteenth-century

United States, political elites and social movements went one step further, struggling to gain the right not only to handle financial instruments from which they had been excluded but also to set up their own banks: this was the case especially in the North, where banking was more democratized than in the South, and thus the process of further opening it up to new constituencies faced less resistance. In nineteenth-century Italy (and other cases as well; see Ingham 1984), the struggle over what industries should have access to what kinds of financing was similarly understood as a political struggle, not one about the efficient allocation of credit.

The idea that credit is allocated to those who deserve it, or what I call the "myth of creditworthiness," in short, must be challenged. This also means that we must consider the banking system a source of inequalities independent of other systems of stratification. And to do this, finally, we must move conflicting banking groups to the center of our understanding of money.

The Road Ahead

The three myths I have discussed above—fungible money, neutral banking, and creditworthiness—must be considered three aspects of the same underlying problem before the centrality of financial conflict to capitalism can be recognized. To be sure, since Zelizer's ethnography of multiple monies, the myth of money's fungibility has been debunked, but only for certain kinds of currencies, and without a systematic treatment of how differentiation impacts the larger financial system. Thus neochartalists like Ingham make a strong case against the importance and even relevance of what they consider privately issued quasi-money to the analysis of money in general. Only if one understands that such quasi-moneys, especially when produced within the financial system, increase overall instability because they circulate among new constituencies, and constitute a threat to established ways of doing banking, then their importance and relevance to finance in general can no longer be underestimated, and processes of monetary differentiation become crucial.

Similarly, if banks are considered neutral institutions, charged with the primary task of moving money from regions where it is plentiful to regions where it is scarce—independently of the analysts' ideological position on the desirability of so-called financial development, the role banks play in it is inevitably misunderstood. Banks become secondary to other

TABLE 1.1

Mainstream and Financial Conflict Views of Credit Allocation

Mainstream View	Finance as Organized Conflict View
• Banker screens the client to assess the likelihood that the debt will be paid back.	• Depending on the prestige of the client, the banker devises appropriate credit and financial instruments.
• Criteria of creditworthiness must be discerning, exacting, and objective.	• Criteria of creditworthiness sustain the prestige hierarchy of both clients and bankers.
• Certain criteria of creditworthiness are functional to a healthy financial system.	• Criteria are contested by less prestigious bankers in search of clients; they are undermined as prestigious actors begin selling the instruments in their possession to less prestigious actors.
• Money is homogenous.	• Money is stratified.

processes, and the centrality of money to capitalism is as a result down-played. But just as heterodox economists insist that money cannot be neutral, so too we should insist that banks cannot be neutral. Debunking the myth of banking as the business of intermediation means understanding how centrally implicated are conflicts among different banking factions in the valuation and circulation of financial instruments.

Finally, an argument about prestige and power radiating from financial markets and acting as sources of financial value would be incomplete without a serious engagement with another widespread assumption about credit—that its stratifying effects are the result of an imperfect application of market principles rather than a necessary result of its inner logic. But this myth of creditworthiness is as analytically misleading as the myth of fungible money and intermediatory banking. Rather, I suggest that judgments of creditworthiness be considered as political, by which I mean, as implicated in the constitution of financial circuits where shared instruments and shared practices and understandings of how those instruments should be used increase the status of the circuit, its exclusivity, and thus its potential ability to command opportunities and resources.

Table 1.1 schematizes the financial conflict view on credit that I develop in the rest of the book. The table highlights in what ways considerations of prestige are constitutive of financial relations; how central hierarchy and stratification are to the credit process; and finally, how inherently dynamic the credit process is due to the varying porosity (or permeability) of the boundaries constructed around different financial instruments.

In summary, I propose that the value of money be understood in terms of the *social experience and the social recognition* afforded by wielding money in a particular form. An analysis of money, then, must begin with the social arenas in which the possession of particular instruments acquires relevance and value: financial markets. And because bankers are the specialized actors who create money in the process of lending, and as a result occupy a dominant position in financial markets, the experience of wielding money is patterned by the structural and cultural cohesion of the banking system. It is to these *proximate* processes that allow money to be reproduced over time as a network of instruments more or less tightly linked to each other that this book pays attention.[8]

A narrow focus on the state, along the lines of neochartalism, would inevitably "black-box" the mechanisms that determine if and the extent to which money will be differentiated; and second, it would ignore whether and the extent to which that differentiation will threaten the stability of the financial system as a whole.[9] By the same token, analyses that take for granted the differentiation of money ignore the mechanisms that under certain conditions turn money into a more homogenous instrument. The monetary forms and financial instruments through which money circulates do not, in fact, emerge at random, nor do they all have the same degree of acceptability and facility to be converted into other instruments (that is, the same liquidity). Ultimately, just as the state involves itself in the day-to-day operations of credit markets to ensure the smooth circulation of its currency, users of more localized instruments also turn to credit markets to endow their instruments with more general circulation. This suggests that it is from credit markets that an analysis of money must begin. Credit markets (or, as I explain in the following chapter, *financial fields*) are the black box we need to unpack in order to understand how and to what extent money is differentiated (see Figure 1).

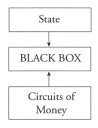

Fig. 1.1. Credit Markets as Black Box

2

Banking and Finance as Organized Conflict

AS WE SAW in the previous chapter, the myths of fungible money, of banks as institutions of intermediation, and of objective creditworthiness are not neutral. Yet they paint a portrait of an economic reality "out there" that financial activities allegedly reflect (see Knorr Cetina and Bruegger 2002; MacKenzie 2006). The myths allow financial actors to blame any problem arising from financial activities on errors in judgment, misaligned incentives, or in some cases, excessive regulation. These myths, in other words, constitute the categories of practice through which financial actors strive to legitimize their behavior, while supporting a functionalist approach to finance. They deflect attention away from the investigation of finance as a social process with dynamics of its own.

Such functionalist stories miss the collective action problems into which financial communities inevitably run when they organize for the appropriation of resources. Thus they downplay the importance of politics to the organization of status groups. But, as argued by Simmel, a strong proponent of the myth of fungible money, no individual can be entrusted with producing a *medium of exchange* that will be accepted by all: a currency is a token of membership in the financial community. It will be accepted only to the extent that a financial community secures it. Exchanging money, as well as more specific financial instruments, is a means of building solidarity at the group level with those who possess similar instruments. But financial instruments and money are also means of personal appropriation, often at the expense of whatever group one belongs to. Two questions are particularly relevant: what logic should *govern* financial exchange and circulation? How should the boundaries of a financial community be patrolled, so that outsiders will not subvert the *meanings* invested in the currency, and threaten the collective basis upon which a status group/circuit is based?

In this chapter, I provide a framework that replaces the three myths surrounding money, credit, and banking with a more sociologically sound set of concepts. This alternative view entails a shift from methodological individualism to a group-level perspective; and an attendant shift from the demand for credit to its supply, and more specifically, to the practices whereby demand for and supply of financial instruments constitute, support, and balance each other. These practices are characterized by a collective action problem: how the circulation of a financial instrument— whether restricted to specific, exclusive groups, or widely exchanged with little regard as to the identity of the traders—influences a group's ability to appropriate resources collectively. Financial actors and organizations manage this tension between individual and collective uses of instruments by specializing in different strategies. By embracing conservative banking, they draw strict boundaries around those who are deserving of credit, and those who are not, and police them through ideologies of sound money. By embracing "wildcat banking," by contrast, they specialize in transgressing the boundaries set by the conservatives, often in the name of expansion and financial democracy. In the previous chapter I made several references to Max Weber's sociology of status groups in this regard, and this chapter systematizes these observations by building a neo-Weberian theory of financial conflict. After delineating the dynamics internal to the field of finance, I proceed to consider how the larger political context may affect them.

From Economic Community to Circuit

We have discussed Simmel's theory of money in the context of a larger analysis of state-centered theories (neochartalism). It is now appropriate to return to Simmel in order to highlight one important inconsistency in his argument, an inconsistency that opens the door for a new theory of financial conflict. This is the inconsistency between Simmel's conceptualization of money as an equalizer or leveler of distinctions, and money as a token of membership in an economic community.

On the one hand, Simmel understands money to be a leveler of social distinctions, and as a result a tool of incommensurability and cold rationality. Some of his most famous statements on the "colorlessness" and "lack of gravity" of money, and on the "emptying out" of social relations by the monetary medium, are drawn from this part of his discussion (see, esp., his essay "Metropolis and the Mental Life," in Simmel 1950). On the other hand, because he is aware of the momentous social transformations that underlie the development of money, Simmel also emphasizes how money has to be backed by an authoritative economic community, so that users of a currency can rid themselves of the responsibility to guarantee its acceptability, and rely instead on the economic community, which functions as a third party. Simmel (1990: 177) writes:

The abstraction of the process of exchange from specific real exchanges, and its embodiment in a distinctive form, can happen only if exchange has become something other than a private process between two individuals which is confined to individual actions. This new and broader character of exchange is established when the value of exchange given by one party has no direct value for the other party, but is merely a claim upon other definite values; a claim whose realization depends upon the economic community as a whole or upon the government as its representative.

The contradiction between the two views is that the economic community, while certainly contributing to certain social distinctions and "private processes" that are irrelevant to the exchange at hand, also adds distinctions and processes of its own. Put differently, social relations seem to disappear from Simmel's *phenomenology* of money, only to return in his *sociology*. As we saw earlier, when financial instruments are exchanged, the fact that they are ultimately denominated in a national currency, and thus guaranteed by a national economic community, is a necessary but not sufficient condition for their acceptability. Rather, instruments are exchanged and accepted because they give exclusive access to particular resources, both material and symbolic, that those who do not hold that specific financial instrument are denied. Therefore, within the larger economic community represented by the government, several other economic communities can coexist and thrive—some smaller, some larger than the national community. In nineteenth-century Italy and the United States (and in a host of other countries as well), the problem of who should be allowed to issue currency, and in what form, was contentious not simply because bankers, and the new financial instruments they produced (such as checks) were still unfamiliar to most people, but also because there was widespread mistrust in the government's ability to serve the public interest. In cases in which the national community was weak, the fact that non-national communities backed the acceptability of differentiated financial instruments was comforting. While making certain *personal* characteristics of those who exchange money irrelevant, as Simmel has it, a currency simultaneously makes other *social* characteristics highly relevant to an exchange. Possession signals social membership in the community where a currency is issued and accepted; the money itself serves as a social marker.[1]

A focus on the collective determinants of money reveals a similarity between Simmel's theory of money and Viviana Zelizer's that is worth pointing out. Simmel connects the kind of trust, underlying the exchange and acceptance of money, to the guarantees an economic community provides for it. He goes on to idealize the general-purpose nature of money, using it as a prism to understand money in general. Zelizer begins from similar premises: she writes of money as a token of exchange that circulates only within circuits—once those circuits have established a set of meanings and earmarks for its uses. But then she treats the emergence of more general currencies as a contingent, and relatively infrequent, accomplishment: her ethnographies of the uses of money show precisely how powerful and pervasive the forces of differentiation and personalization of money can be. These theoretical differences can be reconciled by drawing a parallel between Zelizer's concept of the circuit and Simmel's term, the economic community.

The concept of the circuit points to several sources of money's acceptability and circulation that Simmel unnecessarily conflates, but that are not inconsistent with his general theoretical approach. Zelizer emphasizes meaningful social relations in setting up boundaries between insiders and outsiders; the emergence of abstract systems of accounting for value; and the creation of specific, "earmarked" media of exchange as implicated in the constitution of commercial relations. Zelizer's insight (2005a) that a more fluid organizational form—the circuit—characterizes monetary exchange significantly improves upon Simmel's rigid "economic community." We see convergence in Zelizer's and Simmel's approaches to money once we recognize the social processes that invest money, in the form of specific, differentiated financial instruments, with the power to signal membership.

Pointing to this convergence may also be particularly useful because it introduces a dynamic, if not *dialectical* aspect to the analysis. Here, it is

Simmel who recognizes and best articulates this point. Simmel sees that, once the economic community/circuit develops the power to make its currency acceptable, with the state serving as the ultimate guarantor, the individual holders of the currency gain enormous social power. In addition to the wealth already under their control, they become entitled to the future stream of revenue that other members of the community help to generate; the instrument, that is, reinforces the community and its collective ability to appropriate resources. As it circulates, the instrument also reinforces the sense of membership among members of the community. It thereby tightens the boundaries that define social belonging in the community, it increases commitment of the members to one another, and it reinforces mutual understandings about appropriate and inappropriate uses of the instrument among circuit members. What Simmel emphasizes more than Zelizer is that no circuit will command the kind of commitment necessary to enforce such earmarks once and for all. More specifically, as individuals become involved in multiple circuits, the commitment requested by each circuit may lose some of its binding power; commitments may even turn out to be incompatible with each other, forcing the individual to devise new strategies to accommodate them, or prioritize among them.

While Zelizer focuses on intergroup struggles over the meaning of money, then, Simmel alerts us to the contrasting pressures that bear upon individual users of money within any given circuit. This is the dialectical aspect of money: the more it serves as a marker of membership in a prestigious circuit, the more it becomes subject to contestation and conflict because membership in the circuit, and the boundaries erected to delineate it, require more intense commitment. But the individual members of the community are simultaneously less willing to extend this commitment, and find it more advantageous, at least potentially, to break those boundaries and trade with nonmembers.

Now, let us return to Max Weber, and in particular his writings on status groups (Weber 1978: 306; 341–43), to understand that individuals can use an instrument in ways that clash with the collective conditions that guarantee the money's acceptability and stability. But those private uses can, over time, generate new collective practices, earmarks, and circuits. There is no good reason why an instrument, once removed from the circuit that originated it, should not be subjected to new processes of earmarking. To put it in Weber's terms, we should not confuse the exhaustion of a *process* of status-group formation and monopolization of resources with the exhaustion of the *strategy* of status-group formation and monopoliza-tion as a whole. Rather, the status groups are dynamic: the weakening of one status group may set the stage for the formation of a new one, with the instrument originally devised to sustain the former being retrofitted to sustain the new status group (Collins 1986: esp. 137–40).

This is, then, to say that the problem of individual appropriation of social power that is guaranteed by the status-group's backing of a currency (or instrument) is also a recurrent issue. It is the classic Weberian problem of the closed economic group: as success of the group becomes evident, its members find it personally advantageous to exchange tokens of member-ship in open markets, but by doing so they also, simultaneously, undercut the collective basis upon which they appropriate resources to begin with. The status group, then, must devise ways to recapture the commitment of its members.

In the case of money, focusing on the "specialized circuits inhabited by persons whose social motivation is to promote local solidarity while invidiously excluding or dominating others," at the expense of the "wide-ranging networks that underlie the colorless, neutral monies of econom-ic utilitarianism" (Collins 1995: 74), can be only half the story. Money is potentially transcendental; under certain conditions, however, money reinforces, even creates, distinctions. We need to take the further step of theorizing whether, how, and under what conditions the potentially disag-gregating forces generated by such collective endeavors find organizational outlets. We need a theory, that is, of the agents who specialize in subvert-ing the boundaries set up by established status groups (see Tilly 2005 for a related discussion of de-democratization).

From Producers Markets to Financial Markets

The problems revealed by a reading of Zelizer, with Simmel's and Weber's frameworks as a backdrop, are not unfamiliar to economic so-ciology. They are the problem of theorizing how members of the status group impose boundaries on economic exchange, so as to avoid competi-tive pressure; the problem of illuminating how competitors build niches in the context of open markets; and the final, complementary problem of theorizing how competing social groups organize themselves to chal-lenge those boundaries and distinctions. Zelizer and Simmel, to be sure, do not set this final task to themselves: their focus remains on processes of exchange. And, insofar as Simmel theorizes the boundary-transgressive qualities of money, he does so only at the level of individual users. The organizations that are explicitly invested in policing the boundaries that regulate the circulation of these financial instruments remain out of focus. In other words, neither Simmel nor Zelizer probes the structural sources of monetary circuits.

For this, we need to step into "financial markets," for which a loose definition will suffice. Financial markets may be seen not as specific institutional arenas (such as the stock or futures exchange) but rather as "organizational fields"—namely, the sum total of financial transactions between the "producer" and the "user" of any given currency, ranging from a private credit line from a bank ("producer") to its customer ("user") to the sale of government bonds (with the government/treasury as "producer") in open auctions (with authorized buyers as "users"). This expansive definition of financial markets serves to focus attention on the variable identities of both producers and issuers, and thus on the boundaries erected around the circulation of the currency, as well as on the variable identities of those who control exchanges across those boundaries.[2] To put it somewhat differently: by understanding financial markets as fields, we can focus on the mechanisms that structure the social experience and the social recognition of wielding money in a particular form.

Understanding financial markets as fields allows us to see not only that financial instruments are differentiated but also that differentiation has social significance. Each financial issuer produces differentiated financial products that it allows certain clients, and not others, to hold. Each financial issuer, moreover, differentiates itself from others in terms of prestige (Podolny 1993). Each financial issuer, in other words, constructs its identity in terms of the kinds of services it provides, the kind of clientele it serves, and the kind of clientele it excludes. In financial markets, issuers of financial instruments both monitor each other and exert control over access to financial instruments; they struggle to define both what actors and strategies can be legitimately employed within the field, and what actors and strategies are to be deemed inappropriate. Financial instruments thereby become specialized social experiences—they are "produced" in the particular sense of being earmarked and then exchanged in specialized arenas, where financial actors who recognize each other as legitimate incumbents meet and communicate, and where they invest those financial instruments with meanings so as to signal membership and prestige.

One example, taken from studies of the historical sociology of the Chicago Board of Exchange (MacKenzie 2006; MacKenzie and Millo 2003), may help illustrate this process. In the 1960s, when the idea began to circulate in academic and financial circles that a market for derivatives would revitalize financial markets, a group of capitalists (Edmund O'Connor, Irwin Eisen, Patrick Hennessy, David Goldberg, and Paul McGuire, among others) undertook a strenuous lobbying effort to set up such a market. They understood the new derivatives exchange to be a public good, but why then, asks MacKenzie, did any of them dedicate any time to this pursuit, rather than free-riding on the efforts of others? MacKenzie explicitly argues that the financial community worked like a status group: proponents of the Chicago Board of Exchange knew each other as traders on the Chicago Board of Trade, where they had long interacted and where they had built their reputations. Those mutual commitments bound them to a collective project from which they stood to benefit privately, to be sure, but only after incurring great costs. Ironically, another contributor, Leo Melamed, even "cited the influence of his father, a socialist and Bundist, who taught him to 'work for society as a whole. My father had instilled in me [the] idea that you gain immortality by tying yourself up with an idea, or a movement, or an institution that transcends mortality.'" Another capitalist, Irwin Eisen, reiterated, "'You owe it to your community.' We had all done very nicely, thank you, and we felt that we had an obligation to the Exchange and this is how you pay your obligations" (MacKenzie and Millo 2003: 116). These are, in short, collective processes at work.

Another, more counterintuitive example comes from my later discussion of the Italian case. In the first decade of the twentieth century, the Italian banking system was dominated by two large, so-called universal banks that certain political and industrial elites considered opposed to their interests. The fact that universal banks had several branches, which collected deposits, throughout the Italian territory, but also supported industry by procuring financial resources on the stock market, made them the target of vitriolic criticism: were they speculating on the wealth of ordinary citizens? Rather than criticizing the credit and financial practices of the universal banks on the basis of economic arguments, however, the elites that opposed them mobilized nationalist arguments—because nationalism was a growing political movement in that period, and carried a kind of collective prestige that technical arguments could not match. To be sure, the universal banks had been financed through the inflow of German capital in the 1890s, and thus invited such criticism; but the banks of the elites who opposed them were themselves the product of international finance (in their case, mostly French) (Della Loggia 1970; Falchero 1981). Nationalism allowed rival financial elites to couch their quest for power within the demands of a larger, moralized community. Through nationalism, the boundaries of the financial field could be redrawn in ways that not only served but also helped *define* the collective interests of challenging elites.

Understanding the stratification of credit markets in terms of the collective processes whereby financial communities are constituted and reproduced over time as status groups sets the ground for a theory of the agents invested in the production, distribution, and control of financial instruments. But we are now in a position to be more specific, and to focus on the agents who have a primary role in this process—namely, bankers.

From Financial Markets to Bankers

Bankers control the forms in which monetary transactions take place: as Schumpeter puts it in his *Theory of Economic Development*, in the capitalist system, the most important "method of obtaining money [is through] the creation of purchasing power by banks."

It is always a question, not of transforming purchasing power which already exists in someone's possession, but of the creation of new purchasing power out of nothing— out of nothing even if the credit contract by which the new purchasing power is created is supported by securities which are not themselves circulating media—which is added to the existing circulation. And this is the source from which new combinations are often financed, and from which they would have to be financed always, if results of previous development did not actually exist at any moment. (1911: 73)

Bankers, in other words, control not only the allocation of credit, as exclusively intermediary institutions also do: they control its creation. One of the reasons that banks tend to be central to financial systems is that they are particularly good at turning to their advantage the collective dilemmas intrinsic to finance.

The fact that banks create money by claiming a share of the revenue their financing will help generate has several important implications. These are what Schumpeter refers to as the "results of previous development"—results that, once realized, can be reinvested or, more important, appropriated by the bankers in remuneration for their services. For this reason bankers, as Schumpeter puts it, must have authority, in the sense of being selective in terms of whom they lend money to. They must not be easily impressed by empty promises, resisting grandiose claims by entrepreneurs, especially if they are not convinced that these plans can be realized in some near future. (Schumpeter, in fact, does not draw a sharp distinction between political entrepreneurs and private ones; the more important distinction is between bankers and entrepreneurs.) Schumpeter, then, recognizes a *conservative* stance among bankers, in the face of entrepreneurial demands for credit, as desirable and functional to the smooth working of the financial system—a point to which I shall return in a moment. Simultaneously, Schumpeter shifts our attention from the view that the allocation of credit is an exercise of rational calculation—as if financing was a matter of deciding how to allocate limited resources—to the alternative view that the construction and negotiation of creditworthy categories are preconditions for the allocation of credit.

Crucial to success in banking, Schumpeter argues, is a banker's willingness to deny credit to those who he/she thinks of as undeserving. Just as important is that bankers design appropriate instruments to finance appropriate undertakings, so that they can exercise control. Financing, that is, entails shared expectations that commit the borrower to a given course of action; and most important, that inform the borrower as to how the instrument should be used, and whether and under what terms it can be exchanged for other instruments.

The unit of analysis in Schumpeter's scheme seems to be the individual, but in light of my previous discussion, it can be easily inferred that individual bankers will have little power or influence over their individual customers without the financial field backing up those decisions. Control then, has to be a collective achievement within the field. When bankers organize into groups, they can more easily and efficiently erect boundaries around the circulation and exchange of instruments, as well as enforce shared expectations about the uses of those instruments. Most important, bankers can commit one another to respecting the "earmarks" they develop around those instruments. This is the kind of work that sound banking principles do.

Internal Sources of Sound Banking

What is sound banking? Read through the lenses of the myth of banking as the mobilization of resources, and its attendant myth of creditworthiness, the term "sound banking" suggests a set of neutral criteria and practices aimed at adjudicating between efficient, productive, and non-speculative uses of financial resources, and inefficient, unproductive, and speculative ones. Sound banking principles, abstracted from their socio-political context, could be easily understood as the rules and regulations that relevant actors develop in order to stabilize the business of banking and ensure it follows ethical standards.

I submit that the importance of sound banking principles lies elsewhere. It lies in the work that bankers do to enforce shared understandings of what uses are appropriate for financial instruments, thus creating shared, collective commitments. Because sound banking principles are devices to create collective commitments, their power, moreover, cannot be taken for granted: it does not derive from the intrinsic quality of the principles. Rather, sound banking principles must change how bankers understand and act upon interest. They must command loyalty, solidarity, attachment: they must, in short, generate the kind of collective energy that those who subscribe to sound banking come to value in its own terms. The effectiveness of sound banking principles is not a result of how well they fit an economic reality; rather, as political compromises among potentially rival banking factions, the primary goal of sound banking principles is to stifle the emergence of alternative sources of credit, or uses of credit (that has already been issued) that do not correspond to the creditor's intents. They do so insofar as the principles help to create constituencies that are committed to sound banking.

Just as we used an expansive definition of financial markets, let us also use an expansive definition of sound banking principles, one that focuses not on narrow rules and regulations, such as, say, those dictating how much capital any given bank should set aside to back its outstanding loans (that is, reserve requirements), or what indicators should be used to gauge the viability and profitability of any given financial investment. Rather, let us think of sound banking principles as the frames, scripts, and rules that constitute the "political culture" of stable banking fields (see, esp., Fligstein 1996, 2001a, 2001b). Under this guise, they would include the rules of thumb and tacit practices that bankers have historically been loath to disclose, but that form a central aspect of their business—perhaps even more so than in professions where the materiality of what they produce, and the less ambiguous status of the services they provide, serve as ready justifications of the legitimacy of the field (Ferguson 1999). By agreeing to conceptualize sound banking principles as frames, scripts, and rules (formal and informal), we focus attention not only on how interactions between insiders or issuers of instruments (bankers) and outsiders or users of instruments (borrowers, debtors) are regulated, but also on how interactions among insiders are stabilized; and on the potential contradictions that may emerge to challenge this status quo.

Sound banking principles, in short, can be conceptualized as the means whereby financial stability is ensured and reproduced. They both entail control over the ways that the currencies/financial instruments bankers produce are used, and, more directly, they specify what kinds of institutions will be accepted into the financial field by banks that already occupy a dominant position within it. Sound banking principles are crucial to the workings of the banking system because they justify certain practices of credit allocation, while impeding others; they stabilize relations among financial firms; and, ultimately, they create boundaries between insiders and outsiders, between deserving producers and users of a given set of "currencies" or financial instruments and undeserving ones—such as speculators or unsophisticated victims of financial predators. Whether, and the extent to which, sound banking principles support the social relations that tie bankers to one another also determines the durability and stability of financial arrangements.[3]

Not by virtue of their specific content, but by virtue of the collective effervescence and the moral solidarity, sound banking principles help bankers to delineate the boundaries of the financial field. They help bankers sort out the thorny issues of where to draw the line between creditworthy and undeserving borrowers. But just as important, they rally the collective prestige of the banking system to justify individual decisions of credit allocation, and rally potentially rival firms to respect the spirit of those decisions. Insofar as the loan remains within the banking circuit, the earmarks that sound banking principles attach to it help the creditor control how that loan subsequently circulates. It is once again in Schumpeter, as I mentioned, that the disciplinary aspects of such a logic are explicitly developed, so to Schumpeter's argument I now return.

Having drawn his famous distinction between the "circular flow"—

the normal state of the economy in which resources are being constantly committed to specific uses and routines—and economic development, Schumpeter focuses on the peculiar role of bankers in this process. Then, after pointing to the centrality of the banking system to capitalism, Schumpeter argues that bankers must retain some distance from the entrepreneurs they finance because of the importance of impartiality in their judgments. And after recognizing the "critical, checking, admonitory function" (1939: 118) with respect to credit exercised by the banker, Schumpeter quickly goes on to discuss the basis for the detachment between entrepreneurs and financiers:

> The banker must not only know what the transaction is which he is asked to finance and how it is likely to turn out, but he must also know the customer, his business, and even his private habits, and get, by frequently "talking things" over with him, a clear picture of his situation. (1939: 116)

This is the essence of sound banking, argues Schumpeter. Conservative bankers use intrusive screening practices; they inspect the customer, probe the soundness of the customer's judgment, assess the credibility and viability of the customer's propositions. This is not a one-time decision, as bankers continue exercising this admonitory function "from the cradle to the grave," as Gerschenkron (1962) had it in his description of the German banking system.

Schumpeter, though, excessively relies on an individualistic framework here. The individual banker is powerless if the customer can simply use the loan just received as collateral for further loans from other bankers. The system as a whole, rather, must be drawn into the credit relation. Individual bankers must rely on each other to ensure that whatever money they allocate to outsiders will not be used for purposes they did not envision. They of course cannot control how the money will be spent: but they can regulate the terms upon which borrowers will be allowed to continue their long-term financial relations. Schumpeter recognizes this collective aspect of credit, if only with some lack of precision. He adds that the impartiality of bankers in assessing business propositions cannot be simply a function of superior knowledge. Rather, it flows from what he defines as "intellectual and moral qualities" that the banking profession as a whole must nurture within its own ranks. These intellectual and moral qualities represent a "very high mark" that bankers violate not only at their own peril but also with deleterious outcomes for society as a whole.

In the case of bankers . . . failure to be up to what is a very high mark interferes with the working of the system as a whole. Moreover, bankers may at some times and in some countries, fail to be up to the mark corporatively: that is to say, tradition and standards may be absent to such a degree that practically anyone, however lacking in aptitude and training, can drift into the banking business, find customers, and deal with them according to his own ideas. In such countries and times, wildcat banking—incidentally, also wildcat theory about banking—develops. This in itself—whatever the legal rules about collateral and so on may be—is sufficient to turn the history of capitalist evolution into a history of catastrophes. (Schumpeter 1939: 117)

By discussing the negative case of sound banking, or what he calls "wildcat banking," Schumpeter better delineates the kinds of processes he sees as characteristic of "traditional" or *conservative* banking. Conservative bankers apply sound banking traditions that lead them to thoroughly inquire about the nature of what is being financed, with an eye to control the circuit thereby created. Wildcat bankers are more cavalier in their financing decisions. To the conservatism of sound bankers, they oppose a vision of financial innovation and expansion. Schumpeter's analysis thus shifts to the systemic level: sound banking is a moral aspect of banking that characterizes the profession as a whole, whose impact can be best recognized when the system lacks it. This distinction between "sound" or "conservative" banking and "speculative" or "wildcat" banking, to use Schumpeter's terms, shifts from an individualistic reading—as if it were merely the result of differences in how bankers go about financing outsiders—to a deeper one that emphasizes collective action.

Closer attention to Schumpeter's description of the tension between banking conservatism and wildcat banking reveals a dynamic aspect to the business of banking. Schumpeter's insight is that cultural forms and moral solidarity enable conservative bankers to exercise dominance within the banking system, noting that both cultural forms and moral solidarity are levers to control *access* to the banking system—namely, to impede a situation in which "practically anyone, however lacking in aptitude and training, can drift into the banking business, find customers, and deal with them according to his own ideas." This becomes particularly evident in times of trouble, when banks, by virtue of their ongoing relationships with one another, are more likely to support other banks than they are nonfinancial institutions. For instance, the 1907 financial crisis in the United States was precipitated by the failure of the Knickerbocker Trust

Company, a financial institution (though an unregulated one) that could not rely on clearinghouse privileges available to banks. J. P. Morgan had to personally step in to alleviate the crisis, impressing upon fellow bankers the urgency of the situation and thus persuading them to commit financial resources toward emergency credit channels (Bruner and Carr 2009).

Conservative banking—banking based on sound banking principles—refers not merely to good or better ways of doing banking, but to the ability to construct different kinds of experiences around the uses of different kinds of "monies," experiences that exclude the undeserving while energizing the creditworthy. Conservative banking, that is, produces credit instruments steeped in banking tradition, instruments that indicate austerity and thoroughness, competence and thoughtfulness, strict adherence to prudence and principles. These moral and cultural earmarks serve to give shape to the circuits of money that are generated through the lending process.

Two examples may serve to illustrate the social dynamics that characterize sound banking. John Pierpont Morgan, the quintessential corporate consolidator of the late-nineteenth-century United States—immortalized by Matthew Josephson (the author who popularized the term "robber barons") as a "famous innovator" with the "boldness of character" that made him fit for the new interventionist roles banks were then taking (see Josephson 1962: 291)—was in fact known for his *conservative* stance on business. Morgan realized that cut-throat competition among robber barons was undercutting the profits of the manufacturing industry and the banks that controlled it; his solution was the imposition of "administered prices" (administered by banks, that is) on manufactured products. But to couch this directive role of bankers in the language of instrumental rationality was not politically viable, for two reasons: why should rival bankers entrust Pierpont Morgan with the defense of the putatively general interests of the financial community (Livingston 1986)? And why should the public believe that bankers, rather than the government, were best suited for this role (Sklar 1987)? Morgan, thus, used the language of conservative banking as a way to strengthen, solidify, and then defend the reputation of his firm (at the time, Drexel & Morgan), and so in turn make a claim for his and his firm's ability to speak for, and act in, the general interest. For instance, he would stress the importance of keeping liquid assets at hand, in 1877 proudly writing to his father Junius, at a time when rumors circulated about Drexel & Morgan's being overstretched:

[At] the time then under discussion we had in Bank and Call-loans money enough to pay in two hours every dollar we owed to everyone, assuming that every depositor we had should draw every cent of money out instantly without notice—consequently our whole business was being conducted with our own means in our business without any regard to what any of the partners might have outside. How many partners you suppose, doing such a business as we are, could make such a statement? (Carosso 1987: 144–45)

Pierpont Morgan would similarly insist that the firms under Drexel & Morgan's control be subjected to scrutiny and strict accounting rules. And his dedication to austere and sound business practices was mirrored by his socially conservative lifestyle. "Pierpont Morgan's leisure interests, like his life at home and at the office, conformed to his own standards, which were conservative and patrician, those of the great merchant banking houses of Victorian London. Pierpont identified with them and not the nouveaux riches of New York in the Gilded Age" (ibid.: 143). Commitment to sound banking, prudence, and austerity was in other words the basis upon which Pierpont Morgan built his claim to the specialized honor of the status group.

It is not only in the rarified realm of financial elites that sound banking facilitates the formation of new status groups, unified by common understandings about how the instruments that circulate within them should be regulated. Consider a second example from the post–New Deal United States, in particular after World War II, when "embedded liberalism" in international relations was coupled with interventionist Keynesianism at home. A pillar of the new arrangement was the creation of a market for home mortgages, financed by private banks but backed by agencies such as the Home Owner's Loan Corporation, followed in 1936 by the Federal National Mortgage Association (Green and Wachter 2005). Access to credit—and not just for large purchases such as a home but for all sorts of consumer goods—became an integral part of the American dream, that elusive, idealistic, yet simultaneously materialistic notion that included "the house in the suburbs with a backyard for the kids to play in, a patio for barbecues, a shady street, bright and obedient kids, camping trips, fishing, two family cars, seeing the kids taking part in school and church plays, and online access to the world." That description is taken from a 1999 syndicated newspaper column, and it mirrors a similar depiction from forty years earlier—with the addition of online access, of course (Calder 1999: 3). The dream of mass consumerism and access to mainstream goods was the cultural expression of Fordism, with its emphasis on stability and the creation of a middle class employed by the corporation (Harvey 1991; Aglietta 2000). Until the 1970s, credit was similarly granted only to those who possessed Fordist credentials: primarily, and predictably, employment in the corporation (Davis 2009). Creditworthiness was thus a function of one's involvement in the institutions that stabilized the U.S. economy. The exclusionary boundary between creditworthy and outsiders was, furthermore, overlaid with racial boundaries: the 1950s and 1960s were periods of red-lining and credit discrimination based on race (Overby 1994; Rugh and Massey 2010).

How did bankers act within this context? Regulated from the federal government, until the late 1970s/early 80s the banking sector remained fragmented into thousands of local institutions. Yet, since it financed local communities in the name of high screening standards and specific uses for credit (such as the aforementioned mortgages), it was also unified and cohesive in its upholding of financial rigor. At the higher levels of finance, similarly, a handful of banks occupied a central, directing role—provoking important debates on the degree to which banks controlled industry (Mizruchi 2004). It took a tremendous amount of effort before more speculative practices, such as unsolicited credit cards, took root in the United States (Guseva and Rona-Tas 2001: 524). The market for mortgages itself boomed only once banks began developing innovative financial instruments so that they could offload risk onto others—a strategy that ultimately failed (Lewis 2010).

The point of these examples is that both Pierpont Morgan at the turn of the century, and the domestic U.S. banking system in the post–World War II period, shared a commitment to restrictive credit practices. To be sure, they did it for different reasons: Morgan was in the process of creating new rules to solidify his recently acquired hegemony in Gilded Age America, whereas the local bankers of the post–World War II United States were, to some degree, in a more subordinate position to political power and were thus using their control over credit to forestall further challenges to their position, while the large commercial bankers were intimately connected to industrial corporations. Banking conservatism took different, specific aspects because of the larger context in which it was articulated: in Morgan's case, it was characterized by strict attention to accounting rules coupled with a rejection of the crass, worldly pursuits of his competitors. In the case of the post–World War II bankers, conservative banking was modeled on criteria of membership in mainstream society (employment in the corporation, race) that bankers could easily turn into sources of categorical inequality (Tilly 1998). They shared, however, a common commitment to sound banking: both kinds of bankers deployed the sound banking strategy articulated by Schumpeter.

As Schumpeter (1939: 118) suggests, the defining aspects of sound banking are best seen in contrast with those of wildcat credit. Rather than expressing concerns with social honor and conformity to established rules of stratification and propriety, which are the norms espoused by conservative bankers, wildcat banking is predicated on the creation of altogether new moralities, within which wildcats create new forms of money and invest them with a new kind of prestige. "Wildcat banking" is then, in Schumpeter's scheme, a state of generalized financial innovation, in which existing "traditions and standards" are replaced by new ways of granting credit: that is, a state in which "practically anyone" can enter the banking business and grant loans according to terms and criteria that do not build on the accumulated experience of bankers—the only "school" in which this "highly skilled work" can be learned. In wildcat banking, then, inclusion, rather than exclusion, becomes the primary mechanism whereby the experience of membership is generated. As a result, wildcat banking systems tend to lose cohesion.[4]

In sum, where conservative banking creates exclusivity and prestige in the name of discipline and coherence, austerity and prudence, wildcat banking pursues inclusion and leveling, in the name of innovation and change, and, most important, in the name of transgression. The two typologies of banking, thus, are locked in a conflictual relationship of mutual dependence. A cohesive banking system defines and imposes strict boundaries between those who are worthy of credit and those who are not; it also makes further, finer-grained distinctions between different degrees of creditworthiness, themselves marked by appropriate instruments. While this stabilizes the financial field, it also opens up the ground for wildcat banking—a form of extending credit that constructs prestige out of violating the exclusionary boundaries built around a particular instrument, or what one might call the prestige of *transgressive* inclusion. Wildcats rally against conservative bankers, accusing them of acting as advocates for the preservation of privileges and advantages, and as gatekeepers of economic status groups. Wildcats struggle in the name of a more diffuse distribution of financial instruments to larger constituencies. By attacking exclusivity, they create opportunities for members of established status groups to break ranks and profit from the distribution of advantages over an exclusive boundary. Importantly, wildcat bankers threaten the collective rationality of the status group, as they make possible for its members to sell their instruments in open markets, and in the process find new customers for those instruments. Wildcats, that is, feed on the tension between the collective rationality of the group, and the individual rationality of its members.

The importance, indeed the centrality, of wildcat banking to financial markets should not be underestimated. In any given money of account, financial instruments are distributed along the two dimensions of exclusivity and financial control that I have identified in previous chapters. Access to the most prestigious instruments is restricted to select elite players; by the same token, these elite players prohibit the creation of open markets in the instruments by way of retaining financial control. Conservative banking facilitates this process of control and exclusion. Wildcats, by contrast, act against this tendency: they strategize to give new customers access to instruments, decreasing their exclusivity, and eventually replacing old criteria and practices of exclusion with new ones. Wildcat banking is thus the essence of financial innovation.[5] The recombination of existing resources into new instruments, and the creation of superordinate markets in which instruments composed of other instruments are traded, are the bread and butter of wildcat banking: they are grounded on new ideas about how value should be assigned, about who should be holding those instruments, and about what kinds of operations the possessor of the new instrument should be entitled to.[6]

The relationship between conservative and wildcat bankers is conflictual. The fact that conservative and wildcat bankers respond to the moves, challenges, attacks, and compromises of the other camp means that only indirectly do they respond to the demand for credit generated outside the financial field. In other words, the conflict within the financial system always mediates whatever demand for credit may originate from the outside. When Schumpeter (1911: 88) writes of the conflictual relationship between bankers and entrepreneurs, with the latter convincing the former (and the general public) of the importance of their business propositions "more by will than by intellect," more by "authority," "personal weight," and so forth than by "original ideas," he rightly focuses attention on conflict. But he also misses the importance of the balance of power within the financial field itself, before entrepreneurial demands will be met.

An important question I propose that arises from the distinction between conservative and wildcat bankers is whether their opposing claims—to exclusion and austerity on the part of conservative bankers, to inclusion and expansion on the part of the wildcats—effectively translate into financial fields that are more or less closed off to outsiders. In fact, if this were the case—if wildcats did actually serve as instruments of inclusion—such a conclusion would support the claim of neoliberal theories (see, for example, Rajan and Zingales 2004) that more open financial markets are tools of redistribution and increased access to opportunities. If, conversely, as Schumpeter had it, conservative banking is a necessary condition for the stability of the capitalist system, financial markets should remained tightly controlled.

Two points make both inferences unwarranted. First, if the nature of money is differentiated, and if these distinctions emerge in the course of transactions, money will always be a system of stratification and boundaries—which means that money always affords the opportunity for conservative banking to re-emerge after wildcat attacks. This follows from the more general Weberian point that specific status groups wax and wane, but the opportunity for the monopolistic appropriation of resources under capitalism is intrinsic to the system.[7]

Second, a view of finance as a field focuses on its internal dynamics first, and its external aspects second, which is to say that it identifies the specific boundaries and collective identities created by conservative bankers, not the boundaries through which social inequality as a whole is articulated as the targets of wildcat attacks. This implies that wildcat bankers may reinforce larger systems of inequality, and mobilize on the basis of them, even as they claim to fight for more open access to financial fields. We will see in my empirical discussion of the U.S. case that wildcats during the Jacksonian era reinforced racial inequality by explicitly drawing on racist ideologies, even as they advocated for the democratization of banking.

My thesis that conflict is the core aspect of finance, in conclusion, yields several propositions. To the extent that conservative bankers impose sound banking principles on the banking field, they will reinforce its cohesion and tighten the boundaries around the extension of credit. They will solve the collective action dilemma that always underlies the ex-

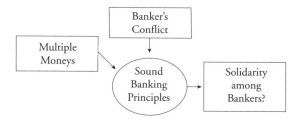

Fig. 2.1. Sound Banking and Solidarity

change of instruments by committing their holders to shared, exclusionary principles. To the extent that wildcat bankers successfully challenge those boundaries and principles, by contrast, they will both weaken the commitment of holders of prestigious financial instruments to keep them circulating in exclusive circuits, and will generate a new set of principles to subvert the financial status quo. The Schumpeterian metaphor of banking as "headquarters" of capitalism is, then, somewhat misguided. It assumes the cohesion of the headquarters. But conservative and wildcat bankers struggle with each other, using instruments couched in competing, antagonistic, but ultimately interdependent ideologies. More generally, it is the activity of organizing financial conflict that structures banking. The source of financial power, as Schumpeter argues, derives from the bankers' unique control over the credit process, but that, in turn, depends on the social cohesion of banking networks. Neither bankers, nor analysts of the banking system, can take that cohesion for granted.

A sociology of financial conflict opens up the analysis of finance to new questions: To what extent will the principles of sound banking, which regulate and discipline the experience of holding different financial instruments, enhance the cohesion of conservative bankers? Sound banking principles, in fact, will not always succeed at increasing solidarity within the financial field; it is an empirical question whether, and to what extent, bankers will organize around them, to see each other as members of a collectivity, their actions becoming concerned with the reproduction of the collective interests of the banking community. Under what conditions, then, do conservative bankers succeed in institutionalizing sound banking principles? Under what conditions do wildcats gain the upper hand, opening up the field to previously excluded outsiders, thus tilting it toward speculation? And finally, which coalition tends to be more stable—that of conservative bankers, or that of wildcat bankers? Both the differentiation of money, and the intensity of the conflicts that characterize the financial system, affect the likelihood that sound banking principles will succeed in focusing the collective attention of banking actors on common identities, through which these bankers can cooperate. And it is an empirical question as to how these processes will interact, and what outcome these interactions will have on the shape of the financial system.

The rest of the book will seek to answer these questions by investigating the financial conflict in two national case studies. In Italy and the United States in the nineteenth century, the struggle between conservative and wildcat bankers took different forms because of differences in the organization of money, with Italian financial instruments becoming increasingly linked to the financial activities of the state, while U.S. financial instruments were instead emancipated from networks of public finance and constituted networks of private debt. We will also see that varying degrees of compatibility among the different social identities of conservative bankers—with Italian bankers becoming increasingly divided on the basis of national origin, and U.S. bankers forging common identities by drawing from traditions of commercial lending—impacted the fate of banking at the time. These distinctions will highlight the fact that an empirical investigation of money necessarily involves a sustained analysis of the social and political context in which money is produced. Understanding the dynamics endogenous to financial systems gives us a renewed appreciation of the role played by forces outside of them. Before we turn fully to the empirical material, however, I want to introduce a more systematic argument about how forces external to the financial field may affect internal financial dynamics.

External Sources of Sound Banking

The expansion of government increases social power, and that social power can be appropriated for new purposes, unintended—and often outright opposed—by the authorities responsible for its initial expansion. (*Policies make policy*, an influential literature reminds us: Steinmo 1989; Skocpol 1992; Pierson 1996; Thelen 2003; Martin, Mehrotra, and Prasad 2009.) Budgets generate new political identities that, in turn, sustain and reproduce the financial commitments authorized by the government. Just as states affect policies, and in turn politics, through the budget, they also affect credit. Budgets entail a material redistribution of resources

(O'Connor 2001), but, more specifically, they detach resources from current uses, to then commit them to new uses. Public finance provides the raw material that bankers then use in support of their collective projects of domination.

Taxes, much like the credit instruments with which bankers remove resources from the circular flow, remove "goods or services" from existing circuits and redirect them to new uses and purposes. They are "one-sided" because the extraction of taxes is not usually justified in terms of how that money will be spent: to put it in simpler terms, "taxation consists of the obligation to contribute money and goods to the state in exchange for nothing in particular," with the resources thus entering in possession of the state becoming *fungible*, since "the resources extracted through taxation are exchangeable for other resources; they make possible not just one state action, but most if not all of the state's activities" (Martin et al. 2009: 3–4).

The fungibility of resources enforced by taxation is consequential. As Weber argues, it is the ultimate guarantee of state support that the status group fights for in defense of its privileges, and so taxes, if they challenge those privileges, can have important effects on the dynamics of status group formation. Resources extracted through taxation become fungible once the state succeeds in removing the boundaries that the status groups, previously in control of those resources, had erected around them. The budget of the state is then a focal point of struggle: potentially, it erases existing social distinctions to then assert new ones. And once a compromise over the budget is reached, that compromise will tend to constitute entrenched interests, invested in the continuation of state spending; invested, that is, in the meanings and earmarks of the circuits that originate with the state's budget.

How the fiscal process affects bankers, then, is a crucial aspect of the bankers' ability to impose sound banking. States tax different sources of revenue, such as personal income and capital gains, differently (Steinmo 1989), thus affecting the likelihood that certain kinds of economic and social policies will be sustainable over time. Most important for my purposes, states often strive to control who has access to credit by promoting goals, such as diffuse home ownership, that require the creation of specialized financial instruments, such as the thirty-year mortgage loan, that the private sector is often resistant to accept (Calder 1999; Benmelech and Dlugosz 2009; Gabriel and Rosenthal 2005; Green and Wachter 2005;

Snowden 1995). States, then, intervene in credit markets both indirectly, by making certain kinds of economic activities more prevalent than others through taxation, and directly, by promoting the creation of new financial circuits altogether.

Conservative bankers are forced to adapt to such changes. If conservative bankers draw their power in the financial field from the financial control and the exclusivity they confer to the instruments they issue, the fiscal and financial expansion of the state can have two contradictory effects. Taxation and debt can reinforce existing relationships of power (Carruthers 1996), as long as conservative bankers serve as the government's primary and preferred intermediaries. Conservative bankers, for instance, may consent to the expansion of government debt to finance new programs, and will help the government in its attempt to extend access to credit for particular purposes, so long as the government never violates its commitment to long-term fiscal austerity. A commitment on the part of the government to balance the budget, in fact, will help conservative bankers negotiate the government's temporary expansion of its balance sheet. Conservative bankers may even hold some of the new debt to offset (or "leverage") their riskier investments. As a result, when properly managed (from the point of view of conservative banking), the fiscal and financial activities of the state will help rationalize finance.[8]

Yet the fiscal and financial expansion of the state does not always lead to more rationalization. Often, government expansion leads to the *transgression* of existing boundaries around the circulation and possession of financial instruments, and thereby of existing financial relations. Fiscal activities affect the dynamics of banking by encouraging financial innovation, both when governments issue too much debt and when they issue too little.[9]

Once the government has a larger financial presence, and further expands its indebtedness, the bankers, faced by new quantities of government debt to market, may be forced to coordinate their activities with the central bank; this relationship becomes constraining (De Cecco 1987). Under the threat of losing their autonomy to the demands for coordination of the central banks, banks thus begin to innovate. They search for new instruments that the state is less able to monitor effectively, such as derivatives. And they are met by borrowers, who now demand assets similar to government debt, which, moreover, they can use as collateral for other operations. In nineteenth-century Italy, for instance, universal banks, formally dedicated to the financing of industry, increasingly resorted to the issuance of more complex financial instruments, such as contango loans, to command resources on the stock market instead.

Governments may not only devise programs with the specific intent of granting larger audiences access to credit institutions, but they may also directly issue the instruments with which such increased access is to be achieved. Historically, state debt was often used in such a way: a strategy that, to be sure, became prevalent only in the late nineteenth century, when sale of debt though public subscription became less risky and thus more widespread. But even before that, when governments were much more likely to rely on elite international bankers for the placement and underwriting of the debt, with the Rothschilds, for instance, playing a dominant role with respect to British finance until the 1850s (Ferguson 2001: 116–17), one strategy that governments often employed was to force financial institutions to compete with each other. Late-nineteenth-century Italy, for instance, attempted on various occasions to play off German financial houses against the Rothschilds and the Barings (De Cecco 1993). Earlier in the century, France had similarly attempted to build up a new, domestic financial elite that would compete with Haute Finance (Kindleberger 1984). Governments, in sum, often refused to rely on established channels, using practices such as competitive auctions for the placement and management of the debt. They attempted, whenever they could, to enlarge the pool of intermediaries authorized to deal with its borrowing to thus gain more advantageous terms. By acting in such a fashion, governments transgressed the earmarks that conservative bankers had built around current uses of money. Britain was, in this case, the exception, with the emergence of a specialized professional group, the "jobbers." But Britain was also exceptional for the general cohesion of its state, banking, and merchant elites. In other states, no similarly unified elite had such exclusive control over both state and private finances (see Ingham 1984; Carruthers 1994). The expansion of public debt through the involvement of new financial institutions was thus a major determinant of wildcat banking.

Wildcat banking becomes more viable in the opposite situation too, when governments carry out contractive monetary policies—when the debt issued by the government is too small. Now conservative bankers experience shrinking balance sheets. As the government calls its debt back, the financial circuits in which the debt previously circulated contract. And especially if debt reduction is accomplished through government surpluses, and thereby through higher taxation, less state money altogether is available for private use. Conservative bankers, as a consequence, begin engaging in new financial practices. Rather than cutting credit to their most established clientele, conservative bankers devise new instruments with which they can continue this relationship (Stiglitz and Weiss 1981; Stiglitz 2011). So, as they devise new methods to extend credit, they become more like wildcat bankers. The create "shadow banking systems" outside public purview and control, which in turn spawn more innovative practices that conservative bankers themselves find difficult to control. De Cecco's history (1974) of the relationship between merchant bankers and the British political elite at the turn of the twentieth century shows how the cultural cohesion that resulted from that relationship served to neutralize the challenge from outsider joint-stock banks.

By expanding its fiscal and financial reach, the state, in short, also becomes increasingly open to social demands—as it acts neither like an "autonomous actor" nor a "passive place" but rather an "active place," to use Michael Mann's felicitous expression (1993: 53). States with democratic regimes, by this logic, are particularly prone to undermining the exclusionary categories of creditworthiness through which conservative bankers attempt to control the process of credit creation. The more the state becomes open to societal interests, the more the budget serves to subvert the existing earmarks, boundaries, and exclusionary systems built around the allocation and circulation of credit, and the more likely that speculation and wildcat banking will take hold. The paradox of the *democratic* state is that it becomes itself vulnerable to financial speculation, more so than when the politics of the budget unfolds in more authoritarian settings. Sociologists of the caliber of Pareto (esp. Pareto 1968; Pareto and Powers 1984) recognized in this dynamic a contradiction of democratic systems. But this is not a question I intend to answer on moral or philosophical grounds, as Pareto attempted to do. This book is intended, rather, to investigate the empirical nuances of this relationship.

Since banking is a system of exclusions and boundaries, conservative bankers are, in sum, particularly threatened by political projects that threaten the durability of the boundaries they erect around credit. When they can control the means whereby the state expands its balance sheet, conservative bankers succeed in neutralizing the wildcat challenges posed by the debt. But even here, as De Cecco (1987) and Seabrooke (2006) both remind us, conservative bankers run the risk of turning into rentiers—namely, into simple managers of state debt. On the other end of the continuum, when conservative bankers are faced with restrictive monetary policy, they often resort to innovation, which in turn challenges the principles of sound banking through which they exert their dominance. This means that, with respect to the politics of the budget, the role of bankers is often simply reactive.

Conclusions

At this stage, we have identified two sources of prestige that underlie the production, possession, and exchange of financial instruments, giving rise to processes that are in contradiction to each other. On the one hand, certain financial instruments guarantee its holder exclusive access to a particular social experience that others, barred form holding the instrument, are denied; on the other hand, other financial instruments allow the holder to breach and transgress exclusive boundaries, and thus to make that experience more available, possibly constituting the springboard for the construction of altogether new boundaries.

The contradiction between these two sources of prestige has important implications for how financial systems are structured. It implies that the stability of banking depends on the ability and success of the banking faction that fights in the name of banking conservatism, against the banking faction that espouses financial inclusion. More specifically, it depends on the ability of conservative bankers to move to the center of the financial field and redefine its culture—the principles, understandings, worldviews by which it operates. The main implication of this scheme is that the stability of finance is predicated on *exclusion,* because it is through exclusion that the financial instruments of sound banking acquire prestige and afford their holder financial control; and that exclusion works insofar as conservative bankers develop solidarity with one another, and act as a collective.

The second implication is that the basic opposition between the two typologies of banking—conservative and wildcat—is a structural one, one that draws from the complex nature of money; from the fact that, just as money, in the shape of differentiated financial instruments, can become a marker of prestige and exclusion, it can also be turned into an instrument of *speculative democratization and inclusion.* The differentiation of money into multiple financial instruments, in other words, accounts both for the complexity of financial fields, and for the instability that characterizes them, because behind these differentiated financial instruments are rival banking factions.

Shifts in external conditions, by which I have meant the resources and constituencies that bankers have been able to draw power from, lead to shifts in the financial status quo. In particular, the politics of the budget can be a source of instability both to the extent that new financial agents become involved in the financial expansion of the state—so that, rather than being managed by conservative bankers according to principles of austerity and sound banking, the new debt is used for new purposes, held by new actors, in short, circulated in new circuits—and to the extent that conservative bankers react to projects of increased state control over money by innovating, by creating new financial instruments whereby that control can be circumvented. These are the main ingredients of financial conflict.

As we move into the second part of this book, we will investigate the unfolding of these processes in real historical contexts. Our analysis will take us to sociopolitical settings where the boundaries built around money's circulation could not be defended; where conservative bankers, initially able to win legal privileges that granted them a certain degree of monopoly over financial resources, subsequently found themselves challenged on the grounds of inclusion; where, finally, wildcat bankers fought to don the mantle of innovation and democratization, couching those claims in culturally specific rhetoric, yet, at the same time, responding to the basic structural constraints and opportunities offered by financial fields. Our journey will reveal the deep connections between democracy and financial speculation, and so it will equip us with a long-term perspective with which, finally, we will be able better to appreciate the nature of our current predicament.

3

Institutions and the Struggle over Creditworthiness in the Nineteenth-Century United States

ANY ORGANIZED ACTOR who draws prestige and resources from the systematic appropriation of economic advantages will face several challenges. A particularly difficult one is that of defining what behaviors are appropriate to the pursuit of those advantages, and what behaviors should be sanctioned; what strategies are supposed to lead to what outcomes; and more generally, where the boundaries defining membership in the status group in charge of resource appropriation should lie. Actors often construe cultural and normative systems to this effect, or what sociologists call a "political culture" (Dobbin 1994; Fligstein 2001b).

Conservative bankers are invested in stabilizing the financial field. Like other status groups, they prefer to rely on more forceful distinctions and systems of exclusion than cultural ones: privileges sanctioned by a political authority can be more easily and effectively defended than privileges communicated through culture. Where political support is uncertain, however, political culture takes up a central role in their efforts. The less the conservative bankers manage to rally the support of political elites in sanctioning their methods of credit assessment, the more they must rely on explicit principles through which they can justify sound banking. These general principles, moreover, will be taken up in the struggle between conservative and wildcat bankers. So in democratic settings, especially where power is decentralized, and where the support of political elites cannot be counted on, conservative bankers will strive to make those principles appear *apolitical*, referring not to collective membership in a political or cultural community but to personal and seemingly objective traits of character, personality, and individual conduct. The criteria whereby creditworthiness is adjudicated, that is, will be explicitly moralized, because they will refer to creditworthiness as a signal of membership into an ethical community larger than a political or cultural group.

To the question of what affects the allocation of credit, scholars tend to provide individualistic answers. For the most part, they emphasize aspects that reduce credit to a relationship between two parties. Think about the myth of creditworthiness, the idea that credit depends on reliable criteria, through which the risk of a loan can be calculated, so that it can be reflected in its price (in the interest rate, that is, paid by the borrower); as well as on appropriate collateral, so that, should the borrower default, the creditor will be able to lay claim to some assets, at least partially cutting losses. The view of credit that underlies these concerns sees it as a relationship plagued by scarce and asymmetric information, as lenders always know less than do borrowers about the true risk of a loan (Stiglitz and Weiss 1981; Arnott and Stiglitz 1991; Stiglitz 2011; Carruthers 2005).

The goal of this chapter is to show that, indeed, debates about creditworthiness in the late-eighteenth- to early-nineteenth-century United States were characterized by serious preoccupations about the connection between credit and character. North American credit-raters, for instance, proposed the idea that creditworthiness was a character trait, self-evident to those who devised the right tools to assess it, and in general reliable as a guide to credit decisions; they began selling credit reports informed by this approach (Olegario 2006). Perhaps the most famous celebration of the importance of character to credit was J. P. Morgan's dictum at the Pujo hearings in 1912: "[To gain credit] [t]he first thing is character. . . . A man I do not trust could not get the money from me on all the bonds in Christendom" (Morgan 1913: 1084). But, in spite of the intuitive appeal of this argument, which locates in the assessment of individual creditworthiness the ultimate challenge facing bankers, I caution against such a reading. Bankers belong to different circuits than merchants and credit-raters do. Approaches that emphasize information, because they take the individual creditor-borrower relationship as their unit of analysis, necessarily ignore the nature of the problems facing bankers, and so tend to see creditworthiness as a passive reflection of an objective quality of borrowers. Here, instead, I claim that creditworthiness is an active, political construction, leading, when successful, to the imposition and enforcement of collective criteria to control financial behavior.[1]

Nineteenth-century North America is an ideal case to investigate how the boundaries that define creditworthiness are delineated in democratic regimes. In the decentralized polity of the United States, bankers sought the support of local political authorities to protect themselves against political challenges. Since the eighteenth century, banking had been a business regulated by state governments (and so, more generally, were corporations: see Seavoy 1978); like any other status group, bankers attempted to back their privileges with the force of the law. In the states of the North, where state governments were democratic, bankers particularly benefited from political patronage. But they were also subjected to important (certainly weak to contemporary eyes, but strong for the time) democratic constraints. They were, most important of all, taxed. So, unlike the financial and monetary media that people used in their everyday transactions, which they considered as private, the status of banks was more ambiguous; indeed their public nature was often debated. The idea that creditworthiness was a function of one's character and reputation for honesty, and that bankers, aided by other specialized institutions, were invested with the unique authority to screen character and reputation, increasingly became the basis for the collective identity of sound bankers, so as to relieve them from the public scrutiny that their ambiguous status inevitably attracted. This chapter investigates and discusses the historical evolution of this financial process.

Creditworthiness as an Individual Trait

There are several ways of deciding whether an individual is worthy of credit (Carruthers 2005, 2011; Carruthers and Ariovich 2010), and how creditworthiness was understood in nineteenth-century America is a subject of important studies (esp. Olegario 2006). In his famous discussion of the Protestant sects of the American Midwest and Upper South, Weber noted, for instance, how religious affiliation could serve as a powerful signal of the creditworthiness of a potential borrower. Weber (1946: 305) argued that this is because:

[a]dmission to the local Baptist congregation follows only upon the most careful "probation" and after closest inquiries into conduct going back to early childhood (Disorderly conduct? Frequenting taverns? Dance? Theater? Card playing? Untimely meeting of liability? Other frivolities?) . . . . Admission to the congregation is recognized as an absolute guarantee of the moral qualities of a gentleman, especially of those qualities required in business matters. Baptism secures to the individual the deposits of the whole region and unlimited credit without any competition.

Membership in a religious community, according to Weber, guaranteed both the moral standards of the debtor, and access to the resources of his fellow church-members should the debtor get into business trouble. And as society secularized, Weber added, other indicators, such as the "little badge[s] (of varying color)" that the American middle classes often displayed in their jacket buttonhole, came to serve similar purposes: in this case, the purpose of publicly displaying the membership of the individual in a larger "brotherhood," ready to help should the need arise.

Weber's characterization of creditworthiness in North America has, however, been questioned. Studies of bankruptcy (B. H. Mann 2002) and, more explicitly, of credit reporting agencies (Olegario 2006; Atherton 1946), show that in early America, it was more common for creditworthiness to be understood not as a function of one's religious, political, or to some extent even ethnic affiliation, but as a direct function of one's character and reputation for honesty, punctuality, and hard work (see also Hilkey 1997). One can read Benjamin Franklin, who insisted in his 1748 *Advice to a Young Tradesman* on the importance of communicating one's creditworthiness through "trifling Actions," in this vein. Franklin famously argued: "The Sound of your Hammer at Five in the Morning or Nine at Night, heard by a Creditor, makes him easy Six Months longer. But if he sees you at a Billiard Table, or hears your Voice in a Tavern, when you should be at Work, he sends for his Money the next Day."[2] Implied in this advice was the idea that one's background, even one's social networks, were secondary to visible commitment to hard, sustained work—a Protestant idea, one that squarely depicted creditworthiness as an individual characteristic.

While one's industriousness may have opened new sources of credit, access to reliable sources of credit was central to trade transactions as well, in which one's dedication to trade was more difficult to communicate, as mercantile transactions took place through long chains of relations, necessarily involving people who did not know each other. The credit that financed trade—at the time far more important to the economy than the virtually nonexistent consumer credit (Calder 1999)—was thereby directly dependent on promises, and "[o]ften the promise to pay is merely implied. Orders are placed most generally without any definite promise to pay. The transaction is largely one of faith, supplemented by information the seller has as to the character, reputation, financial standing and ability of the buyer to pay" (Charles A. Meyer, 1919, quoted in Olegario 2006: 1). Lesser-known figures than Franklin thus insisted on emphasizing the qualities of character that merchants had to possess: as an anonymous Boston merchant (1839) put it in the *Merchant's Magazine and Commercial Review,* "[T]he good merchant is scrupulously just and upright in all his transactions. Integrity, good faith, exactness in fulfilling his engagements, are the distinctive features of his character. . . . Knowing that credit is the soul of business, he sustains the integrity of the mercantile character. Accordingly, his word is as good as his bond." One Richard Smith, writing in the *Cincinnati Price Current* (1839, quoted in ibid.: 81), concurred that character "to a man of business, and indeed to every person, is as dear as life itself."

Membership in a religious, political, or cultural community did not figure explicitly in such conceptualizations of creditworthiness. In fact, understandings of creditworthiness as a private trait, and of credit as intimately connected to reputation and character, were far from being North American inventions. In the *doux commerce* thesis articulated during the Enlightenment and so carefully delineated by Hirschman (1977, 1982), creditworthiness and the larger engagement with the market economy it made possible were understood both as catalysts of virtuous behavior, and as signals of moral rectitude and reputation (McCloskey 2006)—as both determinants and symptoms of character. Craig Muldrew (1998) puts the creation of a link, indeed of a mutual dependence on each other, between credit and reputation sometime in the late sixteenth century, when, in England in particular, the expansion of market relations went hand in hand with a transformation in the ways that social relations were articulated. A language connecting honesty, reputation, and access to material resources arose in this period, argues Muldrew: instead of leading to an atomization of social relations, market expansion was associated with new ways of communicating one's trustworthiness.

Historian Bruce Mann (2002), through a careful study of debates and legislation around bankruptcy in early America, is similarly able to show that ideas about insolvency, and about failure to live up to expectations about one's creditworthiness—much as they shifted away from the religious and moral framework that characterized them in the 1700s—never completely shed their association with a "moral economy of debt." For instance, this conceptualization of creditworthiness as a character attribute, surprisingly, survived the rise of a market for corporate securities, even though corporations seriously challenged the idea that personal character and reputation were as central to the new economy as they had been in the previous era of face-to-face merchant transactions. As late as 1905, in an address with a subtly metaphysical title, "Securities That Are not Securities," First National Bank of Kansas cashier J. T. Bradley would claim: "Any note, bond, warrant, order, draft, or other evidence of indebtedness, which is secured by a person, corporation or municipality . . . is security that secures. . . . When security is individual, not only all the property of the signer, but honor as well is pledged; but the pledge is general and gives no preference to creditors." As a result, "There is a moral as well as a physical element to be considered in the loaning of money, and generally the moral element is paramount." While proposing a number of rules of thumb to assess what securities in fact "secured," prominent on the cashier's list was that the requirement that "pledger's character for integrity, prudence, industry, and ability should be favorable" (in Hull 1907: 63–64).

In sum, creditworthiness, in nineteenth-century America and elsewhere, was understood as a quality of individual debtors, observable through behavior and inscribed over time in reputations. To be sure, if there were moral connotations to such ideas about creditworthiness, they tended to weaken over time, for the related idea that reputation in one's dealings was a matter of "business," and thus one with little relevance for the moral worth of the person was also taking root. Whether one's conduct in business was a reflection of one's moral character was, over time, becoming much more of an open question (B. H. Mann 2002).

Similarly, arguments have been made that this period witnessed the beginning of a shift from interpersonal to impersonal or institutional trust—and that, while some social overhead sector becomes necessary to facilitate this shift, the importance of personal reputation not only did not decline, but even increased, especially as it began to be codified in credit reports. The United States was a diverse and complex world, and the communications revolution of the early nineteenth century, followed by spread of a national railroad network, and the economic and industrial boom to which it was connected (Howe 2007), posed serious challenges to the assessment of reputations.[3] Nineteenth-century U.S. commentators became quite concerned with such dynamics: once it came to devising institutional mechanisms whereby the creditworthiness of individual debtors would be translated into actual quantities of credit, analysts realized that the matter was considerably more complicated than Benjamin Franklin's test of recording the frequency of the hammer's cocking early in the morning or late at night.

While wholesale merchants on the East Coast had required customers from the interior to produce "respectable letters" from businessmen and professionals since the early 1800s (Atherton 1946: 536), more formal organizations such as credit reporting agencies began appearing in the 1830s (Olegario 2006). By the end of the century, industries specialized in intermediating between economic actors who did not know each other, and who thus had to devise new means to know whether to trust each other, now formed a recognizable "social overhead sector" made up of such diverse professions as finance, law, insurance, and real estate (Zucker 1986: 96–101). Credit rating agencies were quite central to this sector, and invariably their guidelines entailed focusing on personal characteristics, not religious, political, or otherwise "moral" ones.[4]

At this stage, I wish to pose one question and address it in two ways. Were the concerns that motivated credit-raters to emphasize character— and thereby apolitical traits—to capture the creditworthiness of a client the same concerns motivating bankers? To answer positively means assuming that the task carried out by bankers is the same as that carried out by credit-raters or more specialized lenders, like wholesale trade creditors. But bankers are faced by other kinds of concerns and problems, of which how to lend safely to reputable borrowers is certainly one, but political concerns, such as how to face wildcat threats, often take priority.

Two main points emerge from this reorientation of the dynamics of banking as dictated not by the intermediating role that commercial creditors occupy, but by the conflictual nature of finance. The first is that, in the nineteenth-century United States, the banks' very right to engage in the operations from which they profited (issuing banknotes, extending credit, and so affecting the allocation and use of financial resources) depended on the kinds of political, cultural, and technical resources they could mobilize. Different political factions would consider banking as a privilege or an entitlement, as a public function or a private matter. Bankers walked a fine line in devising criteria whereby they would accept certain demands for credit, and deny others. Were they acting independently of political authority, critics often wondered aloud, or did they draw the line around partisanship? Did they have at heart the interest of the community in which they operated, or their narrower status as bankers, when they made credit decisions? Did they arbitrarily discriminate against certain classes and occupations, for instance farmers, or were the terms they attached to loans fair? The important point is that the organization of the banking system in nineteenth-century America, while certainly affected by shifting conceptualizations of what it meant to be creditworthy, cannot be understood in teleological terms as gradually approximating an ideal of efficient intermediation of resources, thanks to the ability of bankers to bridge the information asymmetries that plague creditworthiness. Stories that tell its evolution from a publicly regulated to a privately run business as a matter of obeying the laws of the markets—and as a gradual shedding of political constraints on how reputation and creditworthiness were to be assessed—are bound to miss how fundamental politics was, and always is, to the unfolding of financial activities. They are thus also bound to discount the challenges faced by banking systems that do not have political backing.

Second, while creditworthiness came to be understood as a character trait of individuals for several complex reasons, one important factor was the collective attempt by conservative bankers to *depoliticize* the debate about banking altogether. Understandings of creditworthiness as a character trait that the banking system and the agencies around it were allegedly dedicated to detect and assess were reinforced over time because of the political advantages conservative bankers could exact from them. These advantages had important limits, as they did not allow bankers to secure control in the same way a political alliance would have. But they were advantages nonetheless. Creditworthiness, in short, was less a problem that banks set out to solve, inventing over the course of the nineteenth century ever more appropriate techniques to do so, than a set of identities that bankers attempted to reinforce so as to control how credit was allocated and used. The conflict between conservative and wildcat bankers was central, I argue here, to setting the grounds on which this process took place.

The Organization of Banking

To understand the role of banks in the economy of the nineteenth-century United States, we must first spend some time discussing the nature of the operations in which they were involved. The nineteenth century was a time in which deposit banking, and the use of checks on which deposit banks rely, were not diffuse practices. So the business of banking consisted of two main kinds of activities, of which the issue of banknotes in exchange for specie was one, and the "discounting" of notes, which we will take up next, the other. The nature of both kinds of activities raised several problems, and so bankers faced important challenges.

First, for a bank to acquire the important (and profitable) right to issue banknotes, it needed a charter from the state legislature, and it also needed to fulfill certain reserve and capital requirements that were supposed to guarantee the solvency of the institution. Let us discuss reserve and capital first. Banks would, in the main, collect precious metals and issue paper certificates in return that were convertible into specie (gold or silver) upon presentation at the bank. The specie thus collected was part of the bank's reserve, which allowed the bank to expand its business, since it could issue three times as much in liabilities (the principle is called one of fractional reserve. Hammond [1957: 132] argues that the ratio was around three to one throughout the nineteenth century).

The idea of a reserve-backed currency derived, of course, from eighteenth-century monetary orthodoxy, which considered the value of paper money to be derivative of the value of the specie into which it could be converted upon demand (Eichengreen 1996). Interestingly, however, the very notion of reserves was much more complicated than some of the economic literature makes it out to be (see, for example, Bodenhorn 2000), because it was not clear to whom the specie deposited in a bank in fact belonged. Hammond (1957: 137) argues, for instance, that throughout the eighteenth and the early nineteenth centuries, "[D]epositors wished to draw out the same thing they had to put in and thought of a bank as a warehouse which provided safekeeping under earmark. The banks resisted this view of their liability but rather for practical than legal reasons." So it was not simply, as Davis and Gallman perceptively put it, that "the saver . . . gradually became willing to hold scraps of paper representing real assets located far away in both space and experience" (quoted in Bodenhorn 2000: 7), but also that the "saver" had to radically rethink in the process what "representation of real assets" in fact entailed. Hence, "There was a twilight between practice and law, with the depositor prone to think of the specie as *his* specie lying in the bank for safekeeping, and with the bank forced by the facts to consider it bank property, for which, however, the bank was in debt" (Hammond 1957: 138).[5] The myth of fungible money, one that characterizes more modern understandings of the role and function of money in capitalist economies, was fiercely contested in the nineteenth century.

The issue of reserves was intertwined with the issue of whether state banks could issue banknotes. This issue remained constitutionally dubious, as the federal government was by law the only political authority invested with the power to issue money: states, therefore, were banned from doing so. But the constitution was silent on whether private firms could print money. States, then, circumvented the constitutional restriction on their authority over money by chartering banks that in turn could issue money. By one authoritative account, up to six thousand different kinds of banknotes circulated in the United States in the antebellum period. And while they were denominated in one money of account, the dollar (with other currencies, such as the Mexican peso, circulating alongside them), quite strikingly, the market value of banknotes depended on the financial soundness of the issuing institution. Market value could thus vary quite dramatically from face-value (Helleiner 2003). This allowed the nineteenth-century United States to become a "nation of counterfeiters," as Mihm (2007) puts it, precisely because the bewildering variety in monetary instruments made the line between legitimate and fraudulent issues of money very blurry indeed. Further, with hundreds of banks (as well as other kinds of firms, such as insurance and mercantile companies) issuing their own notes, and with the absence of a centralized clearing system that could ensure that the institutions issuing those notes were in fact able to redeem them for specie, the value of money was fluctuating, ambiguous, and problematic.

If the issuance and circulation of money raised several questions, doubts, and suspicions, the important set of activities that defined the business of banking—its lending operations—further confused public perceptions of the nature of banking, and contributed to the multiplication of monetary and financial instruments. With credit, the problem was not so much whether the institution that issued it was solvent, but whether the client to whom the bank granted credit was, in fact, creditworthy. Banks at the time granted credit primarily through the "discounting" of bills (primarily promissory notes and accommodation paper). The value of the note derived from the value of the underlying transaction from which the note originated—for instance, merchants selling and delivering goods in distant localities would sign a note issued by the buyer that, upon completion of the transaction, was worth the value of the goods. "Discounting" was the practice of buying a bill or note issued by a party to a transaction in goods at below its face-value, while receiving the full face-value upon maturity (with the discount applied to the note serving the same function as interest rates on loans). Notes were generally short-term (such as commercial paper), and could be classified into two main types depending on how strong the guarantee for payment was. With single-name promissory notes, only the maker of the note was responsible for full payment upon maturity, a fact that made those notes riskier: if the maker refused or was unable to meet his/her obligations, the holder of the note would lose money. The more secure double-name paper, on the other hand, involved both the maker of the bill and an endorser, and the latter was legally responsible to pay should the maker default. Both types of notes were used to finance trade, and were thus desirable instruments for banks to discount (James 1978: 54–55; Broz 1997: 40). Yet, the general problem with such instruments is that they were only as valuable as the underlying transaction they financed—so they were only as good as the reputation of the parties that issued them and guaranteed the transaction.

Competition for good commercial paper was fierce, as good notes were scarce. But the demand for notes was high also because lending practices were justified through a banking ideology named the real bills doctrine. Championed "by nearly every notable contemporary writer," this approach to banking defined short-term mercantile credit for transactions involving the buying and selling of goods as the only appropriate function for bankers (Bodenhorn 2003: 45). Banks' "immediate and principal operations," wrote University of Virginia professor of political economy George Tucker, "consist in discounting promissory notes and bills of exchange not yet due, that is, in lending money on the credit of these negotiable papers" (Tucker 1839: 161). It was believed that, by limiting banking activities to the finance of trade, banks would be automatically restrained from abetting speculation, especially in times of economic expansion. In other words, the real bills doctrine undergirded what I have called the "myth of banking as institutions of intermediation." In the nineteenth-century United States, that is, the role of banks was understood to be primarily that of intermediating commercial transactions.

Like the attendant myth of fungible money, however, the myth of banking that characterized U.S. credit was contested. One problem was the inability of creditors to control how borrowers used credit. For instance, comparing the American system to the Scottish, in which bankers "who confined their business to the discounting of trade paper, could draw valid conclusions as to the prudence or lack of wisdom with which they ran their business from the conduct of their clients and from general mercantile information," Edward Clibborn lamented the "inability of the American banker to control his customers in the use which they made of the credit received" (Clibborn 1837, in Redlich 1968: 65–66).

A second, perhaps even more pervasive problem, was the ambiguous status of banking institutions. Were they public or private? And, as a related issue, what should their relationship with political power be? In a social context in which the public nature of money was not fully recognized, the role of banks was similarly ill defined, and thus contested. And as we shall see, how creditworthiness was defined responded to such quintessentially political considerations.

The Public Nature of Banking

In his important legal history of the United States, Horwitz (1979: 110) notes a basic ambiguity surrounding the status of corporate charters: on the one hand, there was the idea that a chartered organization was thereby protected from competition; on the other, there was the idea that such protection was legitimate only when the corporation had an explicitly public character. As a result, "[by] 1800 a pattern of private ownership of banks, insurance companies, and transportation facilities had become dominant in America, although existing legal theory continued to enable judges and jurists to regard those enterprises as arms of the state."[6]

The status of banks was particularly ambiguous. On the one hand, banks seemed to have a private nature. As associations of businessmen or "investors' clubs" (Lamoreaux 1994), they seemed to fit such a characterization: the early supporters of Andrew Jackson often thought of banks (and criticized them for it) as the "partial instruments of the favored few . . . for the advancement of their private interests, rather than great public blessings, of universal participation" (ibid.: 31). To the Jacksonians, as we shall see in the next chapter, the privilege of banknote-issue that state charters granted banks was particularly objectionable, because it gave private institutions a monopoly over a public good, as well as giving banks a privilege that other businesses did not enjoy. To the so-called hard-money Jacksonians, moreover, paper-money in and of itself was an abomination, and the fact that banks had the right to issue it at all a social evil.[7] A different interpretation, on the other hand, recognized from the start the public nature of banks. Much like public infrastructure improvement schemes (Scheiber 1975, 1981), banks were understood to be fulfilling important public functions, in particular issuing the circulating medium and providing credit (Bodenhorn 2000). In this view, political involvement in the chartering of banks was absolutely necessary, so as to regulate with fairness their public activities. Some commentators even concluded that banks should not be subjected to competition:

The extension of bank credit . . . may be advantageous to the community, or it may not. Supposing the additional loans to have been made to the prudent, judicious, or even the fortunate, they would be beneficial; but if the increased competition of the banks should have the effect . . . of nourishing a spirit of speculation and over-trading, the wealth of the community would probably be more impaired than augmented. (Tucker 1839: 248)

Because banks were regulated at the state level, and because legislation varied dramatically across states,[8] some commentators interpret such variation as a function of political patronage, and characterize banking as a chaotic, even corrupt business (V. Smith 1990; E. White 1983; Bodenhorn 2000).[9] One important regularity was that, at least in some states, banks were taxed. Those states tended to be Northern states. Understanding the fiscal nature of the relationship between states (at least some of them) and banks is central to understanding how their ambiguous public/private status was negotiated.

Let us first look at the magnitude of such taxes, for which Table 3.1 presents data for selected states. These data represent startling evidence about the degree of interpenetration between government revenue policies and the banking system. For instance, in the 1830s, about 60 percent of current revenue in the state of Massachusetts derived from taxes on banks; in Rhodes Island, the ratio was close to one-third. Comparing Connecticut and Rhodes Island to Virginia and New York reveals how much variation there was in such practices. But the fact that, at least in some states, a large proportion of public revenue could be extracted from banks, instead of other kinds of business, let alone general property taxes, is notable. Wallis, Sylla, and Legler (1995), who have engaged in the ambitious effort to collect reliable data on such aspects, go one step further and argue that, depending on the specific mode of taxation institutionalized by a state, not simply the level of fiscal extraction, the banking system developed differently. State governments could either apply a lump-sum tax on banks, or tax its stocks, dividends, and profit. The former was a one-time tax, which thus limited the relationship between state authorities and banks to the act of chartering. However, states that taxed the latter developed a "fiscal interest" in the organizations they taxed, and as a result encouraged entry into the banking business so as to maximize their

TABLE 3.1

Percentage of Current Revenue from Taxes on Banks, Selected States

	1800	1810	1820	1830	1840	1850	1860
CT	0	9%	9%	27%	37%	34%	45%
MA				61	45	34	21
NY	4	6	6	1	1	1	1
PA	42	38	53	23	9	4	6
RI	0	2	2	24	41	46	46
VT	0	0	3	8	10	4	2
DE	1	12	44	43	56	52	40
KY		6	4	7	8	6	2
MD		29	5	9	18	4	3
NC			31	34	44	1	0
SC	5	9	13	1	5	0	0
TN					0	0	14
VA	0	12	2	0	9	13	10

SOURCE: Sylla, Legler and Wallis (1995).

revenue. This happened in Massachusetts after 1812; Maryland between 1812 and 1830; Missouri in the 1860s. Where they had direct ownership over banking institutions, on the contrary, states restricted entry—with Pennsylvania being the most remarkable case. Where they had mixed sources of revenue, states simply limited entry, as happened in New York (before the 1830s, when free banking, liberal registration was enacted to open up the banking system to competition).

In sum, Wallis and colleagues tell a causal story about the relationship between fiscal/regulatory regime and the shape of the banking system. This story unearths as much variation within regions as it does across regions, but in the Southern cases they discuss, South Carolina and Virginia, the authors point nonetheless to one commonality: the centrality of the plantation economy to the workings of the banking system. So South Carolina began as a mixed system, with a large, state-owned bank in Charleston (the Bank of the State of South Carolina), serving the plantation elite of the interior, and in turn competing with private, chartered banks, which tended not to do business in the interior. (When the Charleston branch of the Bank of the United States closed, a new Bank of Charleston was set up, and the Bank of the State of South Carolina acquired a large part of its stock.) The difference between South Carolina and the Northeast was that South Carolina's banks were allowed to have branches (by contrast, antibranching laws were widespread in the North). That in turn was a result of the urban-rural division of the state, which allowed Charleston banks to specialize in different lines of business than the state bank, and thus not to compete against them for the same clientele. Virginia, by contrast, remained a laggard. It also had branch banking, with the Bank of Virginia initially monopolizing the banking business, joined in 1811 by a new "mother bank with branches," and with the state investing in both banks. Free banking (the abolition of chartering) was introduced only in 1851, with the predictable result of increasing the number of banks. We will return to such sectional differences in a moment.

Two important aspects must be noticed first. One, taxes on banks were, in some ways, alternatives to other kinds of taxes, such as taxes on property (it would be anachronistic to speak of income taxes in the early nineteenth century). State legislatures understood them as means to arrive at the "cameralist" ideal they upheld, an ideal whereby the revenue generated by productive investments would make the imposition of taxes on the people of the state unnecessary. And for some periods, they were successful. "At one time or another between 1820 and 1840, for example, New York, Massachusetts, Maryland, Pennsylvania, Delaware, Rhode Island, and South Carolina had all eliminated their property taxes" (Sylla and Wallis 1998: 279).

Second, even though differences in the share of revenue states extracted from banks did not seem to vary cross-sectionally in significant ways, the fiscal regimes of Northern and Southern states were in fact dramatically different. Table 3.2 provides a summary of those differences.

Property and poll taxes were the main sources of revenue in the nineteenth-century United States (the federal government relied primarily on the tariff).[10] Table 3.2, with data on the magnitude of property taxes, tells several complex stories. One is a story of *new states* (Ohio, Indiana, Illinois, Michigan, Arkansas, and Missouri) exacting higher property taxes per capita than older states. In the 1810s, for instance, Ohio exacted the second highest property tax per capita, at 54 cents: compare it to Virginia, at 1 cent per capita, or Pennsylvania, for which the figure is uncertain but likely did not even reach 1 cent. The newly settled states, the explanation goes, did not have sufficient administrative capacity, and so they could not tax economic activities they were not able to measure, such as trade; moreover, they needed money relatively quickly, so instead of taxing fixed

TABLE 3.2
State Property Tax Revenues, per Capita, in Dollars (Decade Averages)

	1800	1810	1820	1830	1840	1850	1860
Northeast	**0.14**	**0.18**	**0.1**	**0.08**	**0.15**	**0.29**	**1**
CT	0.18	0.32	0.16	0.13	0.15	0.19	0.23
MA				0.12	0.07	0.46	2.01
NH			0.14	0.19	0.2	0.21	1.17
NY	0.07	0.27	0.16	0.02	0.14	0.42	1.52
PA	0	0	0	0.04	0.53	0.7	0.51
RI	0.28	0.16	0.1	0	0.05	0.26	1.61
VT	0.19	0.17	0.16	0.19	0.24	0.37	1.99
Northwest		**0.54**	**0.2**	**0.25**	**0.47**	**1.01**	**1.05**
CA						4.37	3.48
IL			0	0.35	0.52	0.69	0.45
IN			0.18	0.2	0.47	0.62	1.84
IO					0.38	0	0.01
MI				0.2	0.41	0.21	0.56
OH		0.54	0.21	0.26	0.55	1.15	0
Upper South	**0**	**0.02**	**0.03**	**0.02**	**0.07**	**0.14**	**0.25**
DE	0	0	0	0	0	0	0
KY	0	0.01	0.01	0	0	0	0
MD	0	0.01	0.08	0.03	0.04	0.04	0.04
NC	0	0.07	0.06	0.06	0	0.33	0.96
TN	0	0	0	0	0.3	0.37	0.47
VA	0	0.01	0	0	0	0.09	0.06
Lower South	**0.39**	**0.48**	**0.4**	**0.61**	**0.26**	**0.61**	**4.43**
AK				1.93	0.54	1.26	0.36
AL			0	0	0	0	0.68
GA	0	0.38	0.29	0	0.26	0	0
KA							2.27
LA			0	0	0	0.03	0
MS			0.73	0.52	0.74	0.57	0
SC	0.39	0.58	0.57	0	0	0	0

SOURCE: Sylla et al. (1995).

investments that would take time to generate profits and thus revenue, they taxed property instead.

New states followed one pattern of taxation; the impact of war on other states caused a different pattern. For instance, in the 1810s South Carolina topped Ohio's rate by about 4 cents per capita, but South Carolina was neither a recently settled nor a free state. This is the second story the table supports: a story of ratcheting fiscal extraction in conditions of war—specifically, the 1812 War, a war for which Southern states in general had to pay by raising taxes. But note how tax rates in South Carolina hovered at a high level in the decade after the war to then plummet to less than 1 cent per head in the 1840s. A similar story can be told about Georgia, expanding its fiscal apparatus to then dramatically retract it.

This leads to a third, important story: a story of low fiscal extraction in the Upper South, the core of slave-holding states (and similarly low taxes in the Lower South, if one considers that the spikes in extraction in Georgia and South Carolina coincided with the mobilization for the 1812 War and were as a result emergency measures). And this is a complementary story of moderate but steady increases in taxation in the Northern states, where democracy and fiscal extraction seemed to coexist in a mutually beneficial relationship. To be sure, in states like New York, rates increased in the first three decades of the century, then decreased, then picked up again. But contrast that to the smoother, upward trends in Connecticut, Massachusetts (for which, unfortunately, there are no reliable data prior to 1830), Rhodes Island, or New Hampshire. Taxation rates in the free, Northern states were in the longer trend more stable and higher than those in the slave-owning Southern states. On this kind of evidence, Einhorn (2006) builds an important thesis about the symbiotic relationship between taxes and democracy, a relationship she contrasts to the European path of state formation, where higher taxes *were* associated with more coercive regimes. But not so in the United States, where the most oppressive regimes were regimes with low fiscal power, because submitting taxes to the political process would have brought about inevitable debates about the nature of property, and thus would have undermined the authority of slave-holding elites.

It is not only the presence of more democratic institutions that correlates with higher taxes. It is also the development of credit institutions. Table 3.3 shows the distribution of bank money per capita across regions and selected states over the 1820–60 period. New England states appear

TABLE 3.3

Bank Money (Circulation + Deposits) per Capita, 1820–60

Region/State	1820	1830	1840	1850	1860
New England	$7.14	$9.56	$11.36	$15.99	$26.72
ME	5.54	2.4	3.51	6.33	10.12
NH	2.23	3.3	5.08	6.59	13.52
VT	0.98	3.71	4.33	10.43	14.41
MA	11.07	16.56	21.18	24.27	40.21
RI	13.6	17.37	20.71	23.75	35.14
CT	9.09	4.93	9.77	18.66	27.89
Middle Atlantic	2.61	7.71	9.08	15.46	22.77
NY		4.62	9.35	20.73	33.95
NJ		0.59	5.27	8.29	14.72
PA		9.94	8.23	10.51	12.05
South Atlantic	5.51	4.39	7.26	10	11.29
VA		4.53	7.34	8.97	10.18
Old Northwest	0.6	1.41	4.69	4.8	4.95
Old Southwest	4.85	3.65	14.98	7.35	13.74

SOURCES: Bodenhorn (2000): 63–64; Bodenhorn (2003): 79.

to have had the most monetized economies, with every resident there being able on average to dispose of about $7 both in banknotes and bank deposits for economic transactions, whereas residents in other regions had between $2 and $5.50 at their disposal in the 1820s.

While the gap between the Northeast and the other regions seems to close in the 1850s, it widens again in the decade of the Civil War. Within New England, moreover, there is great variation, with Massachusetts and Rhodes Island the most monetized states, Maine and New Hampshire lagging behind, and Connecticut exhibiting increasing monetization over time. Compare nonetheless Connecticut to Virginia: both states begin with similar levels of monetization, but by the 1850s residents of Connecticut had twice the amount of money per capita as residents of Virginia.

The evidence in Table 3.3, in sum, suggests that the New England states had more money with which to carry out economic transactions than other states. This is not surprising, considering that the Northeast was also the most commercialized and industrialized U.S. region. But the debate that exists about measuring differences in wealth between Southern and Northern states reveals no clear-cut line dividing the two regions (Pessen 1980). To be sure, the North was more industrialized, but whether its economy was significantly larger than the economy of the South (especially during the rise of King Cotton) is unclear (Schweikart 1987b). At any rate, the more unexpected relationship is revealed by returning to Table 3.2. The Northeast was the most monetized region, but it was also the region with the highest tax rates. One would expect higher levels of extraction to have dampened the diffusion of credit institutions. The opposite seems to have been the case. Consider once again a few examples. Connecticut: in the 1840s, at 15 cents of property taxes per capita, the state's level of fiscal extraction could be considered as moderate to high. Its circulation and deposits, at $9.77, put Connecticut just below the average for New England. Or take New York in the 1850s, with a steep (relative to other states) 52 cents of property taxes per capita, and a high $20.73 of bank money per capita (just below Massachusetts). In both cases, high levels of extraction and high levels of monetization appear simultaneously.

This, of course, raises a question of causation and temporal ordering: were more monetized states simply better able to impose taxes? Or were states with more developed fiscal apparatuses more favorable to monetization and the development of a banking system? Massachusetts, which seems to be an exception to this relationship between high taxes and high monetization, may provide some clues for an answer. With relatively lower levels of extraction than other Northeastern states, the Bay State exhibited the highest level of monetization. But as we have seen, Massachusetts relied specifically on taxes on banks to cover more than half its revenue needs for twenty years. As Einhorn convincingly shows, the extraction of taxes implied capacity of assessment of wealth; it politicized the budget, as rates were often agreed upon through intense negotiation between political officials and taxpayers—a tradition particularly developed in Massachusetts. Taxes, in short, reflected the democratic makeup of the state.

Additional evidence in support of an association between higher taxes in democratic states and an expansion of credit is provided in Table 3.4, in which I combine the data in the previous two tables with data on the number of banks per 100,000 inhabitant in each state/region (for which data are available). In the 1830s, for instance, among the six high-bank-tax states (let us take 20 percent as a cutoff)—Massachusetts, Rhode Island, Connecticut, Pennsylvania, Delaware, and North Carolina—Connecticut and North Carolina are the two states in which neither the number of

TABLE 3.4
Bank Taxes, Number of Banks, $ per Capita, 1820–60

Region/State	1820			1830		
	Bank as Revenue (Share)	# of Banks per 100K ppl.	$ per capita	Bank as Revenue (Share)	# of Banks per 100K ppl.	$ per capita
New England	**0.02**	**15.25**	**$7.14**	**0.21**	**19.07**	**$9.56**
ME	0	6	5.54	0	9	2.4
NH	0	7.4	2.23	.03	9.7	3.3
VT	.03	4.2	0.98	.08	6.4	3.71
MA		12.6	11.07	.61	17.2	16.56
RI	.02	56.6	13.6	.24	61.7	17.37
CT	.09	4.7	9.09	.27	10.4	4.93
Middle Atlantic	**0.27**	**4**	**2.61**	**0.19**	**4.78**	**7.71**
NY	.06	2.7		.01	4.5	4.62
NJ		6.5			7.5	0.59
PA	.53	2.1		.23	3.3	9.94
DE	.44	5.5		.43	5.2	14.37
MD	.05	3.2		.09	3.4	6.84
South Atlantic	**0.15**	**1.13**	**5.51**	**0.11**	**1.2**	**4.39**
VA	.02	.4		0	.4	4.53
NC	.31	.5		.34	.5	2.10
SC	.13	1		.01	1.4	3.48
GA		2.6			2.5	7.52
FL						
Old Northwest	**0**	**1.9**	**0.6**	**.02**	**1.4**	**1.41**
OH	0	1.9		.01	3.3	0.28
IN				.03	.3	1.47
IL				.03	.6	5.86
WI						
MI					22.1	1.53
Old Southwest		**1.1**	**4.85**		**5.4**	**3.65**
KY					6	0.80
TN		.2			3	0.33
MS		1.3			5	7.33
AL		1.4			2	2.42
LA		2.6			11	4.49
MO						8.18

Region/State	1850			1860		
	Bank as Revenue (Share)	# of Banks per 100K ppl.	$ per capita	Bank as Revenue (Share)	# of Banks per 100K ppl.	$ per capita
New England	**.20**	**14.1**	**$15.99**	**.19**	**20.6**	**$26.72**
ME	0	5.5	6.33	0	10.8	10.12
NH	0	7.2	6.59	0	15.9	13.52
VT	.04	7.3	10.43	.02	14.6	14.41
MA	.34	12	24.27	.21	14.1	40.21
RI	.46	41.3	23.75	.46	52.1	35.14
CT	.34	11.3	18.66	.45	16.1	27.89
Middle Atlantic	**.12**	**5.36**	**15.46**	**.11**	**6.8**	**22.97**
NY	.01	6	20.73	.01	7.8	33.95
NJ	0	4.9	8.29	.03	7.3	14.72
PA	.04	2	10.51	.06	2.8	12.05
DE	.52	9.8	14.40	.40	11.6	17.73
MD	.04	4.1	12.84	.03	4.5	16.13
South Atlantic	**.05**	**1.76**	**10**	**.04**	**2.84**	**11.29**
VA	.13	2.5	8.97	.10	4.3	10.18
NC	.01	2.2	4.30	.02	3	6.53
SC	0	2.1	16.98	0	2.8	21.60
GA		2	12.91		2.7	11.78
FL		0	0		1.4	2.06
Old Northwest	**.02**	**3.86**	**4.8**	**.01**	**4.72**	**4.95**
OH	.01	2.8	7.27	.02	2.2	4.76
IN	.07	1.3	3.91	0	2.7	4.94
IL	0	0	1.93	0	4.3	5.45
WI		13.9	3.24		13.9	8.49
MI	.01	1.3	2.10	.01	.5	0.74
Old Southwest		**1.7**	**7.35**	**.06**	**4.34**	**13.74**
KY	0	1.6	8.34	.04	4.1	15.92
TN	0	2.2	4.72	.14	3.3	8.44
MS	0	0	0.27	0	.5	0.28
AL		.1	4.81		.8	12.12
LA		5.4	24.70		13	44.29
MO	.13	0.9	5.77	.06		8.63

SOURCES: Sylla (1975): 249–52. Bodenhorn (2000): 63. Gilbart (1837): 43–48.

banks per 100,000 people, nor the quantity of currency per capita, exceeds regional averages (Connecticut's number of banks, of course, is high relative to other regions). By the 1850s, Connecticut too experiences financial expansion (measured through money per capita); North Carolina drops its bank taxes but remains a financial laggard.

In summary, even though the evidence is subject to the important caveats I have discussed, as well as to the inevitable unreliability of historical data collected with the imprecise reporting standards of the time, it seems to support a generalization.

It suggests a robust relationship between taxes on banking and the very development of the banking system. Democracy made the nature of banking public not in some abstract legal sense but in the practical sense of subjecting the business to taxation and thus making visible the public impact of banking practices. Banks thrived in the Northeast even though, or perhaps precisely because, they were also subject to political negotiation, to compromises—to politics, in short, that made their business relevant to the concerns of the population at large and as a result allowed them sometimes to win privileges, rights, and entitlements, while sometimes having to submit to popular demands for taxation.

More specifically, banks multiplied in states where the political system was not centered on the protection of the institution of slavery. By contrast, in states where, given the nondemocratic political regime, political debate (let alone political freedom) and thus the political jockeying of taxes were stunted, banks and the instruments they produced (banknotes and deposits) were less diffused. Lack of democracy made banking private in nature. Even though the nondemocratic states of the South were more directly involved in banking than their Northern counterparts were, that involvement subordinated banking to the interests and needs of the planter elite. Thus in one important historical interpretation,

Southern banks were primarily designed to lend the planters money for outlays that were economically feasible and socially acceptable in a slave society: the movement of crops, the purchase of land and slaves, and little else. . . . Planters wanted their banks only to facilitate cotton shipments and maintain sound money. [Especially after the bank failures of 1837,] [s]ound money and sound banking became the cries of the slave-holders as a class. Southern banking tied the planters to the banks, but more important, tied the bankers to the plantations. The banks often found it necessary to add prominent planters to their boards of directors and were closely supervised by the planter-dominated state legislatures. In this relationship the bankers could not emerge as a middle-class counterweight to the planters but could merely serve as their auxiliaries. (Genovese 1989: 21–22)

Having highlighted the institutional differences between the North and the South, I must now introduce a more specific way of characterizing how banking was affected by them, and the quotation from Genovese goes some way in providing an adequate framework: *sound bankers* thrived in the South, wildcats, by contrast, in the North.

An Example of Banking in the North: New England

Lamoreaux's fascinating study (1994) of New England banks in the nineteenth century, which she describes as "associations of debtors rather than creditors," relying for their profits not on the collection of deposits but on the capital investments by restricted circles of entrepreneurs organized on the basis of kinship (23), provides an invaluable window into the politics of credit in democratic states.

In New England, notes Lamoreaux, it was often entrepreneurial families who founded banks. Banks were means of creating investment opportunities for entrepreneurial capital, as they practiced what Lamoreaux terms "insider lending": that is, a bank collected money from several sources and then put it at the disposal of its own directors, who were not only bankers but also local industrialists and businessmen. Lamoreaux asks not simply how and why debtors gained access to credit but also how and why savers—and quite often, savers with no kinship connection to the entrepreneurs—became willing to entrust their resources to banks. A related question is why insider lending was not frowned upon as an illegitimate practice, but was, in fact, taken for granted.

Lamoreaux claims:

Because the practice of insider lending was common knowledge, purchasers of bank stock knew that they were for all practical purposes investing in the enterprises of the institution's directors. As a result, early nineteenth-century banks functioned more like investment clubs than like modern commercial institutions. They provided a relatively safe way for ordinary savers to invest in the economic development of their communities. (Ibid.: 52)

That investors would know in advance that those investments were safe, though, seems hardly to be the case, especially since large purchases of stock were made by companies controlled by the same group of men who controlled the banks. In other words, the very beneficiaries of bank loans were also responsible for raising capital for the institutions that lent to them. This would seem at first sight a recipe for risky if not predatory lending—a speculative scheme to rob investors of their hard-earned money. Surprisingly, Lamoreaux shows that, on the contrary, market yields on bank stock were comparable to those of riskless securities, to the extent that even savings institutions, the most conservative banking elements, invested in private bank stock. The evidence thus suggests that, in spite of evident opportunities for malfeasance, New England banks were for the most part prudent, soundly run, and profitable institutions. The question, once again, is what made this possible.

The answer to these dilemmas, argues Lamoreaux, is reputation. The New England banks, much like the Protestant sects that Weber would study in 1904, devised numerous ways not only to assess but also to communicate the moral probity of their officers; and, just as important, to make sure that, once that reputation was established, it was not squandered through dubious business decisions. For example, the authority of directors was under the strict supervision of the board, which made sure that their personal interests were not in conflict with the interests of the bank at large. Moreover, banks would devise restrictions on insider lending if it seemed to be excessive. Most important, because the directors of any given bank were tied to each other through kinship, they would act in the general interest of the bank even though each of them was likely to be involved in different lines of business. As a result, outside stock purchasers knew what to expect in terms of lending practices: by buying bank stock, "they were investing in the diversified enterprises of the particular group that controlled the bank, not in some anonymous diversified portfolio" (ibid.: 79). Lamoreaux sees a great advantage to this arrangement—it allowed capitalists big and small to diversify their investments (ibid.: 82–83). We shall return to the implications of this strategy in the next chapter.

Like the Protestant sects emphasized by Weber, then, New England banks devised strategies to turn the personal standing of their directors into a means of access to valued opportunities and resources. Unlike Weber's argument, however, where impersonal trust is guaranteed by strict moral standards that qualify one as creditworthy, standards that are upheld by religious congregations, Lamoreaux's analysis recognizes the importance of personal relationships. Bankers' reputations were circulated in communities that were small enough to sustain personal networks. Insider lending, and the diversification of portfolios allowed by it, worked only insofar as bankers were known to be respectable members of the community. As a result, however, once the banking business became too large, bankers had to resort to new techniques of judging and broadcasting creditworthiness. In the same way in which Weber points out that, with the increase in competition among different sects for new members, the very strategies that guaranteed the probity of the members (selectivity predicated upon careful consideration of character) ceased to work as effectively, Lamoreaux notes that bankers were faced with similar challenges once the financial sector became larger, more competitive, and less selective. Sects, argued Weber, relaxed their standards of admission in the face of competitive pressures that threatened their survival and success. Ironically, this very relaxation of standards ended up posing a more difficult challenge, because it undermined the value of membership in the congregation. Similarly, as credit relations multiplied with economic growth, becoming more available and widespread, the need to rely on personal relations decreased, and the selectivity of the process whereby one gained creditworthiness considerably loosened. The ability of any given bank to turn down applications for credit was constrained by a new need to keep up profitability in the face of competition. New England banks by the end of the nineteenth century thus underwent a transformation: they adopted more formal criteria to assess creditworthiness, which allowed them to extend loans to and accept the deposits of more anonymous clients; they professionalized; and they simultaneously became more conservative in how they used their assets. Lamoreaux laments that, with the end of insider lending, economic development in New England was stunted.

Lamoureaux's analysis, at first sight, seems to highlight important challenges faced by banking in a developing economy, such as that of the nineteenth-century United States, deriving from the uncertainty surrounding credit relations; from the problem of establishing reputation in a context of weak institutions; and from the attendant need to rely on personal relationships rather than less direct means to access credit. Much like Weber's analysis of the Protestant sects, it is a *society-centered* explanation of the rise of credit. But I submit that this society-centered explanation misses the institutional dimensions of credit and is thus incomplete. Lamoreaux describes the kind of strategies that bankers could adopt only in a *strongly* institutionalized context, that of the Northeast, where the infrastructural power of the state was anything but low, and where the democratic openness of the political regime allowed different (elite, to be sure) actors to challenge the privileges of incumbents.

Put differently: the banks described by Lamoreaux may have been prudent and efficiently run, but they were not conservative. Rather, they were wildcats in the Schumpeterian sense of using new practices of allocating credit, such as insider lending, through criteria of creditworthiness that favored its expansion.[11] The fact that, as Lamoreaux argues, they were beneficial to the Northeastern economy is not at odds with such an assessment: whether the kinds of financial innovations devised by wildcats (in this case, the practice of insider lending) led to more growth is an empirical question. But focusing on their conflict with conservative bankers allows us to emphasize the more direct challenge wildcats face: how to overcome the restrictions to credit enforced by their conservative antagonists.

Who, then, were the conservative bankers in the New England contest? With state legislatures generally open to wildcat pressures, no tradition of sound banking could firmly establish itself. Lamoreaux and Glaisek (1991), for instance, identify Rhode Island banks as vehicles of mobility, rather than privilege, suggesting that projects of resource appropriation and financial exclusion were difficult to sustain there. This dynamic can be specified even more starkly by investigating the rise and demise of the Suffolk system, a privately organized clearinghouse system whereby its Boston-based investors would buy up the notes of other banks (normally at a discount) and then present them in bulk to the issuing institution for redemption in specie. The system constituted a conservative project, because it limited the ability of bankers to expand their business beyond their capability for redemption. One way banks could avoid the full cost of redeeming their notes was to join the system, which gave them the privilege of redeeming notes at the same discount as the Suffolk. The system, created in 1824, was initially extremely successful: some authors praise the arrangement it made for note redemption as an efficient case of private coordination (see, for example, Calomiris and Kahn 1996). But it was also very controversial: country banks opposed it, for "its activities were viewed as a war against country banks waged by a 'Holy Alliance' of Boston banks" (Bodenhorn 2003: 119). Suffolk, as a result of these political conflicts, dropped out of the redemption business in 1860. As Goodhart (1988: 38–39) reminds us, Suffolk was a case of commercial bankers incurring unsolvable collective action problems, because of the conflict of interest inherent to such arrangements. The lack of political backing for sound banking intensified these collective action problems.

Banking without Democracy

Discussion of the banking matters in the North, finally, should be contextualized in terms of discussions of banking matters in the South, where such collective action problems were solved by recurring to the power of coercion backed by authoritarian state governments. In the South—where the fiscal apparatus of state governments was weak because of the nondemocratic nature of its state regimes (the paradoxical relationship between low taxes and high coercion highlighted by Einhorn); where slave-owning agrarian elites controlled the political process; where, in short, politics was a matter of defending the privileges of the slave-holding minority at the expense of the oppressed enslaved majority, and in certain areas of the South in competition with the non-slave-holding yeoman majority—practices such as insider lending were not diffused. Or rather, they involved restricted elites with political power. *Banking was organized and controlled in top-down fashion by state governments.* This is paradoxical because the traditional story about agrarian elites is that they distrusted the state and the centralization of power, in particular *financial* power. Banking thrived nonetheless in the South, but it was the kind of banking in which the state had a central, promotional, and even directive role—to put it more precisely, it was *conservative* banking that thrived.

Both general and local interpretations of banking in the antebellum South tend to focus not on the low fiscal capacity of Southern states, a reflection of the slave-based political regimes that governed them, but on the interference of the state in market processes (as in the economic literature), or on the dominance of slave-owners over the economic structure (as in a mostly Marxist literature). To be sure, the debate on whether the South was capitalist or not is enormous (see the review in Pessen 1980); but the early economic history of U.S. banking discounted the importance of banks to the Southern economy altogether; histories of the South, for the most part, emphasized the subordination of bankers to the plantation elite.

A notable effort to provide a more nuanced understanding of the role bankers played in the slave-based political economy of the South comes from Marxist historian Susan Feiner (1982). She argues that slave-holders faced two structural constraints: first, the necessity to extract as much surplus value from slaves as possible; second, the necessity to minimize the share of revenue going to what she calls "subsumed" class positions ("chattel owners, lawmakers, and displayers") (63). Access to credit was crucial, for it allowed slave-owners to expand their purchasing power; but it was cotton factors who, by virtue of their intermediating role in commercial networks, were mostly in control of credit. Masters used their power over state legislatures to charter banks that, by lending to them on favorable terms, would in turn emancipate them from cotton factors:

Masters who had struggled to receive legislative permission to have state banks or their branches operate in their locales could minimize their dealings with factors by using the credit-generating and merchanting services of banks rather than those provided by factors. The laxity of the loan practices of these banks is well known: often when a state or branch bank extended credit to a master it simply printed money after accepting almost any sort of personal or real property as collateral. (Ibid.: 66)

Feiner, then, emphasizes "laxity" in loan practices (an aspect I have associated with wildcat banking) as a defining aspect of Southern banking. Laxity here means, however, deviation from objectively sound standards for the assessment of creditworthiness—except that Feiner gives us little clue as to what such standards may be, as she emphasizes only that Southern bankers were not discerning when allocating credit to slave-owners (banks "simply printed money after accepting almost any sort of personal or real property as collateral"). The problem for Feiner's account is that, had the standards been as lax as she asserts, such a system should have generated instability. But it did not.

Economic historian Schweikart (1987a, 1987b), emphasizing the importance of banks to the development of the antebellum South, thus takes objection to Feiner's characterization that class unity describes the relationship between bankers and slave-owning elites. Rather, he claims that bankers were independent of political elites, especially in the states of the Old South (Virginia, the Carolinas, Georgia, and Louisiana), where they thus tended to be *conservative* in their lending and banknote issue practices. The New Southern states, Arkansas, Alabama, Florida, Mississippi, and Tennessee, by contrast, were more prone to speculation, but this was a function, Schweikart argues, of their very newness, and of the fact that in each of them the state government monopolized the banking business (see also Sylla and Wallis 1998). Further, Schweikart argues that statistics on the number of banks in the South systematically ignore *unchartered bankers*:

A sizable body of businessmen carried out banking and financial operations, but they used banking as an ancillary to mercantile businesses, agricultural pursuits, or commercial brokerage operations. They often considered themselves bankers but for a variety of reasons never went through the process of applying for formal charters. Frequently they were in career transition from managing mercantile operations to establishing their own chartered banks. (Schweikart 1987b: 32)

Scheiwkart ends with a condemnation of state monopolies and a celebration of the free market ("the market operated quite effectively where it was not subject to suffocation by the state or crushed by state monopolies" [ibid., 36]). He goes so far as to say, "Had the South been permitted to reestablish the banks of issue after the war, the level of competition in the antebellum period suggests that the freedmen would have enjoyed real access to credit relatively sooner, and to a much more significant degree, than occurred" (ibid.). In this account, the pervasive legacy of slavery on the political economy of the South disappears—for it is the state, and its encouragement of monopolistic practices, that now is to blame for restricting access to credit.

More balanced accounts have emerged recently, and rather than emphasizing the class unity of banking and political elites, or the alleged independence (in some states) of the two from each other, they argue that it was slavery, not state intervention over the economy, that impaired the economic development of the South. Secondly, they argue that the nondemocratic nature of the Southern states allowed for a high degree of collaboration between different economic and political actors, as long as that collaboration was grounded on slavery, and thus on a boundary that was very restrictive in states where *a majority of the population was enslaved* and a majority of the free population was politically incapacitated from challenging the institution of slavery (Einhorn 2006, 2009).

The first aspect is brought out in the context of railroad development by Majewski (2000), who, through a local comparison between two counties (Albemarle and Cumberland) and the two states in which they were located (Virginia and Pennsylvania), traces the economic processes leading to sectional divergence in transportation schemes. These locales were similar on a number of geographical indicators, but important demographic differences arose from the fact that in Albermarle slavery was dominant, whereas in Cumberland it was not. Both in Albemarle and in Virginia at large, the unequal distribution of wealth that resulted from slavery impeded the emergence of large, densely populated urban centers, and of a vibrant market for consumer goods: as a result, the Old Dominion, while undertaking several internal improvement projects, failed to finance a coherent transportation network. A lack of capital, but also of political will, was responsible for this. Large slave-owners in the small centers scattered around Virginia provided a bulk of the capital for transportation projects, with the state picking up the rest of the tab. But no investor was large enough to buy off the others, no political authority gained the power to mediate local rivalries and strive to rationalize these transportation projects, and local interests, with their provincial ambitions, prevailed. In Pennsylvania, by contrast, where major urban centers did emerge, where capital came from several, smaller investors, and where the state government had more capacity, an integrated railroad network was financed and built, giving the region an economic edge over Virginia. In Majewski's account, in sum, we find no single equation linking markets to development. State capacity and the nature of the political regime played more fundamental roles. A focus on free markets, or on how politics constrains them, would simply miss this story.

If the kind of development undertook by the South varied from Northern development, so did the basis upon which the Southern banking system was constructed. Thus Bodenhorn (2003: 219–48) argues that there was staggering variety in banking practices throughout the South, with bankers mostly involved in the financing of mercantile transactions, and only indirectly in extending loans to farmers. But unlike Feiner and Schweikart, Bodenhorn sees the activities of bankers as complementary to, rather than in competition with, other providers of credit, like the factors. The "southern system" normally entailed the establishment of "a large, well-capitalized mother branch and a rationalized branch network. Some branches tapped local reservoirs of capital, while others distributed it." He adds: "Such practices diffused the bank's notes, monetized the economy, and fostered trust in the institution."[12] In fact, a common leitmotiv in Southern projects of internal improvement and economic development, of which banks were a central component, was the promotion of the "Commonwealth ideal" (ibid.: 239–45; Scheiber 1975), whereby the state took the central, directive role of pursuing the welfare of the "community."

But this seemingly benign ambition hid a much darker reality in

the South: that the community to be protected was that of the slave-holders, and that projects of internal improvement were designed to keep in
check the much feared economic decline of the South, in the face of an
industrializing North whose economic success threatened the most basic
aspect of Southern political economy, slavery (Bensel 1990; Majewski 2000;
Fehrenbacher 2002; Einhorn 2009). Appeals to slavery were mobilized in
the vein of a negative cult, borrowing from Durkheim's (1995) sociology
of religion: they would draw strict boundaries between members of the
sacred community (a racial community, in this case), and its outsiders
(slaves), developing systems of prohibitions and taboos intended to police
those boundaries. But, unlike positive cults, which prescribe how members of the community approach and worship the deity, racist appeals in
the South had fewer prescriptions about relations among whites when it
came to devising economic policies: the Commonwealth ideal was thus,
surprisingly, a hollow one.[13] It could not have been otherwise in states
where the practice of electing rather than appointing officials was relatively new (Einhorn 2006: 219), and where elites not only ensured that
fiscal penetration and the resulting potential for political compromises
over tax rates were underdeveloped but also inscribed such guarantees in
state constitutions by passing "uniformity clauses" intended to protect the
ownership of slaves from excessive taxation (ibid.: ch. 6).

Genovese's assessment (1989: 21–22), one that I quoted at the end of
the previous section, thus turns out to have more than an element of truth
in it: bankers could invest in investments that were "socially acceptable,"
with the slave-owning elites in firm control over how what was socially
acceptable was defined. There were no wildcats in the Southern banking
system, then, given that slavery provided the dominant categorical identity
to which all other identities were subordinated, and that the state was effective at fostering collaboration among different social groups only when
slave-owner interests were not threatened, but was highly ineffective at
mediating conflicts when those interests collided. That is, the state would
simply resort to notions of patriotism, local boosterism, and an apocalyp-
tic scenario of Southern demise to restore unity of political intents.

Conclusions

For libertarian economist Vera Smith (1990: 44), the "foundation of
[early U.S.] banks was much more often based on political influence than

on real commercial necessity." The American system was "decentralized without freedom [because] it lacked the essential characteristics both of central banking and of free banking proper. The distribution of powers between the Federal and the State authorities left legislative control in banking matters in the hands of both" (ibid.: 42), effectively politicizing the banking system and, in her view, making it unresponsive to the needs of the economy. Bray Hammond, a Federal Reserve officer who in the 1950s turned historian of U.S. banking, similarly peppered his classic, 1957 study of early U.S. banks with references to their political affiliations, painting them as examples of cronyism and partisan bias.

Both characterizations certainly have an element of truth in them. But they also assume that the relationship between banking and politics, between government and the economy, is by definition an unhealthy one—that banking and politics belong to institutional spheres that should never be mixed, as if they were "hostile worlds" (Zelizer 2005c). The model behind these historical studies is, in other words, one that considers government interventionism as ineffectual at best, or misguided at worst: either way, government's involvement in the economy is seen as coercive and distortive, and the centralization of power it brings about is expected to be resisted by social groups and societal forces. Society's reaction to excessive centralization, in turn, is said to restore a more balanced relationship between state and society.[14] This is, in short, a society-centered model of social, institutional, and economic change. In the specific case of banking, it also becomes a *market-centered* model.

Over the past twenty or so years, however, historical institutionalism has begun to question common assumptions about the nature of social change—locating historical agency in the very institutions that earlier historians saw as exclusively constraining (John 1997; Balogh 2009). It is from this new perspective that I attempted to solve the puzzle of the fleeting nature of creditworthiness, and more generally of the extent to which the conflict between conservative and wildcat bankers characterizes the development of banking.

Bankers are status groups, and, as Weber pointed out, the criteria with which status groups justify exclusion are always arbitrary. They tend to be informed by categories that elicit minimum resistance from those in power. And so it is from conditions in the larger political environment that bankers draw the power and authority to shape the financial field toward either end of the continuum between exclusion and inclusion.

On the one hand, there is a political culture of banking conservatism, predicated on principles that stabilize the status quo by excluding actors and clients who do not fulfill the criteria implied by those principles. On the other, there is a political culture of wildcat banking, predicated on principles of inclusion regardless of criteria of membership, and thus often leading to speculation and predatory practices. This opposition is made possible by the fact that criteria of creditworthiness can never be objective: rather, they are mobilized in the context of financial struggles in which those who succeed in drawing new boundaries and enforcing shared identities within those boundaries can then command the collective process through which market advantages and market resources are appropriated.

In the U.S. case, wildcat banking was a feature common to more open political systems, where boundaries among competing status groups were less effectively and less strictly demarcated, as well as less moralized because of the flexibility and depth of the fiscal system. In states where the fiscal apparatus of the state was more developed because the state was more democratic, credit was more democratic too. According to Gilje (1996: 164):

Americans did not invent banking, they democratized it. Initially banks even in the United States were elitist institutions. . . . But privilege in the increasingly egalitarian United States was difficult to maintain. Other groups quickly petitioned for their own banks, and although it was a struggle at first, soon almost anyone with capital could form their own bank.

This was true in the North, but patently not true in the South, where banking thrived in the guise of large, state-controlled institutions. There, politics was less open to interactions with societal forces, and as a result taxes were lower, banks were less diffused, they circulated less money, and they tended to rely on state governments directly for their finances. Politics, in other words, was central to the constitution of the banking system in both Southern and Northern states, but where it was more subject to democratic and participatory processes, it also led to more open financial systems.

A focus on the institutional sources of banking, then, serves to suggest a new perspective on the question of the personal nature of creditworthiness that I discussed at the beginning of this chapter. I submit that *the professed attention to character as a signal of creditworthiness was the rhetoric that conservative bankers mobilized in order to legitimize boundaries around credit in conditions of democracy.* A focus on reputation as a precondition to credit worked, that is, in political systems where the business of banking was subject to competitive pressures originating from the political system, not from the economy. The language, as we shall see in the next chapter, took root in the postbellum period, when the number of banks catering to all sorts of credit demands proliferated, and less creditworthy actors had a better chance of petitioning for credit than they did in systems where the boundaries between those deemed worthy of credit and those who were excluded were more rigid. And because credit became more democratic, transgression of those boundaries was also more widespread.

Those criteria could have been articulated on explicitly political terms, to be sure. In fact, there were several instances in which merchants and other economic elites campaigned for new banking institutions precisely by claiming that, under current conditions, they were being denied credit on political grounds (Bodenhorn 2006). Yet widespread uncertainty about the strength of political support for sound banking in the North, and the incompatible political identity that characterized the South, made politics too divisive an issue. And especially after the Civil War, when the banking system was developed on a national framework, depoliticizing credit, in the sense of creating shared identities to regulate its allocation that escape political purview and control, became a priority for U.S. bankers. The concept of creditworthiness as a character trait, rather than the result of one's membership in politically defined groups, became particularly useful as a way of legitimizing the professional roles of bankers. This is the subject of the next chapter.

4

Wildcats, Reputations, and the Formation of the Federal Reserve

THE GUIDING POINT for our discussion so far has been that, while there are numerous, more or less relational (that is, face-to-face) bases upon which creditors can rely to decide whether or not they want to lend money to individual creditors, bankers tend to face challenges to their control over credit of a different nature. These challenges have little to do with the ability to assess the soundness of individual credit decisions. Conservative bankers must mark the boundaries that divide debtors into those creditworthy and those undeserving of credit by constructing shared identities to which debtors and creditors alike commit, and this is a political activity. Whether the criteria by which they assess creditworthiness are rational and objective is beside the point, for even if the criteria could once and for all eliminate the contingencies inherent to the creditor-debtor relationship, it would take a more general mechanism to bind financial providers to those criteria. It is commitment to the collective identities that matters, and that commitment can never be based on a rational foundation. Rather, it has to originate with a shared sense of membership, one that wildcat bankers will find difficult and costly to contest. The grounds on which banking is organized, thus, are political.

The previous chapter suggested that in the Northern states of the United States, where state governments were democratic, bankers were at once recipients of political patronage, *and* subject to democratic constraints, in the form of taxes. In the South, where not only were taxes lower, but, in addition, the system of fiscal extraction was not grounded on deliberation and political jockeying, banking was less developed—but existing bankers were also able to win larger political favors. In neither region did appeals to the functional contribution of banks to the efficient allocation of credit characterize debates about banking at the time, despite the existence of fairly elaborate and increasingly widespread systems for the assessment of creditworthiness, originating in mercantile communities and spreading over time throughout the credit economy (Zucker 1986; Olegario 2006). In the North, it was the banks' relationship with politics and, more precisely, with institutions of public governance, that attracted the attention of analysts, commentators, and political representatives. And in the South, it was the relationship between banks and the plantation economy, and later, their contribution to closing a perceived gap between North and South, that animated public debate.

Having considered the relationship between banks and political authority, this chapter emphasizes challenges to banking conservatism that arise when political representatives and financial challengers—wildcats—join forces in contesting the legitimacy of criteria that emphasize soundness, exclusivity, and strict screening in the allocation of credit. Wildcats tend to challenge the general framework that conservative bankers apply to their credit decisions, and respond by proposing alternative definitions of creditworthiness that emphasize openness and access, but this is a latent feature of financial fields. Wildcats must gain organizational strength for their demands for financial inclusion to become relevant. So they are always ready to exploit opportunities in the larger political environment that afford them a chance to jostle for power within the financial field.

Democratic regimes often offer plenty of political opportunities. In democracies, political parties too jockey for power, and thus are in the business of both responding to and shaping societal demands. Since the boundaries that define creditworthy behavior can be contested, conservative bankers cannot take the support of political authorities for granted. Political representatives tend to have little sympathy for the conservative bankers' demand to regulate the flow of credit; they often find it politically advantageous to give in to, if not altogether encourage, demands for financial inclusion. When they attack the strict boundaries that conservative bankers build around the allocation of credit as excessively exclusive, if not altogether discriminatory, their demands become indistinguishable from those of wildcat bankers.

In this chapter, I show that, in the nineteenth-century United States, wildcat bankers, in an alliance with politicians (most famously, Jacksonian Democrats) who shared the wildcats' position against government privileges, increasingly contested and disrupted the activities of conservative bankers. This challenge was motivated not so much on the grounds that bankers allocated credit inefficiently, but by the accusation that they monopolized a power that should be distributed over larger constituencies. The chapter also documents how, faced by this challenge, conservative bankers strove to devise new collective identities in order to commit the banking system as a whole to principles of sound banking and financial austerity. It was not possible for them to protect collective identities they already used to legitimize sound banking, as their calls for more effective systems of financial regulation were rebuked by wildcat arguments against the reinforcement of political authority—ultimately appealing to the need to defend slavery, the system of exclusion and exploitation on which a large part of the U.S. political economy was based. Even in the aftermath of the Civil War, when slavery was formally abolished, strong echoes of sectional divisions still characterized debates about, and legislation on, the proper role of government.[1] The structure of political and financial relations was thus unable to produce shared identities that would command commitment and mutual solidarity among bankers, while securing the political support of relevant authorities to a project of conservative, sound banking. Shared identities to regulate banking would have to come from within the system, and thereby without external political support.

Conservative bankers, accordingly, refashioned themselves as neutral arbiters of character and reputations, couching this role in an ideology that identified the value of money as deriving from commercial transactions (the "real bills" doctrine). They also refashioned private creditworthiness and individual reputation into the basis for a project of privately enforced regulation that eventually constituted the blueprint for the design of the Federal Reserve (even though the Federal Reserve Act imposed an important degree of public control over finance).

Nineteenth-century Wildcats

In the system that preceded the rise to power of Andrew Jackson, both state governments and the federal government had attempted to control the expansion of credit and the nature of economic development. But this mode of governance was superseded, from the 1830s onward, by a more liberal system in which credit and banking became subject to more

TABLE 4.1
Conservative and Wildcat Banking, United States

United States	Conservative Bankers		Wildcat Bankers	
Institutional Basis: Decentralized Polity				
Period:	Antebellum	Postbellum	Antebellum	Postbellum
Identity: Who are they?	State banks in the South; powerful, mostly city-based banks (e.g., Boston) in the North.	Finance capitalists, especially in New York and Boston, increasingly striving to build self-sustaining systems of resource appropriation. Midwestern bankers embedded in commercial circuits.	Jacksonian banks; elites striving for new financial footholds; free bankers.	Unregulated banks and bank-like institutions (e.g., trust companies).
Plan: How do they plan to make money?	Exploited political relationships with state governments (especially in the South) and facilitated entrepreneurial undertakings of urban elites.	Wall Street: Concentrated wealth through stock market manipulation (wildcat phase), then devised ways to exclude others (e.g., clearing house systems). Midwest: Embeddedness in local economy and facilitation of goods transport.	Facilitated mobilization of excluded elites; predatory practices toward more marginal players.	Exploited regulatory gaps deriving from decentralized political power.
Strategy: How do they implement their plan?	Granted credit based on possession of political credentials.	Credit based on degree of integration in elite circles.	Mobilization of excluded elites through populist campaigns.	Dodged systems of public control.
Threat: Who challenges them?	Wildcats: Financial activities of wildcats forced conservatives to give up formal alliances with political authorities.	Wildcats: Deregulated commercial institutions.	Conservative elites with strong financial leverage (e.g., urban-based commercial elites).	Corporate consolidators.
Relationship to new customers	Weak; negotiated through politics.	Weak; negotiated through stock market manipulation on the one hand, and the myth of creditworthiness as personal reputation on the other.	Extensive, predatory, and idealistic (populist mobilization with the Jacksonian movement).	Mediated by state-level politics (deregulation).

formal, abstract rules—the so-called general incorporation rules. Within the framework set out by those rules, state governments distributed their deposits to several small banks, thereby expanding the size of the financial field and giving ample opportunities for wildcats to emerge, while relinquishing control over finance. In this section, I discuss in some detail how these political processes affected the nature of financial conflict in the antebellum United States.

Free banking signaled the beginning of a crisis in the Northern system of doing banking. In the North, the relationship between banking and politics had been subject to political pressure, to contestation, and thus to political compromises. For all their flaws, the circuits of money that characterized the Northern system had originated with a political authority over which citizens had some degree of influence. This had created opportunities for wildcats to contest sound banking practices, and so the weakness of this system, from the point of view of conservative bankers, was that it had given politics too much leeway. From the point of view of constituencies invested in financial expansion, too, politics—which, to them, meant partisanship—had too much sway over the banking sector, but for the opposite reason, that politics was a mechanism of patronage and nepotism. These criticisms came together with Andrew Jackson's ascent to power in 1829, and his subsequent refusal to recharter the Second Bank of the United States (SBUS) in 1832.

The SBUS was the second of the only two federally chartered banks to appear in the antebellum United States. The First Bank had been the brainchild of Hamilton, and part of his larger state-building project: he had decided that the federal government would assume the debt of the individual colonies after the 1776 Revolution, so he set up an institution that would manage the newly constituted federal debt and thus enhance public credit.[2] The First Bank of the United States, however, precisely because it was a federally chartered bank, immediately raised state elite eyebrows. The renewal of its charter was blocked in 1811, but due to the 1812 War and the financial problems it brought about, James Madison, in a reversal of his previous position, succeeded in 1816 in chartering its successor, the SBUS (Savage 1988). Old Hickory and his Democratic supporters made the destruction of this bank a central part of their political platform, just as the Jeffersonians had opposed the First Bank of the United States (Sellers 1994; Howe 2007).

Andrew Jackson's war against the SBUS drew on a suspicion of centralized authority that characterized political debate of the time, and remains a long-standing feature of North American political culture (Dobbin 1994, 2004). In his 1829 presidential message to Congress, Jackson had argued: "Both the constitutionality and the expediency of the law creating this Bank are well questioned by a large portion of our fellow citizens; and it must be admitted by all that it has failed in the great end of establishing a uniform and sound currency" (Hammond 1957: 374). While this war against the SBUS was fueled by the general's antipathy toward central government, and his support of states' rights, the stakes were rather more complex (see, esp., Balogh 2009).

One important objective was the freeing of all banks from political and partisan interference, an objective that embodied the antimonopoly orientation of the Jacksonians. The Jacksonians initially considered rescinding political authority over banking, on the grounds that banks were private institutions, as a way to achieve this: chartering, in this view, was considered a vehicle of monopoly. The more radical wing of the Democratic Party, known as the hard-money wing, went as far as advocating a return to metallic currency: its exponents argued that the right to issue banknotes—one that state laws conferred to chartered banks—was a kind of privilege for which there was no equivalent for other businesses (Formisano 1974). In making this case for the private nature of banks, the Jacksonian position was not so much free-market, laissez faire, as it was antimonopoly. The Jacksonians' "terms of abuse were 'oppression,' 'tyranny,' 'monied power,' 'aristocracy,' 'wealth,' 'privilege,' 'monopoly'; their terms of praise 'the humble,' 'the poor,' 'the simple,' 'the honest and industrious' (Hammond 1957: 328; see also Formisano 1974 and Silbey 1994). From this radically liberal position, charters should be done completely away with, and the right to issue paper money similarly abolished.

The Jacksonians, however, were forced to confront the fact that banks were too entrenched in the economy. Thus they slowly abandoned the private conceptualization of banks that had made them complain about chartering and monopoly as undue privileges. They opted for a regulationist approach instead that recognized their public character (Lamoreaux 1994: 41–48). From this new, publicly oriented conceptualization, they also came to argue for the opposite of their original position—that is, for the regulation of the banking business.[3] The Jacksonians pushed for a reform of the system whereby charters were granted.

Within the context of their acceptance of the public nature of banking, their aversion to centralized authority reasserted itself to take a new, consequential shape.

Free Banking

The Northern states, where the practice of granting charters to multiple institutions was more diffuse, had witnessed a proliferation of banks. Chartering, however, tended to have a partisan character, and quickly became a Jacksonian target. Chartering was at once too top-down to accommodate their demands for financial expansion, because it depended on an act of approval by the state legislature, which to the Jacksonians was an act of elitism. And while chartering, at the same time, was too bottom-up and thus vulnerable to political struggle, for constituencies invested in sound banking, to the Jacksonians this was synonymous with governmental interference. In kind, they began advocating for an alternative system that would subject the business of banking to formal rules, and subsequently remove it from the politics of the states.

The movement for free banking began at the local level, and acquired particular strength in the state of New York. There, the two strands that had characterized Jacksonian liberalism—antimonopoly and laissez-faire—came together with more pragmatic concerns—anti-Republican sentiment and a concern with the importance of banking to growth (Bodenhorn 2003: 191)—to create a regulatory framework based not on politics but on abstract rules: the so-called free banking laws. Free banking consisted of the extension of the right to issue notes to any financial institution meeting certain general requirements (Timberlake 1993). Those requirements concerned the amount of gold and silver that banks were obliged to stock in their vault, as well as government bonds they had to deposit with appropriate state authorities; the laws also imposed some limits on lending to directors; and included transparency requirements.[4]

The laws, due to their focus on formal rules, were an attempt to supersede the existing regulatory regime. They were meant to sever the connection between banks and local politics: to minimize, that is, the role of political jockeying in the development of the banking business. By the same token, free banking weakened patronage and corruption, but simultaneously limited the political accountability of banking. It made no provision for the political control of the banking system.[5] This does not mean, of course, that no authorities at all were involved in the regulation of free banking. For one thing, prior to circulating notes, a bank was required to deposit an appropriate amount of state bonds with a state authority as security for those notes (Rockoff 1974: 141). In the event of the bank's inability to redeem the notes for specie (as the law required), the authority would sell the bonds to raise the money needed to reimburse its noteholders. Careful econometric studies of the Free Banking period attribute the moderate-to-high failure rate of free banks, at least in part, not to the application of general rules to incorporation but to the misguided policy of valuing the bonds deposited with the authority at face rather than at market value—thus making it possible for bankers to overissue currency (Rockoff 1974). Others point to the more general link between note issue and bonds of fluctuating value as a cause of instability (Rolnick and Weber 1983, 1984).

The more general point, though, is that authorities could act only after the fact. They were no longer asked to govern the allocation of credit, precisely because such a responsibility now smacked of corruption. Rather, they were supposed to intervene only once financial trouble had broken out, and then only so as to protect the assets of those who had invested in, or lent to, failing banks. As a result, although free banking laws were meant to achieve the separation between politics and banking in the name of autonomy, responsibility, and accountability, they made only the first goal possible: they meant only that no regulatory, nonbanking body could intervene in adjudicating the soundness of banking practices.

The results were destabilizing. From New York, Michigan, and Georgia, where the laws were passed concurrently in 1837–39, free banking laws spread to Alabama, New Jersey, Illinois, Massachusetts, Ohio, and Vermont by 1851. In the next three years, Connecticut, Indiana, Tennessee, Wisconsin, Florida, and Louisiana passed similar laws. Iowa, Minnesota, and Pennsylvania joined the free banking group by the end of the decade (ibid. 1983: 1082). Redlich (1968: 188) quotes approvingly one Ohio legislator, who quipped in 1839: "Free Banking is the wildest scheme of Utopian speculation prevalent on this subject. It is founded on the fallacious supposition that the business of banking should be conducted solely with a view to private gain and in total disregard of the public interests." Drawing on data on the incidence of bank failures in Ohio, New York, Indiana, and Wisconsin in the 1840–60 period, Hasan and Dwyer (1994) provide support for the proposition that the spread of free banking was associated with more instability. They show that wildcat banking increased the likelihood of runs on banks located in geographical proximity to failing banks, as their customers did not have sufficient information to tell which bank was, in fact, solvent. Paradoxically this led to contagion and widespread failure—the classic case of the "self-fulfilling prophecy" (see Aghion, Bolton, and Dewatripont 2000 for a formal statement).

Faced by wildcat banking, their conservative counterparts were forced to focus their energies on creating shared identities that would commit the banking systems to common principles. They resorted to several private schemes to protect themselves, the most important of which was rudimentary clearinghouses "which resemble clearinghouses' certification of banks during suspensions of convertibility in the last half of the nineteenth century" (Hasan and Dwyer 1994: 284; see also Timberlake 1993). But these were localized and thus limited efforts. They could not provide the broad framework upon which conservative bankers rely in order to manipulate in their favor the shape of existing circuits.[6]

The extent to which the role of conservative and exclusive identities was contested, and how the freedom of banking contributed to the pursuit of private gain at the expense of the very circuits that made that private gain possible to begin with, was reflected in the widespread diffusion of counterfeiting, as Steven Mihm (2007) shows in depth. Counterfeiting, especially of banknotes, had been a common practice in the decentralized polity of the United States from a very early period. Anyone "could use [banknotes]; their worth did not depend on the assets of the individual who presented them, but on confidence in corporate fortunes" (ibid.: 12–13).

But Jacksonian reforms contributed to further atomizing the power to issue money. Now that formal rules dictated what requirements bankers should fulfill before they gained the right to issue notes, there was at least a formal guarantee that the bank was solvent. But with no authority scrutinizing whether the following of rules was sufficient to ensure banking stability, and with a generalized skepticism that any authority was capable of taking an objective and neutral position on regulation, enforcement of free banking provisions was problematic.[7] Jackson himself realized that lack of regulation was a problem in his approach to banking, when he noticed that, instead of ushering in a return to gold coin as the medium of exchange, free banking led to an explosion of paper money. In his farewell address on March 4, 1837, Jackson put it thus:

The paper system being founded on public confidence and having of itself no intrinsic value, it is liable to great and sudden fluctuations, thereby rendering property insecure and the wages of labor unsteady and uncertain. . . . These ebbs and flows in the currency and these indiscreet extensions of credit naturally engender a spirit of speculation injurious to the habits and character of the people. . . . It is not by encouraging this spirit that we shall best preserve public virtue and promote the true interests of our country; but if your currency continues as exclusively paper as it now is, it will foster this eager desire to amass wealth without labor; it will multiply the number of dependents on bank accommodations and bank favors; the temptation to obtain money at any sacrifice will become stronger and stronger, and inevitably lead to corruption, which will find its way into your public councils and destroy at no distant day the purity of your Government.[8]

Free banking without a gold currency, to Jackson, was as corrupt a system as that which had preceded it. But because of his opposition to the authority of the federal government in the management of the monetary system, Jackson could only appeal to an elusive, higher authority—that of the gold standard—as the proper means to regulate the issue of currency. To depoliticize the banking system, in his eyes, meant to entrust money to an international monetary regime. What the Democrats in fact did, however, was to entrust it in the hands of the myriad bankers who, once having fulfilled legal criteria to begin banking operations, had complete freedom in running their business. Mihm (ibid.: 152) thus notes that counterfeiting dramatically *increased* after the passing of free banking laws, and especially after the crisis precipitated by Jackson's monetary policy made paper money the circulating medium: paper money that was printed not just by bankers, but by "oyster cellar owners, tavern keepers, dry goods dealers, import and export firms, to name a few . . . . Every man became a banker, but operated without the slightest sanction from the state."

As far as the organization of credit and finance goes, in sum, the Jacksonian era was one with very limited space for government intervention, both at the local and at the federal level (Watson 2006); and in general, it was also a period in which conservative bankers were on the defense, because the kinds of exclusive identities on which they based sound banking methods were widely contested. The policies of the Democratic successors to Jackson intensified these processes. Once the Second Bank of the United States was stripped of its federal charter, and the federal deposits it held were withdrawn, Van Buren, president after Jackson's second term, instituted what came to be known as the Independent Treasury

System (Temin 1969). The gold deposits the Treasury had previously held with the SBUS were distributed to a large network of smaller institutions (contemporaries called them "pet" banks) (Timberlake 1993). This was another means of debilitating the SBUS—which remained the only powerful U.S. bank with a national scope to its activities. But it was also a way to encourage state banks (especially on the frontier) to expand their activities, with the unintended effect of impairing the liquidity of banks in the East that were more strict in their adherence to conservative banking principles. Drained of gold, Eastern banks found themselves unable to meet demand for coin, and as a result had to restrict credit, precipitating the U.S. economy into a crisis and then a depression. De Cecco (1986: 118) thus assesses Jacksonian policies in strongly negative terms: "From the point of view of monetary management, a series of financial measures nearer to pure folly would be difficult to imagine."[9] Contemporaries were more sanguine: they saluted the financial program of the Democrats as America's "second declaration of Independence" (Silbey 1994).

Folly or not, there was a pragmatic aspect to Jackson's policy against the bank, and to Van Buren's continuation of the war by further concentrating monetary authority in the Treasury while dispersing the resources with which that authority could be exercised: centralized banking was an intolerable challenge to presidential power (Remini 2001: 220–32). The Jacksonians favored the expansion of federal authority only when it came to military issues (such as the Indian Removal policies of Jackson) or repression (John 1998; Fehrenbacher 2002)—issues that reinforced the president's grip on power. But centralized authority in matters of economic regulation was a different matter: it not only meant favoritism, and the undue promotion of certain private interests at the expense of others (Ashworth 1996). It also incubated a potential challenge to presidential authority.

The nature of this challenge was not exclusively direct—even though a centralized banking system could certainly serve as an autonomous and antagonistic power base (Sellers 1994: 322–23). Given how dramatically the political economies of the North and the South differed, and how contentious was the issue of whether political power should be used to boost them (Majewski 2000; Bateman and Weiss 2002), centralized authority also meant having to deal with the intractable problem of slavery (Einhorn 2009). Thus the challenge posed by centralization attacked the very heart of the Democrats' political strategy. The Jacksonians had turned to the issues of decentralization and states' rights as a way of reaffirming and defending the centrality of slavery to U.S. society, and in that way gaining the favor of the lower classes in the North (through demagoguery) and the upper classes in the South. Van Buren embraced this Jacksonian approach in even stronger terms. As it turns out, some prominent Southern elites had been in favor of a more centralized banking system: they benefited from the predictability and regularity in economic exchange that only a large and powerful institution like the Second Bank of the United States could promote (Howe 2007: 390). These were, as we have seen, financially conservative elites, accustomed to using state power to their advantage. And support for the SBUS had been widespread in other states as well, most notably Pennsylvania, where the bank was physically located. In fact, Jackson had had to resort to a presidential veto to remove the charter, since a congressional majority in July 1832 had *approved* the rechartering of the bank. Jackson was weakened, but not defeated, by these potential sources of opposition to his war against the bank. To be sure, he had strong allies of his own (most notably, New York commercial elites who cherished the idea of weakening their rival elites in Philadelphia; Hammond [1957], Rockoff [1974]). More generally, though, his populist message used the appeal of more general, exclusionary identities—in this case, white supremacist ones—than those his conservative opponents were willing, and able, to mobilize. With such appeals, Jackson managed to control the political fallout of his war against the SBUS. For all his support of democracy (Wilentz 2006), Jackson had clear ideas about where the boundaries that limited the enjoyment of its benefit lay, and those were racial boundaries (Richards 2000). His embracement and support of white supremacy were key to his success (Howe 2007: 359). This approach neutralized potential opposition to certain economic measures in the South by appealing to a widely shared, white supremacy identity, the defense of which superseded other considerations (Richards 2000). In Howe's words (2007: 510): "White supremacy remained central to Jacksonian Democracy throughout the second party system, no less pervasively than economic development was to Whiggery."

Jackson's embracement of such general, exclusionary identities must of course be contextualized in the historical period to which he belonged. But a more general theoretical pattern can be detected here. Wildcat strategies are aimed at extending access to credit to actors who were previously marginalized and excluded. Their political allies may make even more general claims about the injustice of existing systems of exclusion. But this should not be confused with the promotion of social justice. The transgression of existing boundaries through which wildcats generate prestige for their own ideas about how banking should take place is nested within a larger system of exclusions that the wildcats have no interest in transcending—exclusions that, in fact, wildcats often reinforce precisely to gain legitimacy for their strategy. These identities are part of the deep structure of exclusions on which status group appropriation is based. Tilly (1998) calls them "categorical" and argues that organizations appropriate them so as to skillfully incorporate the general "scripts" they entail (and thus the boundaries they draw) into the local system of knowledge that characterizes their task environment. Murphy (1984: 555) derives these general identities from "the principal form of exclusion [as] the set of exclusion rules, backed by the legal (and hence ultimately military) apparatus of the state, which is the main determinant of access to or exclusion from power, resources, and opportunities in society." Insofar as the strategy of political elites who gain popular support reinforces general exclusionary boundaries, but contests the more specific ones nested within, the larger system of inequality will be reproduced, even as the boundaries of the financial field shift.

Accordingly, the Jacksonian Democrats became the party of decentralized authority in economic matters, access to credit by the "common man," and slavery, each political position reinforcing the other two. In this endeavor, they were certainly aided by the conservative bankers' reconfiguring of their relationship with political authorities. In the 1840s, the system of state revenue and investment that had preceded Jacksonian financial expansion entered a crisis. States had been directly involved in the financing of canals (and then of railways) (Scheiber 1975, 1981), but in the early 1840s, seven of them—specifically, those that had made bets on such "improvement" schemes to pay for themselves over time, and that had done away with property taxes—failed to meet their financial obligations and defaulted (Sylla and Wallis 1998). Given the considerable share of foreign investment that had flown into these schemes (Wilkins 1989), the most immediate effect was an international crisis of U.S. creditworthiness, and, domestically, a general "revulsion against public improvements" (Goodrich 1950). From then on, state "boosterism" of economic activity was met with severe criticism, to the effect that it favored cronyism and unfairness, and was generally ineffective (Wallis 2000).

The ascent to power of the Whigs—after Van Buren's inability to alleviate the deep economic depression had cost the Democrats the presidency—momentarily seemed to turn events around. The Whigs, unlike the Democrats, were supportive of government planning and interventionism, and even of a third national bank (Holt 2003). Howe (2007: 612) concludes that "from the vantage point of the twenty-first century, we can see that the Whigs, though not the dominant party of their own time, were the party of America's future." But the Whigs' political blunders had the shorter-term effect of stalling national plans for development. The descent of the United States into the Civil War, while forcing both the Union and the Confederacy to centralize power in the government in unprecedented ways as they mobilized for war (and this especially in the South [Bensel 1990]), in some ways and paradoxically also solidified the character of U.S. banking as decentralized banking. In other words, the crisis of local improvement schemes only served to reinforce the Jacksonian thrust toward privatizing the economy and, as a consequence, of the banking system.

The Illegitimacy of Political Authority

When political support fails to materialize, so that politics ceases to be a source of reliable, stable identities with which bankers control credit, we can expect conservative bankers to seek more specialized categories of their own making.[10] This strategy opens them to challenges and conflict yet serves at least partially to insulate them from wildcat bankers, and the political elites allied with them, who are, in any case, already accusing them of elitism and exclusivity. Whether and how successfully conservative bankers in the postbellum United States pursued this strategy can be understood only after considering the effects of the Civil War on U.S. banking.

Two consequences of the war are particularly relevant here: the feeble centralization of the banking system the war brought about, and the continued political support for wildcat banking that this feeble centralization made possible (White 1983; Moen and Tallman 1992, 1999). The feeble centralization of banking was a direct result of Civil War legislation, for that legislation faithfully reflected the free banking approach to credit. With two National Banking Acts, the government of the Union established a system of federally chartered banks, and gave those banks the right to issue notes, a right it took away from state banks. The impetus behind these acts, to be sure, was fiscal. In antebellum America, as we have seen, the collection of taxes was predominantly a local prerogative, so at the outbreak of the Civil War, when the government of the Union needed resources to finance its military efforts, it could only issue massive quantities of debt. As a result, the government first printed a new paper currency, the greenback, that could serve as legal tender and was not convertible into gold (Nussbaum 1957; Unger 1964; Timberlake 1993).[11] Second, to facilitate the marketing of newly issued government bonds, the Union "[transformed] a large part of the financial community into clients of the state," and both "enticed and coerced" financiers into becoming "agents of the Union fiscal policy" (Bensel 1990: 239). The two policies were interrelated, as certain bonds were earmarked to back the issue of currency. Government bonds were also marketed to a wider public. Some of the most famous financiers of the postbellum period, such as Jay Cooke, gained their power and reputation in their role as financial intermediaries precisely in the context of mobilization for war (Bensel 1990).

These policies, even though they created a government-chartered banking system, and thus seemingly contradicted the Jacksonian anti-government approach, simultaneously, and quite neatly, reflected the free banking approach popularized by the Jacksonians in matters of chartering policies. For these newly created national banks to exercise their power to issue notes, they had to fulfill reserve requirements and hold Union (after the war, federal) government bonds equal to 90 percent of the value of outstanding notes as collateral (Sylla 1969).[12] As a result, the centralization of financial power they brought about turned out to be feeble, and the two most centralizing aspects of the system—the national banknote (that is, the greenback) and the role of the Treasury Department in the management of the monetary system—became sources of divisiveness and discord. This is surprising, if one considers how implicated war-making was in projects of state-building, fiscal extraction, and financial centralization in Europe (Tilly 1985, 1992; Sylla et al. 1999). But in the United States, the polity was much too fragmented to sustain similarly visible forms of centralized power (Balogh 2009; Bensel 1990; see Centeno 2002 for a general argument that draws from South America).

Once the Civil War was over, the contentious status of greenbacks became the first stumbling block against the centralization of the banking system. As paper money, greenbacks greatly extended the power of the issuing authority—the federal government—over the market. But greenbacks also polarized economic producers, and more generally debtors and users of money, pitting them against financial actors, creditors, and producers of money, thereby forcing the government to mediate between contrasting demands. The vitriolic monetary debates that rocked the postbellum period, until "Resumption" in 1879, when convertibility of the greenback into gold was reinstated, thus centered precisely on the issue of whether paper should be backed by specie: specifically, should the United States return to the gold standard, or embrace the altogether different regime of "fiat-currency"—that is, paper money? To return the dollar to gold, the outstanding debt of the federal government was to be retired in gold first; without convertibility, the government could simply issue more inconvertible fiat money—more greenbacks (Unger 1964). Predictably, different political coalitions were on the side of each plan. A return to gold would have deflated the economy and favored the holders of federal debt: hence, bankers and more generally financiers, tended to support this option (Bensel 1990). A retirement of Civil War debt in greenbacks, on the contrary, would have increased the money supply and favored debtors: farmers and to some extent industrialists tended to support this option (Goodwyn 1978; Ritter 1997; Sanders 1999). There was an important sectional (East-West) and partisan (Republican-Democrat) dimension to this split (Unger 1964; Carruthers and Babb 1996).

Cross-cutting these divisions was a general perception that, by virtue of their origin as debt to finance the Civil War, greenbacks were politically intractable. Partly, this was because of a widespread suspicion against paper money that the Jacksonians had kindled in the antebellum period, so that remarkably, after Resumption, the greenbackers themselves quickly abandoned their commitment to paper money in favor of silver (Ritter 1997). But more important, the centralization of financial power that greenbacks potentially entailed, created political problems the government was not able to negotiate (see the detailed account of Timberlake 1993). Here the problem was less societal than it was institutional, and it centered on the Treasury.

Since the time that Andrew Jackson and Van Buren had turned it into an independent system, the Treasury had seen its authority in matters of regulation of the financial system widely contested. The Treasury was associated with partisan politics, patronage, and nepotism. "The official importance of the Treasury can hardly be overestimated," noted Henry

Adams. "Not only is his mere political power in the exercise of patronage far greater than that of any other cabinet officer, but in matters of policy almost every conceivable proposition of foreign or domestic interest sooner or later involves financial considerations and requires an opinion from the financial standpoint" (Henry Adams, 1870, quoted in L. D. White 1963: 110). The customhouses, central to the collection of revenue, were even more dramatically implicated in patronage politics (L. D. White 1963: see, for example, 118).[13] Patronage per se, of course, was not sufficient to discredit the Treasury, as the party system of the postbellum United States widely embraced such practices (Shefter 1994). But patronage clashed with the conservative bankers' demand for reliable and predictable credit decisions, especially in the face of the monetary instability that was built into the decentralized U.S. banking system (Bensel 1990: 303–65). This clash resulted in the Treasury's political impasse, as can be seen in the following episodes.

George S. Boutwell, the secretary under Grant's presidency between 1869 and 1873, who supervised a reduction of the national debt, while comfortable with the exercise of monetary authority (which he thought derived from "legal obligation"), was thus struck by the moral character of the Treasury's operations and in particular its use of a $44 million cash reserve to regulate the U.S. money supply:

[W]hen the Secretary of the Treasury came in and issued a portion of the forty-four million, however small, he changed the relations of debtor and creditor. If that were not a great responsibility in a country of forty million people, with various interests locking and interlocking with each other, then I know not what responsibility is. It is not a legal responsibility, but it is a business and moral responsibility of the highest character.

In Boutwell's reasoning, what gave Treasury reserve operations a moral character is that they affected the quantity of money in circulation, and thus caused either contraction or inflation, in both cases changing "every transaction between creditor and debtor" (Congressional Record, Senate, 43rd Congress, 1st Session Anon 1873: 19–20). But recognizing the effects of the Treasury operations was only a first step in devising new criteria for the management of the monetary system. So when those operations kindled the Panic of 1873, as the Treasury failed to plow reserves back into the system, the urgency of monetary reform became once again pressing. The panic, in fact, came to an end when the Treasury, in a fiscal deficit because of a stalling economy, was forced to reissue $26 million of its $44 million reserve. Secretary of Treasury William Richardson could in principle have acted sooner, but he did not, because he demanded that "Congress answer the question" of the Treasury's authority "by a distinct enactment. . . . He was a constitutionalist who did not trust his own judgment in making critical policy decisions" (Timberlake 1993: 106).

For both Richardson and Boutwell, then, the lack of a clearly specific set of criteria through which to define boundaries between creditors and debtors, between those deserving of credit and those to be excluded from it, translated into indecisiveness and uncertainty. Timberlake (ibid.), the most authoritative study in this regard, shows that similar political tensions and questionable decisions characterized the Treasury's response to the banking crisis of 1884; Leslie M. Shaw's policies under Roosevelt; and George B. Cortelyou's fateful indecision in the face of the 1907 financial panic. Carruthers (1994) argues that the lack of cultural autonomy of the Treasury extends to the post–World War II period.

The federal government and the Treasury, in short, were unable to institutionalize their control over money because, in the face of a divided polity, they could not provide morally compelling representations of creditworthiness. Their indecision in sorting monetary matters, and in assigning clear responsibilities and jurisdictions to other institutions and organizations, flowed from a political impasse that discredited the ability of political authorities to deal with monetary matters altogether. Given the Treasury's weak political power and its lack of organizational cohesion, its policies had become a source of strain in the relationship between political and state actors and financiers. "Our government is founded on popular principles. It is not fit to control trade or to manage the money market. It is too free and simple in its nature to adapt itself to the complex work attempted by older governments in Europe, with their bureaucratic habits and centralized power," asserted the *Commercial and Financial Chronicle* in 1873 (quoted in Bensel 1990: 278). So in the crucial decade after the Civil War, financiers came to see the Treasury as unable to fulfill its financial functions with competence, and this had momentous consequences. Incompetence became "the crucial factor in turning finance capital away from a potentially neutral or even favorable attitude toward central state expansion" in general (ibid.: 239).[14] The political price, adds Bensel, was the end of Reconstruction: suspicious of the government's capabilities in steering the economy toward a more stable path, financial elites came to oppose the expansion of the fiscal capacity of the state altogether, severely constraining the political options open to it (see also Foner 2002: 220).

A discredited Treasury at the center of the financial system considerably weakened the political project of creditworthiness of would-be conservative bankers. Conservative bankers, as they search for criteria that allow them to assess creditworthiness and present their assessment as based on legitimate judgment, impose moral boundaries between those who are said to deserve credit, and those who are said not to. Political boundaries can thus be particularly effective in the erecting of boundaries of creditworthiness, because they are backed by the strength of the state, both legal and coercive. But when the political authority invested with the demarcation, maintenance, and defense of those boundaries is itself fraught with controversy, conservative bankers may decide to pursue different routes in order to constitute restricted circuits of money.

Reputation as a Reaction to Financial Expansion

The urgency of finding ways to restrict circuits of money to groups selected through sound banking criteria, without relying on the backing of a political authority, was made more pressing by the wave of financial innovation that, in part, originated with the regulatory gaps in National Banking Acts; and in part, with the take-off of the corporate economy, especially from the 1890s onward. Specifically, national banking laws still allowed states to charter banks that, while forbidden from issuing banknotes, could nonetheless engage in other kinds of operations, most notably, the collection of deposits. In fact, the National Banking Acts required national banks to maintain a relatively large amount of capital, which made them uncompetitive in small communities, where only small institutions could profit; further, the laws forbade national banks to lend on real estate as collateral, thereby also putting them at disadvantage in rural communities. These constraints on national banks were opportunities for state-chartered banks, which were usually subjected to less demanding requirements and could therefore remain competitive even though they could not issue banknotes (Sylla 1969; James 1978). Figure 4.1 thus shows that immediately after the Civil War, banks not chartered by the federal government decrease in number, as existing banks switch their status to fall under the National Banking System. From the mid-1880s

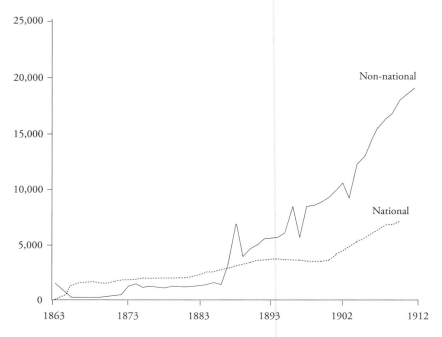

Fig. 4.1. Number of National and Non-National Banks, Postbellum Period. Source: Author's Calculations from Carter, Susan B et al., eds. 2006. "Banks." in Historical Statistics of the United States, Millennial Edition On Line. Cambridge University Press.

onward, however, the number of non-national banks picks up to then quickly overcome the number of nationally chartered banks.

Within this broad, non-nationally chartered bank category, a particularly important kind of bank was the trust company—a type of financial institution that, rather than exploiting the weaknesses of national banks in rural areas, took advantage of loose regulations at the state level to establish a niche in the newly buoyant corporate economy. Initially established as trustees of estates and bond issues, as well as executors and guardians of private wills, by the 1880s trust companies acquired commercial functions. Further, "[T]hey accepted deposits; made loans; participated extensively in reorganizing railroads and consolidating industrial corporations; acted as trustees, underwriters, and distributors of new securities; and served as depositories of stocks, bonds, and titles. Frequently, they acted as attorneys for individuals and companies. Corporations regularly appointed them as registrars or fiscal and transfer agents. Very often they also owned and managed real estate" (Carosso 1970: 99; also quoted in Moen and Tallman 1992: 612). In some states in the Northeast, they completely took over the field of commercial banking (James 1978; White 1983). Remarkably, in New York state, where the largest trust companies operated, their assets grew by 244 percent over the 1897–1907 period, compared to a 97 percent growth in the assets of national banks and an 82 percent growth in the assets of state banks (Moen and Tallman 1992: 612).

The underlying set of processes that was making these new forms of financial institutions profitable originated with the modern business corporation. Interpretations of the emergence of this new business form are numerous. In broad strokes, they have moved from the functionalist analysis best exemplified by the classic Chandler (1977), attributing the rise of the large, multidivisional corporation to the economies of scale and thus the increased efficiency the corporate form made possible (see also Galambos 1970), to the historicist and political analysis of Roy (1997). The latter singled out railroad companies—that is to say, companies that were organized as quasi-public agencies—as archetypal corporations, and then pointed to political movements railing against corruption and favoritism, such as the Jacksonian Democrats with their fights for severing the connection between political authorities and business, as providing the conditions for the transformation of those companies into fully private ones. Once these large capitalized firms were emancipated from public ownership, argues Roy, they could use their sheer market size to structure the economy in their favor, thus growing even further, consolidating rival business into their own corporate structure, and finally branching out from the railroad sector into manufacturing (see also Perrow 2002 for a more general statement).

Importantly, as the more sociologically oriented accounts of the rise of the corporate economy emphasize, the same political environment that had given rise to wildcats in the banking system had, simultaneously, made it possible for corporations to develop as private firms. Within the banking system, however, it had been not domestic wildcats, but private, investment bankers that had seized the opportunity to provide credit to, and then acquire control over, the corporate economy. This was a group of bankers that, in part, had benefited from its dealings in government bonds during the Civil War (I have already mentioned Jay Cooke in this capacity), but that for the most part had derived power from its role as channel of foreign capital into U.S. companies (Wilkins 1989). Private investment bankers thus worked outside the national banking field, which was oriented toward commercial intermediation and, increasingly, deposit banking. But the changes to the banking system brought about by the Civil War did much to change this situation. The system fully institutionalized correspondent banking, which generalized the practice of extending call loans, and connected the domestic finances of chartered banks with those of nonchartered private bankers.

Call loans (also called brokers' loans) were secured loans "representing advances made to brokers by pledging stocks and bonds with the bank as collateral" (James 1978: 63). Prior to the Civil War, country (that is to say, local) bankers had developed the practice of maintaining "bankers' balances" with city banks: they would deposit funds with banks in commercial centers, such as New York, to facilitate trade with the interior. National banking legislation institutionalized this practice into a full-fledged "correspondent banking" system that designated certain city banks as "reserve banks" and allowed some of the funds country banks deposited with those city banks to count toward the fulfillment of their reserve requirements—but also encouraged country banks to deposit additional money in the cities. Country banks, in fact, in order to turn higher profits on those deposits, "as soon as they get any balance in excess of the minimum amount which they feel they must carry, it is in order for them to instruct their city correspondent to loan it" (Frank Vanderlip, personal correspondence, March 23, 1906). Call loans were their favorite investment (James 1978: 118). Frank Vanderlip, at that time vice president of National City Bank, thus continued:

> It looks to me like the most serious rock ahead for banking. It amounts to really giving away our business if we are to make loans like this to everybody. . . . At present it is useless to refuse for every bank here will make them. The First National ordinarily makes a small charge for the business but will do it for nothing rather than permit a correspondent to go elsewhere with the business. (Frank Vanderlip to James Stillman, March 23, 1906)

John James, in a thorough investigation of the postbellum banking system, highlights how what Vanderlip perceived to be a problematic aspect of correspondent banking—the fact that it encouraged competition—was precisely its most positive aspect. Correspondent banking and the "call loans" that mobilized county bank deposits, he claims, served to integrate a capital market that would have otherwise remained regionally fragmented. Moreover, competition over those sources of funds should be considered evidence against the Progressive charge that "the New York market was a noncompetitive one or that a 'Money Trust' in fact existed" (1978: 110). But precisely to the extent that these new practices transgressed previous boundaries around the circulation of money, they also challenged existing definitions of creditworthiness.

We can, in fact, turn James's proposition around and argue that, to the extent that no cohesive group of bankers had control over the allocation of credit, the banking system was "wildcat" in Schumpeter's sense. In this respect, the formation of trust companies was only the latest outcome of a process of financial innovation—of wildcat banking—that the feeble centralization of the banking system had made possible since the Jacksonian period. Just as the free banking system that preceded it had opened the banking field to wildcats at the state level, the National Banking System opened up the banking field to institutions over which no political authority had control. The appearance and increased power of trust companies, though, constituted a formidable challenge to the elite, now increasingly conservative bankers too.

These powerful individuals, and more precisely the organizations they managed, had tamed the corporate economy to their advantage (Dobbin and Dowd 2000), and now presided over a nationally extensive banking system that, through devices like correspondent banking, gave them access to the credit flows of a large, national market (DeLong 1991). Trust companies were outside their control as well. Conservative bankers had devised one solution to the fragmentation of the banking system, one that has been much celebrated by market-sympathizing historians (for example, Timberlake 1993; White 1983): the organization of a private system of clearinghouses, on the Suffolk model, and, most important, on the experience of the New York Clearing House Association, or NYCHA (see, esp., Timberlake 1993). With the reserves of national banks increasingly centralized in select cities, there was the possibility to allocate them to banks in difficulty. But no single institution was invested with the authority to do so, let alone increase the reserves available to the system as a whole, when individual banks experienced a high demand for cash—a function that in Europe had been taken up by central banks (Goodhart 1988). Demand for cash increased regularly, especially in agricultural regions where credit financed harvesting, and where farmers at the end of the cycle would demand payment in cash, forcing banks to sell their as-

sets, contract credit, and thereby putting other banks and financial institutions under the threat of a liquidity crisis (Myers 1971). Clearinghouses
were supposed to relieve this pressure on banks: they pooled the reserves
of member banks and issued loan certificates (backed by those reserves
and other recognized assets) and "emergency currency" to banks that were
experiencing problems of liquidity.

As certain contemporary analysts professed, there was an attractive
logic to clearinghouses, because to be a member, a banker had to prove
that he "is a person of some moral status, and . . . he must see from his
experience that he can make more money, to put it that way, by walking straight than by walking crooked" (Sherer 1913). Crucially, then, the
function of clearinghouses was not purely a technical one; membership
in the clearinghouse had moral and exclusionary purposes as well. But
it was precisely because the distinctions they made between reputable
and disreputable banks could not be enforced, however, that clearinghouses proved to be ineffective. As Goodhart (1969) notes, membership in
clearinghouse associations was certainly restrictive and exclusive, but not
enough. Because the clients of member banks included other banks and
financial institutions, which may or may not have been financially sound;
and because the failure of nonmember banks put member banks at risk
too, it was often the case that clearinghouses extended credit, however indirectly, to nonmember banks as well, in that way undermining their own
exclusivity and prestige. Goodhart argues that this was certainly the case
for the 1907 crisis, precipitated by the failure of the Knickerbocker Trust
Company, an institution that could not rely on clearinghouse privileges
but that forced banks that did business with it, and were members, to turn
to emergency loans. The crisis was stemmed only after J. P. Morgan con-
vened other top U.S. bankers to arrange for private loans, thus revealing
the inadequacy of the clearinghouse in facing the crisis (Bruner and Carr
2009). In a banking system were wildcats wielded enormous resources, in
sum, the setting up of barriers to the participation in private schemes was
insufficient, as those barriers were porous. It was only through a shared
identity to which wildcat bankers too would commit that their conservative counterparts could hope to discipline the credit system.

Without political backing, however, conservative bankers had only
limited means at their disposal to enforce shared identities within the
banking system. The collective action problems inherent to status groups
thereby came to the surface. One particularly clear example is the follow-

ing correspondence between Boston banker Henry Lee Higginson, and J. Lyman of the Webster and Atlas National Bank of Boston—bankers from a city that was a bastion of banking conservatism (Ritter 1997: 244). In a letter written after the 1907 financial panic, at a time when demands for some centralized authority to provide emergency relief to banks were widespread, Lyman argued precisely against such demands. Existing arrangements seem to be working fine, he argued:

Here, we have survived the panic; in some cases with wounds more or less deep, but none mortal and in most cases hardly scathed . . . . I think the Clearing House Committee has sufficient knowledge of the method of any bank in conducting its business to cry halt before anything untoward happens.

Thus, in Lyman's eyes, existing institutions were enough of a guarantee for the stability of the banking system: there was no reason to further increase its internal capacity for self-monitoring. A second concern that Lyman raised against the creation of overarching regulatory authorities was the territorial heterogeneity of banking, which precluded the adoption of a single policy throughout the United States:

It does not follow because certain things are found necessary or expedient in Chicago, or St. Louis, or Kansas City, that they are adaptable to us in Boston. It may be necessary for San Francisco to have a vigilance Committee, but here the police is sufficient.

Third, he predicted that the development of new banking practices to ensure the functioning of the system as a whole would have negative consequences on individual banks, as it would force them to make their business too public.

And again, how far should the good be harried to save the wicked. I have no objection to having my assets called good for what they stand on my books if they so appear, but I do object to their being made a record of piece by piece, showing my customers to whomever and whenever it may seem necessary. Suppose a big toad in the puddle should make it "worth his while" to get from the incorruptible examiner a list of the loans of Boston banks. Here would be a pretty kettle of fish, with onions enough to make a stench in the nostrils of the provider, though a delicious taste in the mouth of the consumer. (Lyman to Higginson, March 14, 1908)

This last concern expressed the bankers' distrust of any system of public disclosure that would reveal precisely how they went about their business.

This was seen as an attack on the professional closure of banking, for the alleged benefit of the "consumer," but with potentially negative repercussions on the bankers themselves. The concern also revealed a lack of mutual trust among bankers: Lyman's worry about a potential "big toad in the puddle" buying off public examiners to gain information about the customers of its competitors spoke volumes about the fragmentation of the financial field, and the lack of commitment to shared identities, backed by political authority, to facilitate a shared sense of solidarity.

Lyman was not alone in expressing such concerns. John Wingate Weeks, chairman of the House of Representatives Committee on Expenditures, in a letter to Higginson, added another dimension to the problem. Reacting to a proposed policy that bank deposits be guaranteed by the federal government, which was hailed as a measure to increase generalized trust in the banking system, Weeks recognized that "the guarantee of deposits would, to a certain extent, prevent runs on banks," but he nonetheless objected to the measure because it

savors so strongly of socialism [that it] does not appeal to me, and I believe would return to plague us in many other ways. . . . I believe that its adoption would cause unsound banking, so that the number of bank failures in the past would be no criterion to those which we would be likely to see in the future. Every bank man knows that loss of confidence means an immediate loss of business. It keys him up to do his best work, and to maintain his bank on a conservative basis. That prop will be entirely removed if a man's deposit is going to be safe anywhere. (Weeks to Higginson, March 6, 1908)[15]

His position against this policy proposal followed from a general principle: "To my mind . . . compelling one man, or a set of men, to be responsible for the lack of wisdom and failures of another man, or set of men, simply because they are engaged in the same business, is fundamentally wrong." The underlying condition that had spurred Lyman to express doubts as to whether collective solutions to the recognized problems afflicting the banking system were possible now too spurred Weeks to express similar concerns (he also hailed from a financial background, as he was cofounder of the Boston-based firm Hornblower and Weeks, an investment bank and brokerage firm). This underlying condition was the lack of a prior, shared identity that would guarantee a collective commitment to common goals. Unable to rally around collective identities whereby responsibilities would be shared along with the advantages that accrued to members of the banking profession, bankers thus recognized the risk they were running in terms of instability and internal conflict. Those like Lyman simply dismissed the problem, while those like Weeks were at a loss to articulate satisfactory principles on which to base a solution.[16]

One possibility that some bankers considered was to give up on the project of conservative banking altogether. In that light Vanderlip of National City Bank suggested in his correspondence with James Stillman to

increase largely the amount of our discounts of commercial paper, using every endeavor to get into direct relations with commercial concerns that now market their paper very largely through commercial paper brokers; and, also, to increase our supply of paper by taking a more liberal attitude toward those concerns who are now with us whose credit standing is satisfactory but whose borrowing lines are larger than we are disposed fully to satisfy.

This reflected a more general assessment that wildcat practices were more desirable in a context in which conservative banking was not firmly grounded on shared identities.

It is quite possible that it is the wisest for us to go on undisturbed in the most conservative manner and to wait for a time to come when conservative management will appeal above all things to people with money but we must not lose sight of the fact that there are coming into the banking situation radically new methods. (Vanderlip, February 1, 1907)[17]

Although the spread of wildcat practices at the local level made more conservative practices difficult to institutionalize, conservative bankers recognized the high cost they would face should they embrace wildcat practices themselves. The sources of their current advantages—their grip over the corporate economy in the case of Wall Street bankers, and their dominance of internal commerce in the case of Midwestern banks—was at stake.[18] Increasingly, U.S. bankers were also gaining international prestige, a factor to which Broz's recent account (1997) of business mobilization for financial reform stresses as the most important in overcoming collective action dilemmas, something to which I will return in a moment. The point is that conservative bankers now fought for stability, and charged outsiders to the formal banking system with speculation and crisis-inducing behavior (Wiebe 1962, 1967). Thus, throughout the last decade of the nineteenth century, different factions of bankers, representing the diverse constituencies in the U.S. banking field, organized movements for banking reform, commissions for sound money, and meetings with legislators and scholars to devise plans for the reorganization of the banking system (West 1977; Livingston 1986). But in general, those plans did not produce the desired reforms, for they never enjoyed the support of the entire banking community (Broz 1997: 33–34).

Matters changed in the wake of the devastating 1907 panic (Bruner and Carr 2009). At that point, claims Broz (1997), bankers set aside their differences to pursue the "public good" of banking reform, because of new, "selective incentives" to do so. It is the general view of historians of the period that the opposition of New York bankers to Midwestern proposals, tying the issue of the currency to "real assets" (commercial paper used to finance sales and purchases of traded goods) was the main stumbling block to reform. Remember that, under National Banking, banknotes were issued upon possession of government bonds, so, as Livingston (1986: 167) notes, a plan that replaced them with private commercial instruments essentially put the issue of money purely on a *private* basis. To New York bankers, however, commercial paper was too restricted a basis for the issue of currency, precisely because of their operations in public securities. Midwestern bankers held exactly the opposite view: to them, the inclusion of a broader class of assets, such as industrial securities, seemed tantamount to an endorsement of speculation. As Sanders (1999) adds, commercial paper also better encapsulated the agrarian demands that finance better reflect the needs of the "real" economy. After 1907, however, New York bankers warmed up to the idea of discounting a restricted class of assets as the basis of a reformed banking plan, as long as those assets included instruments they could use in international trade, and as long as a more centralized system, ideally a central bank (Warburg 1930), was in charge of such operations. This ideological development was crucial to the passing, some five years later, of the Federal Reserve Act.

Conservative Banking and the Federal Reserve Act

From the perspective that I have developed in this book, one that emphasizes the conflict between conservative and wildcat bankers as constitutive of finance, the significance of the Federal Reserve Act lies less in whether it had positive (Broz 1997) or negative (Meltzer 2004) outcomes, than in what it reveals about the character of financial conflict in the postbellum United States. And U.S. bankers faced difficult challenges as they attempted to establish sound banking traditions in a fragmented field, where their relationship with political authorities was conflictual rather than cooperative. But the movement for banking reform did not simply react to external pressure from political groups, such as the agrarian movement (Sanders 1999); it reacted to forces within the financial field as well.

To be sure, the Federal Reserve Act was the outcome of at least two projects, each of them articulated with great attention to the larger political context. One project, spearheaded by Republican senator Howard Aldrich (RI), involved prominent bankers like Frank Vanderlip (at the time, vice president of National City Bank), Paul Warburg (Kuhn, Loeb & Co.), Henry Davison (Bankers' Trust Company, a Morgan affiliate), Charles Norton (First National Bank), and A. Piatt Andrew (a Harvard economist) (Chernow 2001; Wicker 2005: 4). This group met secretly in 1910 to draw up a plan for a central bank, one that was to inform the Aldrich bill (discussed but not passed by Congress in 1912) but ultimately became the blueprint for the Federal Reserve Act itself (Warburg 1930; West 1977; Broz 1997).[19] The main request of this camp was for a central bank in the European tradition, subject to only slight modifications to make it more appropriate to the U.S. context: this bank was to be centralized, have command over the nation's reserves, and be empowered with the ability to extend emergency loans. This plan had been resisted by New York bankers in the past, but a new generation of bankers more familiar with European traditions, headed by Paul Warburg, a German emigre, made a strong case for it, and eventually the plan received the backing of New York (Moen and Tallman 1999).

The second camp centered around Democratic representative Carter Glass and economist H. Parker Willis. As several contemporaries and historians insist (Warburg 1930; West 1977; Wicker 2005), the proposal emerging from this Democratic group differed from the bankers' (and Republican) plan on two details: first, instead of a centralized institution, it mandated a regionally based system of banks. In Timberlake's colorful language (1993: 220), this is because "any institution that looked like a central bank was politically impossible at this time. A central bank was 'monopolistic.' It was run by bloodsucking bankers who were given special privileges to soak the poor, keep interest rates up, and conspire with Wall Street speculators to cause panics that were profitable to the speculators and themselves." A regionally based system of multiple central banks, on the contrary, would dilute power. For good measure, Glass insisted that the board of governors of these regional banks was to be politically appointed, rather than being selected by the bankers themselves.

The second difference was the explicit reference in the bill to the "real bills" doctrine. This is not surprising, as this part of the bill was the work of Willis, who had been involved in the Indiana Monetary Commission—one of the several attempts in the earlier decade of the century to push for banking reform, and also one that emanated from the Midwest (Willis 1915: vii; Livingston 1986: 22; Broz 1997). The real bills doctrine was particularly popular there because it singled out so-called self-liquidating assets (that is, those originating from a commercial transaction). More generally, the doctrine resonated with agrarian and small-business interests as well. "Though Bryan and his followers had traditionally opposed a currency based on bank assets . . . the Laughlin-Willis doctrine was potentially attractive . . . . The doctrine implied that no strong central control or anti-inflation mechanisms were necessary, and that the issuing of paper currency could be quite decentralized" (Sanders 1999: 242).

The bill presented by Carter and Willis was the one eventually to be passed, and Mehrling (2002: 209) credits the "rhetorical success of the 'real bills doctrine,' introduced into the bill by Willis, in signaling to the country that the new Federal Reserve System would stand for small-business interests against both big government in Washington and big finance in New York." But there was more to the doctrine than rhetorical success. In the decentralized and fragmented financial field of the postbellum United States, alliances with a political authority could have potentially served as a source of cohesion, except that the political authority itself did not enjoy the kind of legitimacy that would have made its control over credit stable and reliable. And "speculative interest would always be tempted to influence officials, which might lead to corrupt political as well as business methods," as Vanderlip pointed out to Aldrich (January 11, 1908). As we have seen, this was the long-term legacy of slavery, one that not even the Civil War had succeeded in overcoming (Bensel 1990). This pathway, then, was closed off.

A centralized system governed by conservative bankers, similarly, could have stabilized the system (as it did, for instance, in Britain: see Ingham 1984). But formidable collective action problems closed off this path as well, as the fragmentation of banking weakened any sense of shared solidarity among bankers and raised instead mutual suspicions and mutual accusations.

The real bills doctrine, by contrast, afforded a more general identity, one that could generate a shared sense of membership and allow conservative bankers to rally together against wildcats. As the ideological glue that allowed a banking coalition to form, the doctrine offered the *moral* and thus collective grounds on which such an alliance could be forged. It did so in at least two ways. First, the real bills doctrine reaffirmed the self-regulating qualities of the banking system. The famed Chicago economist J. Lawrence Laughlin was the most important proponent of this view. Rather than focusing on the Simmelian problem of the standard upon which the currency should be grounded, Laughlin worried about the "inelastic currency," the fact, that is, that the issue of money under the National Banking System was tied to the price of government bonds, and not to the needs of trade (Mehrling 2002). His solution was to give certain classes of assets, which were believed to have a self-liquidating power, the status of banking reserves. The main asset with such qualities was commercial paper, issued among traders as credit upon the sale and delivery of commercial goods. Because trade was trade in physical goods, furthermore, the value of money issued on the basis of those transactions was believed to have a natural grounding in productive activities, not in speculation—a practice that the contemporary National Banking System, on the contrary, ended up favoring. In Laughlin's framework (1903: 5), finally, tying credit to self-regulating and self-liquidating assets made "creditworthiness" secondary: real bills made the distinction between credit and credit transactions redundant, because "if credit is regarded as the transfer of goods, there is no such distinction. Credit appears only in a transaction." Judgments about the creditworthiness of customers, then, could be shown to be only indirectly related to the amount of credit actually in circulation. "What is a man's high credit? It means that his reputation for repayment is high; that he easily gets a transfer of goods" (ibid.).

In Laughlin's characterization, in sum, the ability of commercial paper to regulate itself made the *political* regulation of creditworthiness altogether superfluous. Laughlin found this property of real bills reassuring. By allowing banks to print currency on the basis of their holdings of commercial paper, Laughlin and real bills proponents believed to have found a solution to the problem of decentralization and speculation. The New York faction of the banking reform movement found this aspect of the real bills doctrine "simpleminded" (Sanders 1999: 242).[20] But discussions about the self-regulating properties of commercial paper opened up a space for the discussion of other financial instruments too, in particular those that banks issued in order to transact with one another—instruments that were woefully undertraded in the United States but that enjoyed deep markets in Europe (Warburg 1930). As Broz (1997) documents, these were assets, such as bankers' acceptances, that involved three parties—the two parties to the transaction that underlay the asset, and the bank that discounted it, which functioned as an intermediary and added its own creditworthiness to that of the transacting parties. To be sure, bankers' acceptances were particularly useful in international transactions (where the parties to the transaction were importers and exporters from different countries), and thus internationally oriented bankers were especially keen on creating reliable markets in them (Broz 1997). But the larger goal remained one of creating the conditions for domestic discount markets, in which banks developed not only the capabilities to act but also the authority to become central players in them. It was crucial that bankers articulate a rationale as to why their own creditworthiness was to be believed, for how else would they be able to assess the creditworthiness of individuals? As Warburg put it, "[In] the United States our commercial paper is the old promissory note, *it is a* BILL. . . . If, in the United States, this promissory note has entered the bank, it usually remains there until it falls due; if a New York bank, under normal conditions, would try to rediscount such paper, it would create suspicion and distrust. This means that every dollar invested by a bank in American commercial paper, that is, every dollar invested to satisfy the most legitimate requirements of business, leads, without fail, to a locking up of cash in unsalable assets" (Warburg, "American and European Banking," in Seligman 1908: 125).

Conservative financial elites attempted to articulate such a rationale. Sound banking, in banker Lee Higginson's eyes, was a necessary and inevitable characteristic of credit, because:

[n]othing but character and personality will hold deposits in a bank, whether large or small, for everybody knows that any man may draw out all his money from the bank without notice, and either hide it or put it in another bank. Therefore, the bankers never can be sure of their deposits unless they conduct their corporations properly and with due regard for others . . . . Banking depends entirely on character and fair dealing—the only lasting assets. (Higginson to Woodrow Wilson, February 7, 1913)

While the idea that credit and banking depend on trust resonated with commonly accepted conceptualizations of the nature of credit in the period, as we saw in the previous chapter, Higginson's articulation of the problem lent itself to further political uses. J. P. Morgan seized the opportunity in the context of the Money Trust investigations, the great showdown between the Progressive movement and Wall Street bankers (Chernow 2001). In a banking system, he argued,

the only genuine power which an individual, or a group of individuals, can gain is that arising from the confidence reposed in him or them by the community. Every town, large or small, seems to choose a limited number of men (merchants, manufacturers, lawyers and bankers) to represent it in the management of its chief, local industries. Those men are entrusted with such heavy responsibilities because of the confidence which their records have established, and only so long as their records are unblemished do they retain such trusts.

To this, Morgan added, echoing Higginson:

To banking the confidence of the community is the breath from which it draws its life. The past is full of examples where the slightest suspicion as to the conservatism, or the methods of a bank's management, has destroyed confidence and drawn away its deposits over night. Much, therefore, may be left to the instinct and the force of public opinion; and finally, in urging upon you once more the establishment of a sound banking system. (Morgan 1913, February 25)

Morgan's and Higginson's statements, in essence, reduced banking to the activity of winning the trust of the "community." Morgan's claim rested on an even more microlevel argument about credit.

I know lots of men, business men too, who can borrow any amount, whose credit is unquestioned. . . . It is because people believe in the man. . . . He might not have anything. . . . The first thing is character. . . . Before money or anything else. Money cannot buy it. . . . [A] man I do not trust could not get the money from me on all the bonds in Christendom. (Morgan 1913: 1084)

This conception of banking posited the trust that the community invested in the banker as the precondition for the trust that was to characterize the relationship between customer and banker. Their community was local, rather than national; and the banker was the guarantor of the creditworthiness of those who belonged to that community, which in turn retained the ultimate power to take trust away from bankers who took advantage of this position.

To be sure, by tying monetary processes to local control, Higginson, Morgan, and New York financial elites in general were trying to prevent a national economic community from emerging: articulating a local logic was a way to strongly limit any potential role for the federal government—since it was only the banker, the implication was, that had the trust of the community. This was in direct defiance of Democratic plans to put the banking system under the control of the government, plans that eventually succeeded (Sanders 1999: 232). But by associating creditworthiness with individual reputations (and with the communities in which those reputations developed) and by arguing that the role of bankers was functional to the full development and screening of those reputations, conservative bankers now also had some common ground from which to fight wildcat bankers. As Paul Warburg, the reformer most favorable to centralization, had argued, "responsible" banks were to be allowed to engage in the kinds of operations through which they could stabilize the system.[21] The real bills doctrine thus served as the ideological terrain—as the shared identity—in which a link between banking and community could be articulated and supported, allowing banks to present themselves as enemies of speculation and wildcat banking.[22]

While West (1977) argues that the real bills doctrine was the cornerstone of the Federal Reserve System, Wicker (2005) strongly qualifies this view, arguing that, operationally, Federal Reserve policies were neutral. But this is precisely because the real bills doctrine was less about providing the operational guidelines for monetary policy than about providing a common identity for conservative bankers to rally around. In fact, the real bills doctrine had never worked as a set of operational guidelines. In the antebellum period, strict adherence to the doctrine would have relegated banks to a passive role (Bodenhorn 2000, 2003): rather than seeking new opportunities for investing their capital, real bills doctrine practitioners would have limited themselves to the financing of "prudent [and] judicious" trade, not the riskier and longer-term business propositions that often embodied a "spirit of speculation and over-trading." Bodenhorn shows, in fact, that things worked differently in practice—that nineteenth-century U.S. bankers, while professing adherence to short-term lending, were in fact often involved in longer-term credit relationships that a real bills focus would have avoided (see also L. E. Davis 1960). Real bills had always been more of an ideology justifying and rationalizing ways of allocating credit than an accurate description of lending practices.

In sum, as Moen and Tallman (1999) argue, it is no coincidence that reform efforts came in the wake of the 1907 panic, because the panic made it clear to conservative bankers that they had lost control over the most wildcat representatives of the field, the trust companies, and that united action was necessary to regain that control. Moreover, as accounts of Progressive America have argued, a centralized regulatory institution for the banking system was politically unappealing. But that was not the only reason why the real bills doctrine, with its implications for decentralization, was adopted. The real bills doctrine, rather, provided a compelling moral account for sound banking, and thus an identity around which conservative bankers could rally.

Conclusions

This chapter has covered quite a bit of ground, but its focus has remained firmly on the character of the conflict between conservative and wildcat bankers in the nineteenth-century United States. This conflict encompassed large and varying political constituencies, but ultimately revolved around the issue of where the boundaries around credit should be marked. Conservative bankers were, in the antebellum period, faced by a political movement (Jacksonian democracy) invested in liberalizing the banking business in the name of states rights to be sure, but more generally, in the name of white dominance; and by a sectionally divided polity in which discussions about politics were often veiled discussions about slavery (Einhorn 2009). The seed for presenting creditworthiness as a *private* matter, to be decided by bankers alone, rather than in conjunction with political authorities, was sowed in this context.

Because sectionalism persisted in the postbellum United States, the privatization of banking and creditworthiness maintained its ideological appeal to the conservative financial elites who were trying to build shared identities. In fact, in the period following the spread of free banking laws and the institution of a similarly decentralized system at the federal level, private creditworthiness and individual reputation became the frames through which conservative financial elites mobilized the entire banking community in support of a project of privately enforced regulation, thus providing the blueprint for the design of the Federal Reserve. Because of the balance of political power tipped in favor of antibanking constituencies, the Federal Reserve took a different shape than the bankers had intended, yet the similarities in the bill that was passed were perhaps more striking than the differences.

The conflictual dynamics of banking systems have been at the center of my explanation, on the premise that the claims to objectivity made by bankers—namely, that they strive to perfect the art of credit allocation—are directed not at the solution of some general, technical problem, inevitably leading to some collectively desirable outcome (in the eyes of the economist, more efficient markets, more capital integration, or even better regulation), but as a strategic movement aimed at changing the power dynamics of the field of finance. The central problem for bankers is to devise the conditions whereby they persuade borrowers to value the identity connected to the possession of a financial instrument. What Zelizer (1994) has argued for everyday monetary transactions, such as tipping—namely, that they tend to be regulated by meanings and practices originating from within the circuit in which these transactions take place—may hold, under certain conditions, for other kinds of instruments as well. These conditions are politically determined.

Structurally, financial instruments serve to reinforce a sense of identity for those who hold them, as they facilitate interactions among members of the circuit in which they are traded and thereby reproduce its culture, meanings, and expectations. In the previous chapter, we saw that this was the case particularly in the Southern states, where circuits of credit revolved around the plantation economy. It is crucial that these circuits be exclusive, regulated through what I have called "sound banking": this was not quite the case in the Northern states, where democratic regimes put pressure on conservative bankers not to rely upon exclusionary identities, and so produced systematic deviations from the uses that were intended for the issue and uses of credit, eventually challenging the identity through which circuits were regulated. The collective basis upon which credit circulates was as a result particularly vulnerable to conflict in the U.S. context—a conflict that forced conservative bankers to devise new ways to articulate a shared identity for the field.

From the point of view of the bankers, the assessment of the creditworthiness of a borrower or, more generally, a party to a financial contract, is just one step in a much more complex process, characterized by the more general problem that, once the financial contract is written up and the borrower acquires possession over the financial instrument, the borrower will have to decide whether to keep using the instrument for the purposes for which it was issued, or to devise new uses for it.[23] The boundary between what is traditionally understood as "money"—an instrument with general circulation—and "credit"—a financial contract specific to the two parties who agree to it—is thus porous, or more precisely, can be made so. The borrower may have both the incentive and, depending on how financial agents interpret the institutional context, the means to use credit differently than she had agreed to do. Individual borrowers, to put it differently, will "hold" financial instruments, say, to trade in stock markets, or buy real estate, or, if they act as representatives of an industrial firm, to buy equipment. At least on the surface, they will be under no pressure to conform to appropriate uses for those instruments, as they will have selected those particular instruments (stocks, mortgages, retained earnings) *instrumentally* to carry out specific transactions to start with. But this means only that they are already working within the framework of identities that have been firmly established. Those identities, however, will be challenged if the instruments are used differently than they were intended—as when, for instance, mortgages become assets to trade on stock markets rather than instruments with which to purchase real estate (G. F. Davis 2009).

Creditors have several means at their disposal to ensure that they maintain control over the exchange of the instruments they issue. Thus, for instance, communities and the locally entrenched financial institutions that serve them normally employ face-to-face strategies in order to exercise control over how their debtors make use of financial instruments—with those financial instruments being, in the main, loans. The concepts developed by Viviana Zelizer in her microsociology of money turn out to be particularly useful in describing these dynamics, as locally oriented banks—such as credit unions and cooperatives, the informal credit arrangements of immigrant enclaves, or the local currency schemes of certain towns in places like the UK, Argentina, and the United States—can often rely on personal networks and the particularized commitments such networks engender to control flows of credit. Yet the banking system and the financial agents it contains are too complex and too removed from local circuits of money to rely on "embedded" relations the same way that local creditors would. They must still find ways to commit the members of a circuit to appropriate uses of the instruments that originate with the banking system; they must, in fact, define what such appropriate uses will be in practice. That is primarily so they can restrict the holder's ability to trade with outsiders to the circuit, for we know from analyses of the collective determinants of inequality (see, esp., Tilly 1998) that the organized, collective exploitation of a resource, a market advantage, or a skill generates more effective and durable systems of revenue than individual efforts can; that, however, individual interests rarely align with collective ones; and that it is only by committing members of an organized group to shared goals and strategies that the group will reproduce its advantages.

Boundaries, then, become central to the normal workings of credit systems: boundaries that bind both borrowers and other creditors to common principles, and that in turn justify and feed into larger systems of exclusion; boundaries that, no matter how specific and on a first reading removed from more general boundaries of exclusions—such as racial and gender categories (Tilly 2005)—are nonetheless nested within them. But general categories often delineate too broad a boundary for the circulation of the selective instruments that are normally traded in credit markets, because they do not usually command the kind of allegiance and sense of identification that more specialized categories do. As identities, they are not (usually) sufficiently strong to command commitment. Thus I have argued that bankers, and creditors more generally, specialize in creating narrower categories of exclusion to which they attach moral worth so as to produce that commitment. They mobilize specialized categories, to the extent that they can generate commitment to collective goals in those who fall within those categories. They do so by moralizing the boundaries between those who are included within, and those who are excluded from, those categories.

Yet general categories, under certain circumstances, can be used to challenge the particularized categories that are nested within them. The struggle between slavery, as the overarching framework to which all other political projects should be subordinated, and the "American System" of the Whig Party that, after the Jacksonian presidencies, almost set the United States on a government-orchestrated, comprehensive, national-developmental path, is an instance of this struggle. The general theoretical point is that the kinds of distinctions possible in the social space contained by general categorical distinctions, and the specialized ones that indicate membership in more exclusive communities, is a space of struggle. It is in this space of struggle that conservative and wildcat bankers articulate their financial strategies.

Our analysis of the U.S. financial system unearthed the kinds of strategies that were available to conservative bankers, as politicians increasingly questioned their choices and strategies, and wildcats took advantage of such political opportunities and pushed for the liberalization of the banking system. Politics—which in the nineteenth-century United States meant the securing of political and legal support of state governments for one's monopoly over certain practices—gave way to more privatized means of securing such monopolistic appropriation. This approach was privatized in the sense that it emphasized specialized, technical expertise backed by a form of moral authority as the basis for the carrying out of banking activities. The Federal Reserve Act, because it made the "real bills doctrine" so central to its logic, served this project, if only for a short period, as the onset of World War I changed radically the balance of political power and gave the Federal Reserve a new mission and rationale (Mehrling 2002).

As Thomas Lamont, at the helm of J. P. Morgan & Co after World War I, was to explain to an audience of bankers in 1923, however, the tendency of U.S. bankers to think of their business as governed by ethical imperatives and service to the community, rather than other, more explicitly political considerations, persisted.

Banking, like any other calling, has its critics and detractors. Yet I hear no serious suggestion that the business of banking be abolished . . . . [T]he great bankers have always been—not the hard-headed conservatives and holders-back they are often pictured—but real constructors. The *great* bankers, I say—and what one among the fraternity is lacking in the ambition to be a great banker; great not necessarily in the eyes of the world, but great in the services he renders to the community? Some of us may at times have been bounded by too narrow a horizon; but the number of such bankers is happily, I believe, growing less each year. . . .

"Trust" is an old-fashioned Saxon and Norse word that came into business parlance almost as soon as its cognate word "true" came into colloquial use. Perhaps today we use more the rather technical phrase "to give credit," but all that means is "to trust in," to have faith in. The late Mr. J. P. Morgan's remark, uttered just a few months before his death, to the effect that he would rather loan a million dollars on character than on the best collateral in the world, has been repeated many times, and worthily, because it was a striking phrase to emphasize that quality of trust, of faith.

If the soundness of our business depends upon the extent to which we are able to trust our customers, how much more does the whole system of banking, of which we are a part, rest upon the faith that the community must place in us. And that faith which they have in us is bounded, not simply by their knowledge of our ordinary honesty, not simply by their belief that in our hands their savings and their deposits are safe; it has a far wider range. The community as a whole demands of the banker that he shall be an honest observer of conditions about him, that he shall make constant and careful study of those conditions, financial, economic, social and political, and that he shall have a wide vision over them all. The community does not insist that the banker shall be prophet too; but it does look to him for an intelligence of high order and for a courage fully commensurate with such intelligence. (Lamont, September 21, 1923)

Lamont emphasized intelligence and courage; breadth of vision but also modesty (since the community did not expect the banker to be a prophet, he quipped); prudence but also decisiveness. Around the same time, Schumpeter (1911, 1939) was developing his ideas about the conflictual nature of banking, identifying the main source of the bankers' power in their capacity to act as "headquarters of capitalism": bankers take a more general and objective perspective on the future profitability of business propositions than the entrepreneurs they finance, argued Schumpeter, but they are also subjected to pressure to open up credit to those normally excluded by sound, conservative criteria. In this respect, and in his further, perhaps ironic, characterization of bankers as sitting on the capitalist equivalent of a "socialist planning board," Schumpeter thus departed from Lamont's more self-celebratory description of bankers as the "honest observer" of the economic conditions of the community. For Schumpeter, antagonism and even struggle characterized the banking system; for Lamont, as well as the bankers who inspired him, banking was, by contrast, a matter of moral leadership, "courage," and "intelligence." On a deeper level, however, Schumpeter and Lamont were in fact describing similar issues: Schumpeter, in a more analytical fashion, focused on the kinds of challenges characterizing the business of banking; Lamont, by virtue of his professional prominence more politically savvy, highlighting instead the cultural aspects of the struggle, provided the kind of rationalization of the bankers' activities that would resonate with the decentralized and fragmented banking system of the nineteenth-century United States. A different structure, this implies, would have generated a different set of cultural responses to the challenges inherent to banking. The conflict between conservative and wildcat bankers, that is, would have taken different contours, leading to different financial outcomes.

In order to explore this possibility, it is now time to leave the United

States, moving to a country where, not for lack of banking traditions—Italy was, after all, the birthplace of capitalism (Braudel 1992; Arrighi 1994)—conservative bankers were able to retain the political support of the state and to construct shared identities in the justification of sound banking that had institutional backing. This achievement, however, became possible only at the cost of alienating conservative bankers whose identity did not correspond with the identity sanctioned by the political authorities. In the next two chapters, I document the emergence of the intersection between banking and nationalism in liberal Italy.

5

Italian Elites and the Centralization of Creditworthiness

IT WOULD SEEM TO BE in the bankers' best interest to build a relationship of trust with their clients, so that they "not only know what the transaction is which [they are] asked to finance and how it is likely to turn out, but . . . also know the customer, his business, and even his private habits, and get, by frequently 'talking things' over with him, a clear picture of his situation" (Schumpeter 1939: 116). Credit is, after all, a matter of interpersonal trust, for as Carruthers (2005: 362) perceptively puts it, "[F]or credit to function . . . the creditor has to trust a specific debtor at a particular time: will she repay in a year's time? Trust problems in credit cannot be resolved globally since they arise out of specific debtor-creditor pairings." In the previous two chapters, however, I have argued that the principles that organize the *credit system* are not the same principles that regulate *credit relations* between two parties.

The organization of the credit system requires the articulation of shared identities, to which both debtors and financial providers commit. Those identities may be grounded on the specialized claim that bankers are impartial assessors of reputations and creditworthiness; but they may be grounded on different claims too, so long as the criteria they articulate legitimize the work done by bankers. The political structure in which bankers operate imposes a first set of constraints on creditors; but it is conflicts among creditors that constitute the main challenge to the construction of stable identities, and of stable boundaries around the allocation of credit.

The previous two chapters focused on the shape and character of the conflict between conservative and wildcat bankers in the nineteenth-century United States. In the decentralized and sectionally divided U.S. polity, I argued, conservative bankers were hard-pressed to construct shared identities and traditions of sound banking that, by making access to credit exclusive, would give them control over the circuits they had created. Local politics, too democratic in the North, but more generally, within the racial boundaries imposed by the slave system, too susceptible to wildcat projects of financial inclusion, was not a reliable source of stable, shared identities—thus of the kinds of meanings, practices, and media of exchange that make up the basic infrastructure of conservative banking circuits. Neither was the politics of the federal government, whose authority was illegitimate in the eyes of wide sections of the U.S. population, and whose lack of financial expertise and competence made it illegitimate in the eyes of financial elites as well. Where politics failed, the developing traditions of mercantile networks came to the rescue, so to speak. Understandings of creditworthiness as the activity of assessing individual reputations became the logic through which conservative bankers strove to organize the U.S. financial system. Such understandings of creditworthiness as inhering in the character of the borrower derived only indirectly from the uncertainty that characterizes creditor-debtor relationships, and more directly from the kind of financial conflict produced by the decentralized political system of the United States.

That the reputational strategies for assessing creditworthiness are political illustrates a larger theoretical claim—namely, that there are no objective, neutral, "natural" criteria to underlie the assessment of creditworthiness through which bankers adjudicate demands for finance (the "myth of creditworthiness"). The criteria that guide financial decisions emerge out of political interactions and processes in which debtors participate only indirectly. In addition to delineating the character and limitations of the exclusionary strategy articulated by U.S. conservative bankers, the analysis of the two previous chapters also posed the question as to whether a financial system can be organized differently than it was in the United States, and whether such differences might result from political conditions too, rather than from the putative requirements of the economy. Addressing these questions is the task for the next two chapters, the focus of which is nineteenth-century Italy.

In the Kingdom of Italy, created in 1860 out of a heterogeneous set of smaller political units (Romeo 1959; Ziblatt 2006), just as in the United States, economic and political communities maintained strong, local loyalties (Cafagna 1989; J. A. Davis 1994; Banti 1996; Riall et al. 2007). However, the political bodies that administered them (specifically, communes and provincial administrations) were infrastructurally weak (Ziblatt 2006), especially in the south (Putnam 1993). They lacked credibility, authority, and capacity (Romanelli 1991, 1995). As a result, local authorities could not guarantee the kind of stability that makes conservative banking projects possible. Over the course of the nineteenth century, moreover, local authorities became increasingly open to democratic pressure. This turned them into wildcat strongholds.

The central state had difficulties, too, in supporting banking conservatism. The central political elites' ideological commitment to fiscal austerity—a central tenet of their classical-liberal persuasion—was challenged by the demands of running the newly centralized polity. Central political elites also remained suspicious of the motivations of their local counterparts: why did they spend so lavishly on local improvement? Were they building the foundations of a modern state, or were they distributing resources nepotistically? One way of facing the challenge of managing a centralized polity was to use the credit system in order to centralize resources. This entailed building up new circuits of credit, which, as we will see in this chapter, generated conflict with the local bankers and local elites subsequently excluded from the national circuits of credit. An outcome of this conflict was the emergence of nationalist identities as the basis for excluded bankers to make claims to inclusion (Mori 1977, 1992; Falchero 1981). Nationalism, at that time particularly focused on economic matters (Lanaro 1979), thus acquired prominence as a tool to mobilize banking and political coalitions in support of projects for financial inclusion (Galli Della Loggia 1970). This is the topic of the next chapter.

The Antinomies of Centralization

Born as a union of several regional states (states that, with the exception of Piedmont, were all under foreign influence or domination), the new Italian state was politically weak. The southern regions, kindled by nationalist sentiment, were in a state of insurrection that the moderate Piedmontese elites had no intention of encouraging: they feared the larger political repercussions on national politics (Riall 1998; Tarrow 2001). The Catholic Church was also hostile to the new kingdom, both because of the anticlerical position of some of its new leaders, and because of concerns about the kingdom's ambitions over Rome (Riall 1994: 76–77).

The state's political weakness was mirrored in its fiscal weakness (Luzzatto 1968). With a debt equal to about 40 percent of GDP at unification (in 1860; it escalated to 96 percent in 1870, and remained above 100 percent of GDP from 1880 onward), for its first decade of existence the new state did not have enough fiscal capacity to balance the budget, even though that was an explicit goal of its liberal governments (Zamagni 1998). The fact that central political elites recognized the importance of developing a national infrastructure (Romeo 1959), for which they needed money, did not help; neither did the fact that the past debts of the former, regional states, and Piedmont in particular, had now become the debt of the unitary polity as a whole (Ziblatt 2006: 74–75). Local authority revenue accounted for 3 to 5 percent of GDP in the 1866–1913 period, compared with central state revenue ranging from 7.6 to a maximum of 16 percent. In 1873, the first year for which data on both levels are available, central state securities and debt amounted to about 76 percent of GDP, whereas local political bodies issued debt worth about 5.5 percent of GDP. In 1894, central government debt reached a high of 135 percent of GDP, with local debts at about 15 percent (Zamagni 1998). These factors, coupled with the very newness of the Italian state, decreased the legitimacy of its fiscal authority and undermined its political capacity to develop an apparatus of fiscal extraction, in a vicious circle of low taxes and more deficits (De Cecco 1990).

Centralization had not always been among the political preferences of the state-building elites. At the eve of unification, in fact, Piedmontese elites felt that fiscal and administrative *decentralization,* coupled with banking and financial *centralization,* would set Italy on a virtuous path of fiscal extraction, paired with a reliable credit system capable of mobilizing the resources freed up by the state (Sabetti 2000). They understood that political decentralization and financial centralization would act in such a fashion, insofar as domestic political relations between center and periphery were reconfigured. Specifically, with fiscal and administrative decentralization, central political elites hoped to gain the support of local elites in balancing the state budget and reducing the national debt. With banking and financial centralization, on the other hand, central elites wanted to strengthen the financial leverage of the state. They wanted to increase the scope and depth of its financial system, diverting the flow of finance and credit from regions where capital was abundant to those where it was scarce (Conti and Scatamacchia 2009; Della Torre 2008; Conti 2007; Polsi 1993; Conti 2000).

As Ziblatt (2006) has most explicitly argued, in spite of such ideological preferences, the breakdown of local authorities that preceded unification forced Italian political elites to centralize authority. And once the unitary, centralized state was institutionalized, discussions of federalism became critiques of the remnants of administrative decentralization. Partly that was because in some provinces, especially in the south, in spite of sometimes fierce rhetoric to the contrary, local administrations were dependent on the involvement of the central government for the enforcement of law and order (Riall 2003: 41). And as local challenges to authority continued for at least the first twenty years of the unitary state, central elites were forced to further build up central power as a way to restore control (Riall 1993, 2007).

Central state elites, however, were conscious of their own limits, and especially of the fact that, without developed local institutions, their intervention could not be controlled, and central state resources were thus likely to be channeled into uses that were not congruent with their original intentions. Administration was centralized, since the state relied on prefects who answered directly to the government for the implementation of its policies throughout the territory; but it had pockets of decentralization too, since towns and local provinces also exercised administrative and political power, with significant overlap between their areas of competence and jurisdiction and those of the prefects. The structure of the state was often referred to by contemporary writers as a "monstrous combination," half English, with its emphasis on local sovereignty and self-government, and half French, with its emphasis on administrative and often coercive implementation of orders from the center (Romanelli 1988; Duggan in J. A. Davis 2001: 175). Central political elites were also increasingly conscious of the stark social inequalities that the new kingdom had partly inherited from the Restoration regimes, and partly contributed to exacerbate (Renda 1987). Their logistical constraints were particularly frustrating.

In this context, central state elites couched their critiques of local political authority in the rhetoric of imposing strict budget constraints that would better discipline local administration. Agostino Magliani's important critique of the profligacy of local administrators stands out. Magliani (1824–91), Italian financier, liberal minister of finances under

Depretis (leader of the Historic Left), and co-founder of the Italian Adam Smith Society, pointed to a defect in the governance system of the unitary state that allowed local administrations to go into debt, even as the government had taken fiscal power away from them. This freedom, he added, encouraged speculation. Local debt was excessive relative to the budget of the bodies that issued it, argued Magliani, because local authorities were not controlled by any national regulative body, and thus the decision to issue debt was not only decoupled from their capacity to raise resources but also detached from any concern with the financial cohesion of the new kingdom as a whole. After unification the state had followed the tradition of the autonomous Communes, and the law had empowered them with the administration of their finances, argued Magliani. This shift from direct intervention from above to self-administration had not been coupled, however, with appropriate laws that would restrict the Communes' freedom to go into debt. If there was to be fiscal conservatism, it was to start from the local level.

A balanced budget cannot be said to have been achieved until there will be a similar normalization of the finances of the Communes, on which so many important public services depend, and which are an integral part of the body and life of the nation. (Magliani 1878: 293)

The *Rassegna Settimanale*, a widely circulated liberal weekly, agreed: in a series of editorials, it pointed out that, initially, legislators agreed that to facilitate progress, they should indicate what expenditures were obligatory for the Communes.

The facts now show that this is not enough, that what must be determined are also the kinds of expenditures a Commune should be forbidden from allowing. . . . We limit ourselves to mentioning the need to stop local administrators from spending impatiently and abundantly on broad-walks and public gardens, monumental buildings etc.; and how damaging is the tendency of most of those who run the Communes to see them as means to increase their influence and power rather than managing the public interest. (Anon. 1878a: 246)

The issue was not simply about excessive quantities of local debt: even though central government revenue was between 2.5 and 3 times as large as local revenue throughout the period between unification and World War I, national debt dwarfed local debt. Opposition to local spending, rather, had to do with the *kinds* of expenditures that Communes often

TABLE 5.1
Italian Revenue Structure: Central Government and Local Authorities, 1866–1913
(Millions of current lire)

	State	% of GDP	Local	% of GDP
	(1)	(2)	(3)	(4)
1866	610	*7.4*	241	*2.9*
1868	741	*8.4*	275	*3.1*
1870	787	*9.3*	321	*3.8*
1872	1152	*11.7*	358	*3.6*
1876	1179	*12.5*	399	*4.2*
1880	1297	*12.3*	432	*4.1*
1886	1624	*15.3*	491	*4.6*
1890	1604	*14.9*	534	*5.0*
1896	1646	*15.9*	522	*5.0*
1900	1742	*14.3*	568	*4.7*
1906	2010	*14.0*	682	*4.7*
1912	2495	*13.1*	1015	*5.3*
1913	2573	*13.0*	1040	*5.2*

SOURCE: Zamagni 1993: 173; Zamagni 1998.

TABLE 5.2
*Percentage of Revenue Accruing to Central Government and
Local Authorities, Italy, 1866–1913*

	Central	Local
	(1)	(2)
1866	71.7%	28.3%
1870	71.0	29.0
1872	76.3	23.7
1876	74.7	25.3
1880	75.0	25.0
1886	76.8	23.2
1890	75.0	25.0
1896	75.9	24.1
1900	75.4	24.6
1906	74.7	25.3
1912	71.1	28.9

SOURCE: Zamagni 1993

authorized, for those expenditures indicated just how different from the national level political priorities were at the local level.

Two points stood out in the critique by Magliani (and the central elites he represented), argues Romanelli (1988). First, commentators focused on the danger that the "democratizing" of local administrations posed to the central state. They were quite unsure that their commitment to the unitary state was shared by the larger population. In Duggan's even-handed assessment (in J. A. Davis 2001: 160): "Cavour's successors had faced a monumental task after 1860: how to introduce the practices of freedom to 22 million people, the vast majority of whom had had no experience of liberalism and most of whom were more likely to be deferential to a local priest, a tyrannical landlord, or even some local bandit, than to a high-minded exponent of constitutionalism. In such circumstances, could decentralization and a broader suffrage be justified? Would this not be simply playing into the hands of the enemies of the state?" Magliani (1878), for instance, argued that among the most urgent reforms needed to improve local administration, the design of communal elections so that local interests would be represented was crucial—an apparently democratic move. Yet he also stressed that elections should be carried out as independently as possible from "the agitations of political parties." This should be coupled with more transparency and control over the budget, as well as better accounting procedures. One is here reminded of the fight between Democratic Jacksonians and Whigs in the 1840s, when the transition to a party-competitive system was taking place (Silbey 1994). But the fear in Italy was that, as Romanelli (1988, 1995) points out, in regions that were more progressive, nonlanded majorities would gain political power if given the opportunity to organize against local notables, thus subverting the liberal order from the bottom up by attacking property and demanding land redistribution; whereas, in regions under the domination of more conservative forces, granting authority to local administrations could reinforce opposition to the unitary state.

Second, and perhaps more important, debates on local administration criticized the tendency of local authorities to spend money on the infrastructure that, symbolically, undergirded the new, self-consciously bourgeois status order: from the 1870s onward, the emerging middle classes now claimed a space in public arenas that reflected their newly found confidence (Banti 1996). So the *Rassegna Settimanale*, as we have just seen, complained about "broad-walks," gardens, and monuments. The administration of Naples was there criticized for "happily spending, even though its annual deficit exceeds six million lire, and almost ignoring the need to raise new revenue, while it earmarks even bigger sums for the arts and the press." Liberal, landed elites were quick to characterize such expenditures in terms that referred to nepotism, corruption, and the squandering of resources. "Public works" in reality meant "colossal expenditures on building beautification . . . and under the 'police' category are included many a luxury expenditure," complained an editorial (Anon 1878a). Romanelli suggests that the struggle between the center and the peripheries over expenditures and revenue should be understood as an instance of class conflict, with the emerging bourgeoisie entrenching itself in the cities and engaging in patterns of conspicuous consumption and status display, while the agrarian minority and local notables wanted to practice local fiscal conservatism that would defend their rentier position. But what these loans were raised to finance was as important a source of preoccupation to central political elites as the fact that local loans created financial instability. The *Rassegna Settimanale* continued: "[T]he financial crisis of many communes originates with exaggerated expenditures and *easy access to loans.*" Critics were convinced that Communes could save substantial money if their budget was structured differently.

If local Administrations want to contribute to funding new railroads, they must do so without excessive sacrifices and without suffocating the potential for future development of industry and commerce. (Anon 1878b)

Issuing new debt would simply "stifle" both.

Because they saw cities as sites where new urban elites squandered resources that the state had so carefully earmarked for more important purposes, central elites like Magliani finally wondered:

Would it not be more beneficial for the development of our liberal institutions if Parliament was the referee of those deliberations that will determine the future of our Communes? . . . By pushing them [the Communes] to deal with local affairs, would they not be better known, and better tied to the foundations of our national building, which are nothing but well ordered and prudently administered Communes? (1878: 304)

It was, in sum, a situation of conflict and mutual dependence that characterized the relationship between central political elites and the regional elites that had joined them in the unitary, centralized structure of the new kingdom. Unable to find political solutions to the problem of revenue distribution and allocation of administrative authority, central elites resorted to a decentralized financial and credit system to fulfill the role that they had failed to assign to fiscal penetration and local administration. And just as they were dependent on foreign loans for the accumulation of sufficient resources to spearhead economic development and undertake new military operations, central political elites resorted to loans from the Banca Nazionale and the smaller banks of issue in order to spread the use of new instruments throughout the national territory, in the hope that financial interest would create a more cohesive polity. To these issues we now turn.

The Organization of Banking

After unification, the one solution to the fiscal problems of the new kingdom that was most congruent with the liberal ideology of central political elites lay in raising money in foreign markets, a decision helped by the favorable conditions they offered (De Cecco 1990). Thus in 1866, the Italian government authorized the House of Rothschild to underwrite the issue of government bonds (Fratianni and Spinelli 1997). The loan, however, made Italy dependent on the vagaries of the Parisian stock exchange, with outcomes that did not take long to become visible to Italian authorities.[1] Credit in Paris soon dried up, and Italy was forced to suspend convertibility (or in the parlance of the day, it established a *corso forzoso* for the currency). Exit from gold brought into relief the extent to which the new kingdom, if it wanted to pursue its expansionary policies, needed to build a domestic constituency of creditors over which it would be able to exert stricter control than it ever could on foreign financial houses. Hence the government devised a strategy of building strong local banking institutions as a way to gain more financial autonomy, even though its fiscal structure remained heavily tilted toward the center.

The Banca Nazionale, the product of the merger between the Banca di Genova (funded in 1844) and the Banca di Torino (in 1849), was the largest bank on the Italian peninsula, and, once the Italian Kingdom was formed, the government turned it into the backbone of the financial system. The 1866 royal decree on exit from the gold standard had important implications in this regard.[2] First of all, the exit from gold restrained the outflow of specie from the country. With Italian money no longer convertible into gold, the Banca Nazionale was able to retain a sufficient quantity of reserves to extend a large loan to the government, which in turn authorized the bank to print more paper money. In this transaction alone, the government asked the Banca Nazionale for, and received, 250 million lire (Zamagni 1993: 175–77).

Understandably, central political elites wanted the relationship with the Banca Nazionale to grow stronger, and vied to grant it full monopoly over the issue of notes. Carlo De Cesare, head of a short-lived government agency regulating the issue of new securities, argued:

Banknotes are a most marvelous modern invention, which cannot be comprehended or defined through the lenses of the *idealist school*, which tends to see even matter as spirit; but neither through the coarse claims of the *metallic school*, which only considers precious metals. A banknote is what it is, *a means of exchange that functions as coin*, and as such cannot be left to the arbitrary decisions of private interests. It must be systematized and disciplined by the State. . . . If this were not to happen, the monetary regime of a country, its public credit and national economy would be upset from top to bottom, and the common measure of value and prices would be turned upside down. (De Cesare 1874: 33)

In spite of De Cesare's articulate argument about the public character of money, and thus the need for its supervision by government, however, financial unification, and the centralization of the power to issue money in the hands of the Banca Nazionale, both proved to be difficult projects, taking far longer to be completed than its supporters had expected.

Italian political elites clearly understood that a successful credit system should penetrate the local level. The decree that signaled exit from the gold standard, accordingly, gave legal tender status to all the notes issued by the minor banks (namely, Banca Nazionale Toscana, Banca Toscana di Credito, Banco di Napoli, and Banco di Sicilia), and made them convertible for the notes of the Banca Nazionale, which also had to be held as reserves (one-third of reserves still had to be in gold, whereas the Banca Nazionale was obligated to hold all its reserves in gold). The decree gave issuing privileges to all banks but created a stratified system in which the Banca Nazionale held a hegemonic position by virtue of its control over specie (Cardarelli 1990). For the Banca Nazionale to exercise its power fully, however, it needed to rein in the financial activities of its rivals, which could otherwise exploit the less stringent reserve requirements the law imposed on them and thereby expand at the expense of the Banca

Nazionale. Accordingly, the Banca Nazionale made repeated attempts to merge with the Banca Nazionale Toscana, attempts that spurred much controversy in the first twenty years of the new kingdom (Sannucci, pp. 244–80 in De Cecco and Giovannini 1989; De Mattia 1990).

The Grand Duchy of Tuscany was, along with Lombardy and Piedmont, the most prosperous and commercialized region in the Italian territory. Because of its long tradition of dealing in commercial operations, its Banca Nazionale Toscana discounted (that is, guaranteed and endorsed upon charging a fee) commercial instruments signed by two parties—usually, the buyer and seller of merchant goods. It thereby had a direct relationship with commercial elites and fostered a decentralized system of payments in which it had the role of guarantor. As a result, its notes were widely accepted in Tuscany. The Banca Nazionale, by contrast, because of its central role in the more hierarchical financial system of Piedmont, and because its operations were mostly in the nature of investments, discounted financial instruments bearing three signatures—the signatures of the parties to the transaction, as well as of a banker guaranteeing the transaction itself. It thus had a centralizing function: it established relationships with other bankers rather than building its own clientele (Polsi 1993). Merging the two banks was not only a politically difficult operation: it also entailed choosing a specific kind of financial system, one more oriented toward stability and centralized control, vis-à-vis one more oriented toward commercial development. The struggle between the vision of a centralizer like Cavour,[3] as opposed to the decentralizing ambition of non-Piedmontese elites,[4] that underlay each financial framework, however, resulted in a stalemate. The merging of the two banks was postponed until the financial crisis of 1892–94 (De Mattia 1990).

The conflict over the centralization of the financial system was not limited to the relationship between the Banca Nazionale and the Banca Nazionale Toscana. The Banco di Napoli and the Banco di Sicilia presented equally formidable challenges to any project of financial centralization, especially because the southern regions in which these two banks operated were the theater of intense, antinational opposition. Having just been liberated from the rule of the House of the Bourbons (or, more realistically, forced into a union with Piedmontese elites whose legitimacy they did not recognize), southern regions had agricultural economies increasingly organized around large land-holdings that were dependent on the vagaries of world trade for the export of their products (oil, oranges,

TABLE 5.3

Italian Banks of Issue, Nineteenth Century

Preunification State	Bank of Issue	Year of Formation	Year of Dissolution	Type of Debts	Gold reserve ratio	Paper Circulation	Specie Circulation
						Millions of lire	
Kingdom of Sardinia	Banca di Genova	1844	1849				
	Banca di Torino	1847	1849				
	Banca Nazionale	1849		National, private	1:3	83	175
	Banca di Savoia	1851	1859				
Duchy of Parma	Banca Parmense	1858	1861	Local, private, state	1:3	–	20
Lombardy-Veneto	Banca Nazionale Austriaca	1816				9	112
	Stabil. Mercantile Venezia	1853	1867			19	100
Grand Duchy of Tuscany	Banca Nazionale Toscana	1857	1893	Local, private, state	1:3	20	73
	Banca Toscana di Credito	1860	1893				
Pontifical State	Banca dello Stato Pontificio (Banca Romana)	1850	1893	Local, private, state	1:3	44	30
	Banca per le Quattro Legazioni	1855	1861	Local, private	1:3	3	100
Kingdom of the Two Sicilies	Banco delle Due Sicilie (Banco di Napoli)	1816	1926 (become commercial banks)	Local, private, state	1:2	179	350
	Banco dei Reali Dominii al di là del Faro (Banco di Sicilia)	1850		Local, private, state	1:1	30	107

SOURCE: De Mattia (1990).

lemons) (Cafagna 1989). In the south, moreover, unification had stirred both a rebellion against peasant exploitation and a rebellion against the replacement of old, foreign elites with elites who were perceived to be just as distant. Northern elites were thus conscious that the outright dissolution of the two banks that southern elites used for their financial and commercial operations was simply out of the question. The issue, rather, was to encourage the formation of additional, alternative circuits of money.

The problem with this strategy of increasing the reach of national institutions was that regional elites were excluded from the financial circuits of the Banca Nazionale, so their support for the state building project, weak as it was, could be weakened even more if the issue of financial reform was not dealt with carefully. It was apparent to many that the Banca Nazionale was the nexus of a northern financial oligarchy, as the directors of the Banca Nazionale were involved in other banking ventures as well, concentrating a significant amount of power in their hands.[5] Three main positions on the continuum from centralization to decentralization thereby came to focus elite attention.

According to one position, a centralized financial system, ideally with one bank of issue at the top, was preferable to other, more decentralized arrangements, for three main reasons. First, it would invest one institution with the kind of power and prestige that would make it an equal to its international counterparts (De Cecco 1990). Second, it would facilitate the expansion and penetration of credit relations into regions where credit was scarce: once centralized, that is, credit could be redirected toward areas that needed it most (Polsi 2000). Third, as a consequence, a centralized credit and financial system would increase the overall robustness and capacity of the Italian financial system, while countering its fragmentary tendencies (Romanelli 1988). In this view, in other words, the exigencies of the central state took priority over local demands.

A decentralized financial system was, by contrast, the battle cry of another group of reformers, who played up the importance of the local development of banking institutions. Decentralization, these reformers asserted, by stimulating trade and commercial development, would seamlessly ease the entry of the Italian nation into capitalism and modernity (Conti 2000). Unlike a centralized financial system, moreover, a decentralized financial system would bring about more freedom and equality—thus countering the oligarchic tendencies the unitary state had brought about (Sabetti 2000).

TABLE 5.4

Biographical Sketches of the Protagonists of the Italian Debates

Author	Occupation
Bertolotto, Sebastiano (?)	Genoa stock exchange broker.
Pallavicino, Camillo (?)	Banker: First president of the Banca di Genova.
Boccardo, Gerolamo (1829–1904)	Liberal economist. Senator.
De Cesare, Carlo (1825–87)	Senator (Naples). Director: Commission of Control over Banks (1860s).
Ferrara, Francesco (1810–1900)	Liberal economist, briefly Minister of Finance. Strong believer in laissez-faire. Patriot in Risorgimento.
Grimaldi, Bernardino (1837–97)	Minister of Agriculture, Industry and Commerce (1870s)—Left government.
Luzzatti, Luigi (1841–1927)	Economist. Parliamentary deputy. Protagonist in international monetary arrangements with France. Founder of banking cooperative movement.
Majorana-Catalabiano, Salvatore (1826–97)	Left-liberal deputy (Sicily). Economist.
Martello, Tullio (1841–1918)	Liberal economist. Disciple of Ferrara.
Nisco, Nicola (1816–1901)	Risorgimento patriot and collaborator of Cavour. President of the Banco di Napoli.
Rossi, Alessandro (1819–98)	Industrialist. Protectionist.
Seismit-Doda, Federico (1825–93)	Left politician. Risorgimento patriot.
Semenza, Gaetano (1826–82)	Journalist. Patriot in Risorgimento.
Soria, Beniamino (?)	Economist/journalist.
Stringher, Bonaldo (1854–1930)	Economist. Treasury officer. Bank of Italy governor 1900–1930.

The first group, which I will call "strong state-builders," wanted a governance structure characterized by a strong center aiding the emergence of peripheral banks of deposit only indirectly, through discounting (in that way following the model practiced by the Banca Nazionale). The second group, the "liberal decentralizers," argued that only a system of multiple and numerous banks of issue would help develop the backward and oligarchic Italian credit system into a modern and democratic one. An intermediate position espoused a mildly decentralizing perspective, arguing that multiple (but not numerous) banks of issue would be better suited to spreading the use of money and credit than a unitary bank. Table 5.5 at the end of the chapter provides a synopsis of these debates, as well as listing the primary literature on which the rest of my discussion is based.

In the background of these debates were the recent, failed attempts to decentralize the fiscal system, so that the issue of political decentralization was, for all intents and purposes, off the table. As a result, these debates were marked by a shared skepticism that the centralized fiscal setup of the Italian state provided no opportunity for the development of local banking conservatism.

Centralization and State-Building

Elites invested in the centralization of credit were most directly concerned with the "monetary chaos" created by inconvertibility, which the Italian government had declared in 1866. Exit from gold, to be sure, had advantaged the Banca Nazionale, which, as we saw, in return for a large loan to the government, had gained the right to print paper money as legal tender. This was a step in the centralization of the credit system, albeit one fraught with difficulties, given the instability of paper money. Importantly, though, these elites reasoned that exit from gold had led to even greater outflows of gold and silver from the Italian economy (the technical explanation they proposed was simply that other countries had higher exchange rates and thus tended to attract specie); and it had resulted in a proliferation of "illegal" currencies, especially special coins of small denominational value that were necessary for local transactions.[6]

Elites invested in the centralization of credit, whom I will call "strong state-builders" because of the link they posited between centralized credit and political authority, worried about this state of affairs. They believed that, in a regime of paper money, bankers were forced to compete for scarce, good investments, and would eventually have to undertake risky propositions, compromising the stability of the system and as a result creating problems of public order for political authorities. De Cesare (1874: 80–81), opposed to the privilege of issuing money that the banks of the preunification states had managed to preserve, did not hesitate to describe the Italian financial system as "anarchic": without the discipline of the gold standard, he argued, banks simply issued money for speculative purposes. Like other state-building elites, he favored a centralized bank of issue that, because it was disciplined by the gold standard, would in turn exercise its hegemony and impose discipline over other banks as well.

It was a common eighteenth- and nineteenth-century trope to use organic metaphors involving the body to understand the workings of complex social, and especially economic, systems (see Pasanek and Polillo 2011). Intellectuals who made the case for the superiority of centralized credit arrangements were naturally drawn to such metaphors, as ideas about the credit system as a well-functioning and well-coordinated body served to undergird their preference for stability and good governance. Economist Gerolamo Boccardo (1881: 11) argued, for instance:

From the humble savings banks to the powerful bank of issue, from the modest credit union to the most courageous *crédit mobilier* and investment bank, from the functions of a private banker to the combinations of the most gigantic clearing house, we observe in the modern system of credit an enormous range of entities, which in the whole form a strong body with extraordinary capacity for action, subject to the great and supreme biological law, by virtue of which with the increased differentiation of organs and functions the directive impulse from the center increases too.

In this view, the creation of centralized structures of governance was both desirable and inevitable. It responded to forces operating in ways similar to a "biological law" (see Goodhart [1988] for a modern evolutionary perspective on banking).

Centralization was thought to carry enormous benefits to the development of the financial system as a whole. Bertolotto (1867: 11), for instance, asserted that

the Banca Nazionale fulfills its role particularly well. Through its note it enlarges the circuit of its operations to incalculable advantage to the nation, thanks to the solid conditions it enjoys and to the trust that its able and prudent administration has been able to inspire. This institution is so intimately linked to the economic fate of the nation . . . that it would be a national tragedy to change the conditions in which it operates just to pursue a utopian illusion.

In this vision, state-building and liberalism went hand in hand because of a shared understanding that the bank of issue, given its special relationship with the central government, had been able to build a solid financial reputation for itself. This reputation, in turn, now allowed the Banca Nazionale fully to extend its operations with confidence: Bertolotto thought that the Banca Nazionale could seamlessly move to the role of financing private bankers, rather than the state. By doing so, the bank of issue was supposed to encourage the development of smaller institutions, which Bertolotto understood as crucial to commerce: "The institution of banks of discount and deposit would bring great advantage to small industries and petty trade. . . . Even those with little competence in matters of commerce would readily recognize how discount banks would give impetus to industry and to activity of many small centers." Finally, a central bank would exercise control over national credit: it would replace the multiple, often foreign currencies in which private transactions were previously carried out with a national currency (see also Helleiner 1999).

Strong state-builders, importantly, supported fiscal conservatism. State money was safe only insofar as it was backed by the fiscal machinery of the state, so the issue of debt beyond the means of the state was to be discouraged. Sound budgets would permit the banking system to specialize in private transactions. Whenever debt had to be issued, the government should exercise its moral authority so that those securities would not be used "speculatively." So, according to Luzzatti (1883):

The government must never violate and must in fact protect the inviolability of balanced budgets, so that the healthier its finances, the more austere the technical requirements regulating the budget. This, in order to reach that exquisite point that is the only criterion of truth ... the kind of criterion that any good head of the household respects, according to which revenue pays for actual expenses, leaving an adequate margin to pay off outstanding public debt.

Having a strong, fiscally responsible central government at its core, the Italian financial system, argued these state-building elites, would finally gain the kind of technical competence and prestige that befitted the new Italian nation, as Cavour had long argued.

Mild and Radical Decentralization

Proposals in support of financial centralization were contested. Banks other than the Banca Nazionale, and southern banks in particular, remained strongly opposed to it, and several intellectual and political elites joined them in voicing their aversion to a single bank of issue. They proposed alternative projects of their own that endorsed different degrees of decentralization. One position can be characterized as favoring a mildly decentralized system. These commentators believed that, since money was a fiscal instrument created by the state, and also an instrument abetting the development of other instruments (private banknotes) that facilitated commerce, several kinds of banks should be instituted. They distinguished between the role that the Banca Nazionale and discount banks should each play within the financial system.

Mild decentralizers, much like strong state-builders in this regard, recognized the importance of a central bank of issue, and of provincial banks, in the coordination and diffusion of credit. But within this group, proponents of *central-periphery coordination* supported the establishment of a robust central bank, specialized in discounting the paper of provincial banks. Pallavicino, for instance, distinguished between monarchical regimes, where a single bank of issue worked most effectively, and "popular" regimes, in which plurality of issue was preferred. He thought that Italy should reach a compromise: with "a central or primary Bank, whose notes are accepted by the Treasury of the state, and circulate thanks to the help of secondary, provincial banks, to be instituted autonomously throughout the provinces" (Pallavicino 1864: 321) Through discounting, mild decentralizers claimed that both the center and the periphery of the banking system could develop autonomously and harmoniously. Mimicking the organization of finances in England, the central bank would specialize in financing the state; its private business would be directed exclusively to other bankers, and not to the larger public. The central bank would also become the only institute of issue: provincial banks would not be able to print money, but they would be given full access to the facilities of the central bank and through discounting would be given the opportunity to purchase liquidity. In the longer run, once provincial banks had finally spread to the peripheries of the state, they would also diffuse the use of current accounts and new financial instruments such as checks. Ultimately, deposit banking would replace the issue of money.

Other supporters of decentralization were more radical, partly as a result of their hostile posture toward the Banca Nazionale, and pushed for complete plurality of issue. They can be described as proponents of *peripheral dominance,* because they downplayed the importance of a central coordinating agency, and at most supported the institution of a central clearinghouse that would simply keep the accounts of the provincial banks. More peripherally oriented decentralizers thus believed that the issue of money was to be fully liberalized. Monopoly was the evil they most explicitly wanted to fight:

In Italy the government tried all sorts of strategies in order to turn the economy, finance, and administration into a banking oligarchy, whose effects we can predict will be nefarious to the condition of our country, to the political life of the nation, and to the development and consolidation of our parliamentary institutions. (Seismit-Doda 1873: 59)

A preoccupation with the political effects of the organization credit on the makeup of the Italian nation took center stage in this critique. Given that the Banca Nazionale was politically and financially linked to the government, peripheral decentralizers charged it with neglecting provincial bankers, and even financing speculation at the expense of small investors. The fact that Italian public debt was predominantly held abroad only increased the gravity of the situation, they argued.

While the more radical wing of the decentralizers disagreed on the role that the Banca Nazionale would play in facilitating this integration, it also shared with their moderate counterparts a basic confidence in the "democratizing" effects that the decentralized issue of money and the spread of local banking institutions would have on the polity at large. Local institutions with autonomy of judgment and operation would, at least, counterbalance the centralizing effects of the Banca Nazionale. Some commentators even proposed that local banks would promote harmony among the classes and generalized prosperity. Mild and more radical decentralizers ultimately recognized that a successful and balanced financial system required the integration of means of payments originating from the state with those used by the private sector.

Liberal Decentralization

Other kinds of locally oriented, prodecentralization positions were possible, and the most common one among them resisted even the weak state-building ambitions of mild decentralizers. These *liberal decentralizers* articulated a theory of money based on trust, rather than governance. Thus they were interested less in the institutional design of the Italian banking system than in the macroeconomic conditions for the growth of the private sector. In particular, they believed that the value of money derived from its redeemability into metal (a belief that other positions shared as well, as it derived from the classical, and in the era very popular, argument in favor of the gold standard). Consistently with this position, they argued that inconvertibility was the biggest problem facing the Italian banking system, and that more precisely, through inconvertibility, the Banca Nazionale was enriching itself at the expense of the public. In other words, they mirrored the hostility toward the Banca Nazionale expressed by peripherally oriented mild decentralizers. Finally, they connected this issue to the fact that capital was not flowing evenly throughout the national territory, and did not reach commerce and industry. In even stronger terms than the strong state-builders and their decentralizing counterparts, they understood this as a moral failure that hampered the creation of harmony between the producer classes.

Liberal decentralizers, because they shared a faith in the market as the ultimate and most effective agent of social transformation, could afford to make more pragmatic claims than their counterparts. The market will eventually prevail, they asserted, so a few compromises on the way could not be as detrimental as they seemed to those who did not share their teleological mindset. For instance, they recognized that the amount of money issued by the state was too large to be disposed of at once and replaced with metallic currency. And since, in their eyes, the value of both state and private money was determined by trust, they also conceded that credible governance structures should be put in place to guarantee that the promise to redeem the currency into metal would not be broken, but nothing more. This led them to flexible positions: in conditions of inconvertibility, that is, when a state suspended the gold standard and allowed the printing of paper money not backed by metal, monetary issue should be monopolized by the state because that arrangement offered the best system of guarantees—through the judiciary and legislative apparatus of the state. However, once money was put back onto the gold standard, the issue of money could be liberalized and granted to multiple institutions. The goal was to use the territorial spread of currencies to abet the development of alternative and more "modern" credit instruments as well, such as checks. The social consequences of this process would also be beneficial: the working classes, by entrusting their savings to the banking system, would increase their participation in public life, predicted the liberal decentralizers.

Nonetheless, a utopian philosophy informed their pragmatic public policies. Liberal decentralizers shared a faith in the transformative and socially beneficial effects of the spread of credit, a faith that turned otherwise incompatible commentators into bedfellows. Counterintuitively, an industrialist like Alessandro Rossi, who would later articulate protectionist ideas (Lanaro 1979), found himself essentially agreeing with a liberal economist such as Francesco Ferrara. While their ideas about free trade were very different, the two shared a commitment to diffusing credit relations through banks not connected to the central state. Rossi (1878) called it "popular credit." Similarly Ferrara (1873), echoing the positions of the

English banking school, argued that, in fact, neither banks nor the state could ever control the issue of money, because it was ultimately the public that decided what, and how much, to hold.

Centralization and Creditworthiness

Having discussed the differences between, and similarities among, these three groups, I now want to focus again on a common theme they shared: a recognition of the need to improve peripheral deposit banking—namely, banks that collected the savings of individual customers who lived in the more rural and, in their eyes, undeveloped areas of Italy. Deposit banking was crucial in such accounts: intellectual elites recognized it as the means that would make credit more accessible to a larger population. While state-builders and mild decentralizers emphasized that the state should promote its development through appropriate institutional change, liberal decentralizers were willing to entrust the "market" with the diffusion of new credit instruments—thus they agreed with state-builders on the objective, but disagreed on the means. It was a rather minor disagreement: all three camps saw the financial penetration and development of the peripheries of the state as a desirable outcome. They all understood that a financial system without "depth" and "breadth" was inevitably limited.

This shared concern with deposit banking reveals a common awareness of the linkage between credit and regional development. Commentators were contemporary witnesses to the process of economic development (Fenoaltea 2006). As a result, they explicitly wondered how the establishment of a national credit system would affect the development of the Italian regions they considered more backward, and whether the formation of a strong financial core would facilitate or hamper the spread of credit relations to the provinces. Their concerns, in other words, were of a structural and macroscopic nature. Their solutions to the perceived problems of the Italian financial system, paradoxically, were not necessarily so.

Italian commentators seemed uninterested in issues regarding the creditworthiness of individual borrowers, for they shared a view of the transformative aspects of credit that made creditworthiness an outcome rather than a precondition of credit. Different institutional arrangements, in other words, were thought to create different kinds of creditors and debtors. Rather than believing that creditworthiness was a property of a banking public, of a clientele that bankers had to develop the skills to screen in order to serve most effectively, Italian financial and intellectual elites believed that creditworthiness was a quality that the financial system, if properly set up, would help *produce*.[7]

Such understandings of credit institutions, as possessing the power to transform the identities of those they served, generally failed to specify how to set up such institutions. That is, even though elites shared a deep preoccupation with the potential instability that a growth of the credit system would provoke, supporters of decentralization did not propose institutional alternatives to the central state. Therein lay the paradox of diagnosing the problem of credit as having macroscopic sources, while proposing solutions that were decidedly lacking in institutional content. To be sure, decentralizers understood that the central government was the primary financial actor in the Italian polity; but they were also painfully aware of its weakness and inability in fostering new criteria of membership for local financial circuits that would promote a return to banking conservatism, rather than encouraging speculation.[8] Their concern, then, ended up being with the cultural and moral "preparedness" of the Italian people, and more specifically the middle classes and peasantry, to enter modern financial relationships, not with the political conditions that would make the development of more modern financial behavior possible. Elites were also concerned with the potentially speculative effects of credit instruments spreading to areas that were, allegedly, not ready to use them, so they did not appeal to some ultimate quality that borrowers allegedly possessed as the arbiter of good financial practices. But this was only the flip side of the argument that different institutional arrangements of credit would produce different kinds of creditors. The mode whereby the diffusion of credit would take place was considered crucial, but elites had come to terms with the central state's involvement in this process. Supporters of decentralization could only hope that, once the reform of the banking system was completed, new rules to control speculation would emerge either spontaneously, through market processes, or would be enforced by local banks. But none of these elites would go so far as to tie the reform of finance with a reform of state structures.

This had important implications for the character of financial conflict, which becomes immediately apparent once we remind ourselves that conservative banking is an attempt to delineate strict criteria through which creditworthiness is defined, in ways that protect the exclusivity of an established clientele. These criteria gain support and legitimacy to the extent that they are presented as natural and objective, rather than "arbitrary" and interested—a point that, as we have repeatedly seen, Weber turned into the premise for his argument about the collective dimensions of the economic processes by status groups. The Italian debates about the shape of the credit system, however, started from the premise that existing understandings of creditworthiness were too strict to begin with; that the economic and social development of the new kingdom depended on how effectively those boundaries were opened to new customers; and finally, that new criteria would have to be developed along the way. Strong state-builders, however, were virtually alone in arguing that, given the centralized nature of the Italian polity, a decentralized banking system would be too difficult to control, let alone to direct toward the kind of economic development that central elites envisioned. Other elites, by contrast, simply accepted the administrative setup of the kingdom, however flawed it seemed to them to be.[9] The final showdown between decentralizers and state-builders in which these considerations generated much political conflict can be seen in the context of a legislative debate charged with deciding whether Italian banking should adopt the U.S. model. To this we now turn.

American Dreams

In the 1870s, Italian political and financial elites of the liberal Left attempted to imitate the banking system of the United States, and in particular the Free Banking Laws that had been institutionalized by the Civil War–era National Banking System. Unlike other episodes of cross-national diffusion of legitimate models, there were no strictly geopolitical (Djelic 1998), prestige-oriented (Westney 1987), or professional (Guillén 1994) reasons for Italian political and financial elites to choose the United States as a model to imitate. In fact, in spite of its impressive economic growth, the U.S. financial system was often criticized sharply for the instability it brought to economic and trade relations: it was not by any stretch a legitimate model (De Cecco 1990). But certain Italian elites appealed to the U.S. model selectively, in order to justify their challenge to the power of the Banca Nazionale and gain wider support for their call to decentralize the banking system. U.S. Free Banking Laws, put differently, were appealing for political reasons, as they promised to solve the contradictions of a centralized state with a decentralized financial system. In reality, the debate that surrounded the proposed laws highlighted precisely the incompatibility between free banking and a centralized polity in which local administrations had weak political capacity (Cardarelli 1990; Carocci 1956).

First, it is important to note that in 1874, an important set of laws had already established a more decentralized financial system than that which had followed unification. These laws established a consortium of the six banks of issue, and authorized them to issue inconvertible notes (proper "government notes," printed on behalf of the government), thus breaking the monopoly over the issue of notes that the Banca Nazionale had previously enjoyed. Notes of the consortium were then used to replace the notes through which the Banca Nazionale had monetized the national debt. This was a way of rationalizing the banking system: the consortium checked the proliferation of banknotes not issued by the consortium, and thus ended illegal circulation.[10] More important, law-makers explained that the Banca Nazionale was to have no privileged position in this operation, and authorized the other, smaller banks of issue to open branches in the Italian territory. The rationale was to lay the foundations for the return to convertibility, but also to check the hegemony of the Banca Nazionale and reinforce the connection between local banks and the banks of issue (Fratianni and Spinelli 1997; Luzzatto 1968).

This new set of policies was a precursor to the important change in the balance of power that characterized the second half of the decade. The party of the Right, which had led the country to unification, was replaced in 1876 by what was called the Historic Left, a somewhat amorphous coalition of regional landed elites, free-market liberals, and the new, emerging bourgeoisie (Carocci 2002: 16–17). The very internal incoherence of the Left was to give rise to a notorious practice, *trasformismo*: the creation of ad hoc coalitions held together by the dexterity of the prime minister (in particular Depretis, who was the creator of this system) and thus expressing clientelism and favoritism rather than a distinctive political project (Carocci 1956). One of the issues that held the coalition together was opposition to the Banca Nazionale. And if "the Banca Nazionale always encountered, before and after the 1870s, the hostility of the Left," with the rise to power of the latter this hostility took on a "democratic character" (ibid.: 34), aimed at weakening the boundaries that the Banca Nazionale insisted on imposing on credit.

The debate over free banking played out in a series of legislative proposals by Senator Majorana, who discussed several bills in Parliament on repeated sessions, beginning in 1877 and ending in May 1879 with Majorana's presentation of a bill to the lower chamber. His "free banking" proposal was finally rejected, yet a discussion of the arguments that surrounded it reveals an alternative definition of the power of the state in the economy, and a different view of the integration of the lower classes and the peripheries into the credit system than those that were eventually institutionalized. Importantly, the proposal completely bypassed the issue of the institutional basis for such reform, and was thus easy prey to the criticism of the state-builders.

Just as with other proposals to reform the Italian banking system, two preoccupations informed law-makers and bankers of Majorana's persuasion: first, how to return Italian banknotes to the gold standard, the international monetary regime that not only regulated flows of capital in the pre–World War I period but also enjoyed international legitimacy; and second, how to structure and regulate note-issue, by turning it into either a monopoly (benefiting, in the Italian case, the Banca Nazionale) or some sort of oligopoly (benefiting regional banks) (Cardarelli 2006). As members of the liberal Left, the proponents of U.S.-style banking (who included, along with Majorana, Member of Parliament Seismit-Doda and liberal economist Semenza as well) proposed the devolution of the power to issue money to any bank that could secure its outstanding notes with a certain amount of central state debt. This was, first and foremost, a radical antimonopoly position (Carocci 1956). But it was also (and this is the less remarked upon fact) a position that focused only on the role of the central state in the structuring of the financial system, without making any provision for alternative, more local bases of authority.

Showing a sophisticated understanding of the fiscal reasons why the National Banking System had been established, for instance, Semenza suggested that in the United States, thanks to free-banking, "government stock . . . remained in that country to bear interest and accumulate wealth, while also creating a safe and guaranteed circulation" (Semenza 1879: 4). The implications for state-building were, to him, far-reaching: "This system can be considered as one of the most important financial applications for having turned into circulating value the credit of the nation and having created a large quantity of currency—[it] gave the United States the opportunity to sustain the most gigantic and expensive of all modern wars, and to develop at the same time its resources to an extent that amazes the world." The focus was on the central state-enhancing features of the banking system, especially in connection with the quintessential state-activity: war making. The banking laws had encouraged the "nationalization" of financial circuits, and as they had involved domestic financial institutions in the management and diffusion of government debt, they had contributed to growth, argued Semenza.[11]

The crucial point about the freedom to issue money, rather than the stimulus it would give to economic growth, lay in its political consequences. Majorana saw it as counteracting the institution of "a State Bank, representing a burden to the State because in exchange for the privilege of monopoly, the State would be subject to pressure from the Bank and would find whatever useful services provided by it very dear. The Bank would thus become a bank of speculation" (Majorana-Calatabiano 1879: 31). Tying debt to circulation, on the other hand, would sever the nexus between the Banca Nazionale and the state, and that was the core of the free banking proposals. In this aspect also lay the main reason why Free Banking Laws were attractive to Italian reformers. Free banking was supposed to break the alliance between the Banca Nazionale and the government, in turn freeing up financial resources and thus spurring private investments. As Seismit-Doda (1873) put it, "[N]ew Banks will thus be founded, and they will survive longer since the demand for deposits is increasing in Italy, as shown particularly by the increasing inflow of money into the Savings Bank, that of Milan in particular." In the centralized context of the Italian state, the deposit of government stock with banks as security for the issue of notes was thus supposed to have multiple beneficial effects: act as "a brake against speculation, as a legitimate means of defense on behalf of the banks of issue, and an act of justice toward the Institutes of agrarian credit; this deposit . . . will at the same time be of immense help to the State" (Majorana-Calatabiano 1879: 38).

This reading of the effect of free banking on the U.S. polity was not devoid of merit. The National Banking System had been devised exactly to create a bond between local elites and the state. But that was in the context of a decentralized system, where local elites had already developed strong connections with local banking, and where the legislation was trying to make the federal government more central to their concerns. In the Italian case, the same project was to be applied to a radically different institutional context, where it was meant to break the hold that the Banca Nazionale allegedly had on national finances. Although the most crucial feature U.S. banking system was how it was made to fit the federal organization of the polity, which assigned fiscal power to subnational states, the Italian debate assumed the backdrop of centralized fiscal structures. Free banking proposals were framed as a way to manage the centralized nature of state finances, not to devise ways to make the federal framework more congruent with the organization of the banking system, as had been the case in the United States.

For all its emphasis on freedom in the financial arena, the debate was thus silent about the fiscal structure of the state. Conservative representatives like Salandra were quick to point to this inconsistency, in the context of a larger critique of projects that espoused any kind of decentralization. In the absence of strong authorities, Salandra argued, decentralization could give rise only to strategies of personal enrichment at the expense of the collectivity.

Our economy too is stricken by a conflict, but the fighters are not capital and labor. It is an intimate fight, that our leading classes fight with each other; insofar as they are invested in the prosperity of their individual wealth, and on the other hand, insofar as they govern the coercive institutions of the State all the way down to the Communes, and thus feel the need to foster a level of development in them that is appropriate to the time. (Salandra 1878: 355)

In Salandra's commentary, it was also fundamental that the "confusion between decentralization and freedom" be cleared up, because it was often the case that "local freedom turns into the oppression of individual freedom, which is in fact the only kind of freedom that deserves total guarantees." He was particularly concerned with one of the mistakes that, he argued, flowed from this position: that of "considering the State and its law as eternal rivals of freedom." The "old liberal idea" that weak state power grants more freedom only encouraged specialized groups to vie for a position of power within the state, he added. The state thus had to reassert its autonomy, because "the invasion of the State by society is a certain sign of political decadence." Salandra argued against both the "decentralizing" prejudice that other conservatives were attacking and the "democratic prejudice" that was increasingly becoming the center of the debate on administrative reform. For instance, he claimed that local elections, rather than guaranteeing local representation, gave power to majorities inevitably oppressing the losing minority. Just as the monarchy was a guarantor of the privileges of the few who were not represented in Parliament, at the local level the law should have exercised that same restraining power. Otherwise, democracy would turn into an "oligarchy of the elected, which is possibly the worst of oligarchies" (ibid.: 363). As Magliani also emphasized, the most important guarantees were to be found in a law "limiting debts and expenditures . . . and in the supervision of local administration by the highest state authorities . . . in the most severe case even Parliamentary intervention" (1878: 655).

Given the political structure of the Italian state, attempts by Majorana and Semenza to discredit the financial operations and practices of the Banca Nazionale as speculative, in short, backfired. The Banca Nazionale, uncharacteristically, responded to its attackers by producing a strongly worded parliamentary report in which it vehemently disputed the accusations of the free bankers and reasserted its right not only to exercise control over credit but also to expand geographically into areas where other banks were already operating (Cardarelli 1990). This gave new impetus to the opponents of the adoption of a U.S.-style banking system (political elites who fell in the strong state-building camp I described above), who had long criticized it as "strict and severe, [because] rather than equality in freedom, it sanctions equality in common subordination" (Sella and Castagnola 1870). With the intervention of the Banca Nazionale, the debate could be shifted away from the issue of free banking per se, toward a specification of the particular ways that the U.S. banking system was suitable (or not) to Italian conditions. For instance, the eminent economist Gerolamo Boccardo (1881), who certainly recognized the political expediency of the Banking Act in the context of the Civil War, expressed strong doubts that free banking could be safely implemented in the Italian context, where war was not on the horizon, and where any act that encouraged excessive lending (such as freedom of banking) could actually reverse the progress made toward balancing the budget.

The real strength of the U.S. system was fiscal, according to Boccardo, by which he meant that it lay in the U.S. federal government's ability to restrain spending and thus practice fiscal rigor and resume gold payments. Freedom of issue had neither helped nor hindered this project. By contrast, in a context in which the state budget was not set firmly on a conservative path, such as Italy, the ability to turn government bonds into money could lead bankers to seek out political alliances with the government so as to gain exclusive rights on the purchase and marketing of such bonds. This was to be avoided because:

Among the banking institutions of Italy, some have particular vitality, energy and fertility; they have for so long been rooted and cemented in the most legitimate interests of our country, that I cannot understand why we should not try to find in them the safe and strong foundations for the future organization of our credit and circulation. (Ibid.: 56)

The would-be Bank of Italy governor Bonaldo Stringher, then a high official at the Treasury, agreed with Boccardo, and added a point that summarizes the intellectual charge against free banking and the politicians who espoused it:

[As] far as economic institutions are concerned, the art of a Statesman should be that of capitalizing on the conditions existing in his own country . . . rather than importing systems that have grown in very different environments; we are convinced that nothing would damage the national economy as much as the radical reform of banking institutions, because credit, unlike business—as Bagehot acutely observed—is very similar to trust in matters of government: one must accept what is there and draw as much benefit from it as possible. (Stringher 1879)

To both Boccardo and Stringher, then, the idea that the banking system should be subjected to radical changes that would make it more liberal was simply too risky. Local level institutions were not able to control the diffusion of credit provoked by such changes. The U.S. financial system was inapplicable to the Italian situation, argued opponents of free banking. In spite of its ideological resonance with some intellectuals and politicians, it could not be made to work in a political system that was centralized and in a financial system in which the Banca Nazionale occupied such an important role. The fact that supporters of free banking themselves were preoccupied more with the impact of decentralized banking institutions on central state institutions and practices, such as the allocation and management of government debt, than with the consolidation of power and authority at the local level, revealed the extent to which the political structure of the Italian state strictly limited the kinds of options available to reformers too.

More important, the fact that central government elites were themselves quite suspicious of the fiscal practices of local political authorities foreclosed the possibility of a U.S.-style, bottom-up coalition against the concentration of political and economic power in the central government and a central bank allied with it. In the centralized Italian polity, no equivalent of the Jacksonian attack on the politics of chartering was possible, because local institutions simply did not have the authority and the mobilizing capacity they had in the United States, and so could not serve as a platform from which to launch movements for the liberalization of the banking system. Given the structure of the Italian state, it was thus relatively easy for state-builders to make a case against the decentralizing ambitions of their opponents while rallying the support of the Banca Nazionale. This is, of course, not to suggest that it was purely because of the superiority of the state-builders' argument that free banking was defeated, but to argue that, given the political structure of the Italian Kingdom, support for the kind of decentralization proposed by Majorana was unlikely. In fact Majorana, who had staked his personal reputation to the passing of Free Banking Laws, left the political scene altogether once his proposal was definitively defeated (Carocci 1956: 346; Cardarelli 2006).

It should also be noted that the banking system was not further centralized either, for as we shall see, the administration of the Historic Left shifted its priorities, over this period, toward establishing a rapport with international finance, thus once again bypassing the reform of domestic banking relations—a lack of action that further weakened banking conservatism.

Conclusions

This chapter discussed the positions of those political elites who, over the first two decades of existence of the Kingdom of Italy as a unitary state, debated whether its financial structure should be centralized, and thus organized fully around the finances of the Banca Nazionale; or decentralized, with the right to issue money distributed among several institutions, or, in the argument of certain liberals, rendered completely free. In a manner consistent with the finance-as-organized-conflict perspective that I develop in this book, I have pointed to the political foundations of these different banking arrangements. In particular, I have showed that, given the lack of strong, legitimate local institutions, the Italian central state was forced to play a directive role in the national financial system; that, as a result, proposals to fully decentralize the issue of money, articulated by some on the liberal Left, were met with anxiety on the part of central political elites, who feared the speculative and destabilizing outcomes of decentralization. Whatever decentralization bankers had inherited from the preunification states, local financial elites were unable to turn into the basis for stable systems of appropriation of economic opportunities. We shall see in the next chapter that the 1880s thus witnessed the collapse of the financial system and its restructuring on decidedly national foundations from then on.

In the 1860s–70s, in sum, the boundaries around the distribution of existing political and economic opportunities had been weakened because of the breakdown of local authorities that accompanied (some authors would say spurred) the unification process (Tarrow 2001; Ziblatt 2006). Insofar as the organization of banking was concerned, it was a period characterized by wildcat dynamics, much as the Jacksonian period in the United States had been some thirty years earlier. The boundaries bankers had erected around existing circuits of money and credit, that is, had lost their political backing, and now financial conflict had turned into a general struggle to reconstitute the rules whereby the system would be organized (see also Meriggi, pp. 49–64 in Laven and Riall 2000).

Local elites, however, failed to reconstitute stable systems of authority at the local level. They simply exploited the vacuum of power created by unification and established local systems of patronage to consolidate their ascendance. As the central state continued to put pressure on local administrators to centralize resources further, local elites presided over only an ever-shrinking pool of benefits. And their abysmal performance, especially in the south, in matters of public order discredited them in the eyes of central elites. Among the political elites who supported decentralization few were willing to grant complete autonomy to local administrations. As a result, when the so-called party of the Historic Left gained power in 1876, even though the Left had been more sympathetic to demands for decentralization, it simply turned the central state into the arena in which financial and economic conflict would, from then on, take place. (The party of the Historic Left had acceded to power thanks to the support of southern elites—forming what came to be known as the "historic bloc"—who were searching to gain political strength in the face of local turmoil [see Riall, p. 153, in J. A. Davis 2001].)

Alberto Banti, in an important work on the Italian bourgeoisie (1996), reflects on the emergence of a nationalist-patriotic discourse in liberal Italy throughout the nineteenth century to mediate these shifts in the political loyalties of the nation (see also Banti 2005). He conceptualizes it as a cultural response to the social fragmentation of the Italian nation, as well as a rival discourse to that of class, thought to be too divisive by political elites who, after unification, were both materially and symbolically invested in the consolidation of the new nation. Banti claims that the identity of the Italian nation had to be worked out in cultural rather than institutional or class terms. Nationalism, in this interpretation, did

TABLE 5.5

Italian Monetary Debates, Summary

Authors	Theory of money	Problems of current system	Governance structure	Plural power to issue money
Mild State-Builders (Pallavicino 1863), (Pallavicino 1864); (Bertolotto 1867); (Seismit-Doda 1873); (Semenza 1873); (Majorana-Calatabiano 1874); (Semenza 1879); (Nisco 1879); (Grimaldi 1881).	Fiscal— Government debt as basis of money supply. Credit and money are different: money is state-money, whereas private banknotes are credit that should not enjoy legal tender status and should be subjected to limits. Bank deposits allow accumulation of capital	1) Coexistence of national framework and provincial banks; State is unfairly bankrolling Banca nazionale and financing speculation at the expense of small investors. Banca Nazionale is too tied to government and too little with commerce. 2) Government debt is held abroad.	**Central-Peripheral Coordination:** Robust central bank discounts paper of provincial banks. Provincial banks own shares of central bank. (Bertolotto, Pallavicino). **Peripheral dominance:** At most coordinated clearing house. Otherwise, free banking (Majorana; Seismit-Doda).	**No,** treasury accepts central bank notes only; unitary issue ensures stability. (Pallavicino, Bertolotto). **Moderate Support:** As temporary measure: it is more important to develop deposit banking (Seismit-Doda). **Unconditional Yes:** Market expansion through monetary competition and freedom (Majorana).
Liberal Decentralizers (Ferrara 1866); (Corso Forzoso 1868/1990); (Ferrara 1873a; Ferrara 1873b; Ferrara 1873c); (Rossi 1878); (Soria 1880); (Martello 1881).	"Soft metallism." Redeemability of money produces trust, both in state money and privately issued banknotes. Money as debt of society toward the individual. No difference between money and credit.	1) Inconvertibility; Nazionale enriching itself at the expense of public. 2) Capital does not flow across regions/provinces. It does not reach commerce and industry. This is a moral failure that fails to produce harmony between labor and capital.	Legislators and judiciary and fiscal power of the state guarantee state money. Decentralized, transparent accounting and publicity guarantee soundness of individual banks.	Yes; rather than unitary private issue, however, state money is preferable. Once money is issued by multiple banks, it will lead to development of other instruments. Issue of money must be competitive. Regulation comes from trust individual banks are able to inspire.

Role of central government	Penetration of periphery	Rationale for peripheral penetration	Inspiration from foreign model
Limited to relationship with central bank. State as backseat regulator after setting up system. Central state–appointed prefects responsible for setting up "healthy" provincial banks. Government debt used as security for the issue of private banknotes.	Through independent, local provincial banks which spread of current accounts, discounts, and deposits. New credit instruments such as checks as way to "democratize" credit. Ultimately, deposit banking should replace issue of money.	**Central Peripheral Coordination:** Credit institutions are in the realm of public interest; credit coordinated by a central federation of central bank to mediate local/public needs. State control apparatus to ensure proper functioning at local level. **Peripheral Dominance.** The law is not suited to diffuse money and credit. Those processes should be left to freedom and competition. **Common goals:** Peasant and workers deserve credit. Banking system establishes harmony in the class structure. Banks must be democratized.	Italy as mixture of different traditions. Theory adapted from Corcelle-Seneuill (French free banker). Material inspiration: UK and U.S. because importance of capital is recognized there. U.S. system of banking currency with government debt.
State money preferable to unitary issue because more guarantees. State should create an "idle fund" using the "core quantity" of money, which never goes into circulation. Relationship with state plays to the advantage only of larger banks. Bank-backing of state money is an "insult" to state power.	Through free issue of local currencies. Notes must be issued at local level. Even branch banking is undesirable because not local enough. Banks "naturally" arise in response to needs of particular, delimited areas. Local trust hinders the development of "unnatural" monopolies established by law.	Inconvertible paper redistributes wealth. State issue of money prevents private appropriation of benefits of inconvertible currency. Centralized money issue is seen by the public as a "privilege" and "monopoly." Working classes should "participate in the benefits of credit." Collection of the "humble savings of the people" should motivate the system.	In the future, development along English lines. U.S. is a failure: debt is not reliable backing for paper. Link between government financing and industry unwarranted.

(continued on page 180)

TABLE 5.5 — *continued*

Authors	Theory of money	Problems of current system	Governance structure	Plural power to issue money
Strong State-Builders (De Cesare 1874); (Boccardo 1879); (Stringher 1879); (Boccardo 1881); (Luzzatti 1883)	Means of exchange cannot be left to private interests. Banking school: quantity of money in circulation an effect of production, not a cause of increased economic activity. Gold standard as a standard of "Truth"	Inconvertibility; monetary "chaos." Competition in banking only forces banks to undertake riskier propositions. Legislation (1879) forced interbank acceptance of notes and removed legal tender. Banks could no longer choose which notes to accept, but government and public could.	Strong, single bank at the center supports peripheral banks and thus aids division of labor, specialization, and territorial spread. State must systematize and discipline issue of money Fiscally sound budgets; differentiation of banking system into specialized institutions.	No—unitary issue ensures stability.
The View from the Bank (Stringher, September 18, 1905); (Stringher, October 28, 1907)	Sound money is based on discounting commercial credit, not stock exchange operations. Banks of issue must lend in times of crisis They are the supreme regulators of the money market and the safekeepers of the monetary reserve	Private banks compete with banks of issue over deposits and use those funds to loan money short on the stock market. Interest rates not useful to stem gold outflow because their increase would damage commerce and industry.	Competitive dominance of the bank of Italy. Bank as safekeeper of national credit/ theory of money thus embedded in governance structure.	Not relevant.

the work that institutions were unable to do: it emerged as a common repertoire upon which new identities could be created and subordinated to the larger, national community.

In the specific context of the organization of creditworthiness, I will show in the next chapter that national prestige became the criterion guiding the organization of credit; this emerged from the tensions between different circuits of money, tensions that gave opportunities to different groups of bankers to draw more general boundaries around creditworthi-

Role of central government	Penetration of periphery	Rationale for peripheral penetration	Inspiration from foreign model
Government can back its money through its fiscal machinery.	Local banking institutions and Banca Nazionale play crucial role.	Patriotism should inform private gain. State debt should not be used for speculative motives.	Italian domestic institutional context does not lend itself to imitation of foreign models.
Leading "impulse" from the center integrated in a differentiated "organic" system.	Diffusion of credit only through savings and deposits, not monetary issue.		
Restraint.	Provincial banking centers in the south would "fertilize" local credit.		
	Deposit banking. Through proper banking practices, local economies benefit.	Stability of the system ensured by proper adherence to principles of sound credit.	France: Deposits finance commercial discounting. England: Deposits, not currency, finance commercial activities.
	Discounts of banks of issue must aid local economies.		Bagehot's theory.

ness than the ones that currently existed. Understanding and representing credit as a matter of economic nationalism, and of the financial prestige of the Italian nation, thus became an effective strategy in an institutional context in which the economy was perceived as too fragmented, even centrifugal.

6

Italian Creditworthiness
From Central to National

THE PREVIOUS CHAPTER sketched nineteenth-century Italian debates on political and financial centralization. We have seen that decentralization—in principle the preferred design for the new Italian Kingdom—clashed with the political dynamics facing central elites. Allowing local political authorities to spend freely, in the eyes of those elites, was a dangerous strategy. Only after a strong political and financial center was secured could financial and political relations be extended to the territory: the state was to be built from the top. Consequently, Italian elites began looking for ways to strengthen the domestic banking system. But the central state, in response to the pull from regional elites, was becoming more open to social formations, invested in the extension of credit to new actors. To facilitate the incorporation of these new actors, central political elites had little choice but to increase their issue of state-money and state-debt, in explicit transgression of the principles of sound banking (Cotula 1996).

Conservative bankers found themselves unable negotiate these challenges within the parameters defined by their current identities. When the newly available credit failed to be channeled into state-building projects, such as the boosting of new industrial sectors and, by the end of the century, the military-industrial complex (Webster 1975), going to feed real estate speculation instead, there was little they could do. The Italian financial system collapsed in 1893, leaving the ground open for new actors (foreign capitalists) to gain powerful footholds. The topic of this chapter is how conservative bankers reacted to these dynamics.

This will be a story of how the relatively cosmopolitan identities, from which conservative bankers had previously drawn in order to gauge the extent of their commitment to common financial goals, gave way to nationally oriented identities. Wildcats were the first to embrace them, even if the most vocal proponents of economic nationalism within finance, as we shall see, had themselves strong connections with international finance (Della Loggia 1970; De Rosa 1984). On the basis of nationalism, wildcats could drive a wedge between conservative bankers, turning the financial field into a struggle to prove one's loyalty to the nation. The consequences of this shift were far-reaching. Nationalism provided more general criteria of creditworthiness than the privatized ones that took precedence in de-

TABLE 6.1

Conservative and Wildcat Banking, Italy

Italy	Conservative Bankers	Wildcat Bankers
Institutional Basis: Centralizing Polity		
Identity: Who are they?	Banca Nazionale and Banca d'Italia: Stable financial ties with central government. Savings Deposit Banks: stable financial ties with regional elites (until they invest in government bonds). Universal banks.	Banks of Issue of former states; Investment bankers tied to military industrial complex but excluded from Giolitti's inner circle (e.g., Societa Bancaria Italian).
Plan: How do they make money?	Exploited political relationship (banks of issue) and entrepreneurial activities of industrializing regions (savings banks and mixed banks).	Banks of issue competed with BN with low-interest-rate loans/discounts; corrupt contributions to political elites (Banca Romana); largesse from military spending.
Strategy: How do they do it?	Granted credit based on possession of political credentials.	Speculation on politics; nationalist attack on foreign capital.
Threat: Who challenges them?	Wildcats: Financial activities of wildcats forced conservatives to operate on financial markets.	Conservative elites with strong financial leverage; stalemate.
Relationship to new customers	Forced upon: Banca Nazionale forced to bail out failing banks (Banca Romana, Societa Bancaria Sconto), hence pulled into wildcat camp.	Extensive, Predatory and Idealistic: Nationalist mobilization.

centralized polities, such as the United States. Worth, as a result, became less a matter of personal qualities—of lending money to someone with no means purely on the basis of trust, for instance—than of political loyalties, and of communicating one's allegiance to the nation.[1]

Threats to Banking Conservatism

Let us proceed in steps, resuming the discussion with the coming to power of the Left in 1876—a major transition in the political system of the Italian Kingdom, one that brought new constituencies into the political arena. The Left rallied the support of the producer classes, who were hard hit by the stringent credit conditions created by the government. Tight government budgets were their common enemy, the Left argued, because the increased taxes through which the government balanced its expenses took capital away from production. The inconvertibility of the currency, declared in 1866 by the Historic Right (the liberal party in power since the unification of the kingdom), fueled such complaints. Fiat money made credit less available: foreign capital stayed away from Italy, and banks of issue were forced to use an equivalent amount of their assets as reserves for their issue of notes (Fratianni and Spinelli 1997). The Left also accused the government of widening regional disparities, as government securities were available for purchases only in the markets of the north, while southern capital sat idle. Of the capital that was invested in industrial concerns, the Left claimed that most of it actually financed speculative, not productive, enterprises (Carocci 1956: 41).

The Left undertook a legislative battle in order to restore a more democratic distribution of financial resources—a project that, unlike the greenbackers in the United States, Left politicians believed was congruent with a return to the gold standard. To be sure, the free banking proposals that the more liberal factions of the Left articulated were defeated. But an 1880 bill drafted for the purpose of restoring convertibility succeeded. The bill authorized the government to organize another substantial international loan, to be disbursed in 1881–82, through which the Italian economy would gain adequate supplies of gold to back the Italian lira once again (Zamagni 1993, 1998). The conditions of the loan that the government finally managed to secure proved rather advantageous to Italy—the price of the bonds was low, and the government received the full 644 million lire in specie that it had planned for, which it turned over to the banks of issue, so that they could build up the reserves necessary to re-enter the gold standard.

The Italian government, however, was still torn by a dilemma: should it establish a *conservative* network of bankers, again centered around and controlled by the Banca Nazionale, with which to reap the benefits of the lira's return to convertibility; or should it continue its project of expansion, thus running the risk of destabilizing the system but also expanding its network of patronage and support? An alliance with the Banca Nazionale would give the government more leverage and control over its finances, against both foreign capitalists and domestic speculators. This was at the core of the project of "strong state-builders," elites who eventually prevailed in their intellectual debate with decentralizers. But the political reality conflicted with their lofty ideals. An alliance with the Banca Nazionale, leading to its strengthening, as strong state-builders advocated, was incompatible with the government's project of building a wider, domestic creditor class through financial expansion.

The Banca Nazionale explicitly opposed such a strategy, as we saw in its response to Majorana's free banking proposals. But a diffuse class of creditors and clients of the state, however, was the social basis of the Historic Left now in power (Carocci 1956: 349). One of the purposes of the loan was to increase the strength of this alliance by reinforcing *trasformismo,* Depretis's project of maintaining the status quo by creating a constitutional bloc that merged the moderate Left with the moderate Right, through a clientelistic mode of governing. *Trasformismo* functioned through tariffs, with which the Left attracted the support of southern representatives (Barbagallo 1999; Duggan, in J. A. Davis 2001: 176); tariffs were soon followed by the sale of industries that the state had until then owned and managed, most importantly railroads and commercial shipping (Carocci 1956: 346–50). The intention was to use these new financial resources to "turn around the trend of increasing distance and litigiousness between and within upper echelons of the economic and social structure of the country" (Mori 1992: 35).

The 1881–82 loan, according to Italian historians, delivered an "exceptionally intense stimulus and shock to the whole national economic system and society" (ibid.: 34). First, it was accompanied by the promotion of new, strategic industrial sectors, steel in particular, which part of the loan went to finance (Bonelli 1971b). Secondly, the loan increased the size of the financial sector. Even though the new injection of money into the domestic economy was to be backed by specie, the government instructed the banks of issue not to contract credit, and through repeated legislative decrees, it allowed the banks of issue to issue more money for any given level of reserves (that is, it loosened reserve requirements); it lowered capital requirements; and it even allowed rural and savings banks to decrease their interest rates below the minimum it had until then mandated (ibid.). As Agostino Magliani, the minister of Finances and the Treasury responsible for negotiating the terms of the loan, put it:

It is necessary to prevent a restriction on circulation that would force banks to sell the securities they hold and thus to decrease their help to trade. . . . We shall stop at nothing in supporting the banks, so that they can keep their current circulation. (Quoted in ibid.)

By promising to "stop at nothing," the state committed itself to neutralizing the contraction of credit potentially deriving from a gold-backed currency. This obviously violated the core tenets of conservative banking: that there are prudential practices that must be followed to ensure the stability of credit; that there are limits to just how far the government should go in supporting the banks; that the restriction of credit is a desirable approach, especially relative to an alternative, speculative set of practices.

But, it would be incorrect to say that the government's financial policies were automatically conducive to speculation. Local elites, who were the primary clients of savings banks, were natural recipients of the Left's largesse. If the government could turn them into a loyal constituency of bond-holders, its basis of support would be deepened. Government bonds could even abet the rationalization of local economies, as long as their value remained stable (Masi 1989). In fulfillment of the government's wishes, the deposit banks of the north, most notably the Cassa di Risparmio delle Province Lombarde (CARIPLO), began heavily investing in central government securities. CARIPLO was hailed as the "central bank of the state of Milan," its position within the national financial system described as one of "splendid isolation" (Confalonieri 1974), so its involvement in financing the state was an important success from the point of view of incorporating new actors into the national credit system. However, two aspects of this diffusion of government debt turned out to favor wildcat banking, leading to increased local instability—in stark contrast with Depretis's goal of reasserting the status quo so as to diminish the "litigiousness" of the ruling classes.

First, no single savings bank (not even CARIPLO) was large enough to provide the state with the kind of leverage and control over its debt, through which it could hope to break Italy's dependence on foreign stock exchanges, the Parisian Bourse in particular (ibid.). A significant percentage of the debt, in fact, was held abroad (Zamagni 1998), so foreign intermediaries could easily manipulate the price of the stock in Paris, creating negative effects on the Italian perception of the safety of the debt, and leading to local instability. In short, the fragmented, domestic ownership of Italian government securities did not allow the state to exercise full sovereignty over its finances (De Cecco 1990). The challenge for Italian state-makers remained that of developing financial autonomy from international finance.

Second, the savings banks' orientation toward government debt weakened their ability to command control over local finances. As the stock yielded higher returns than other kinds of investments, savings banks risked becoming mere rentiers, invested in government debt as a way to find a safer outlet for their deposits than those afforded by local economies (Conti 2000; De Cecco 1987).[2] To be sure, this relieved local bankers from the need to assess the soundness of local investments themselves, and thus to articulate and enforce local rules of reputational assessment and credit allocation. The disadvantage of this strategy was that savings banks opened the field to local wildcats, ready to attract customers who did not want membership in circuits of government debt holders. This had already happened a decade early, in the 1870s, when the expansion of public debt had generated a "bankmania," a wave of speculative institutions leveraging risky investments with their holdings of public debt, and promising altogether fictitious rates of return that depositors and investors were willing to believe, being attracted to the opportunity to participate in new investments. Savings banks had remained immune from this practice, and therefore to some extent had been able to counterbalance and contain the effects of speculation (Polsi 1993).

In the 1880s, with the increased availability of government bonds, but a corresponding absence of conservative banking traditions, history repeated itself. About 350 million lire were invested in real estate development in Naples and Rome, with consequences we will soon discuss; an equivalent amount of money went to the construction of warships (Confalonieri 1974: 82). The construction boom quickly attracted the financing of bankers of the old guard, such as the Banca Romana, the bank of issue of the former Papal State (Manacorda 1993), but remained in the hands of minor, speculative banks such as the Banca Tiberina and the Banca di Torino. Confalonieri (1974: 345) sees them as paradigmatic illustrations of the problems that afflicted private bankers in general in this period:

Banca Tiberina and Banca di Torino are, to be sure, and for different reasons, extreme cases; but they are indicative of what appears to be one of the most significant traits of [Italian] banking structures of the 1800s: that they find it difficult to rely on a "tradition" that might give appropriate guidelines to managers of private banking institutions and to the policymakers in charge of monetary policy.

To put it differently, these were wildcat bankers, not so much lacking as *rejecting* the traditions of banking conservatism, in order to privately appropriate the benefits of a financial expansion orchestrated by the central government.

The result of meeting the demands of the regional elites (which, before the rise to power of the Left, had mobilized against their exclusion from national circuits of finance) was that the government undermined its own ability to control financial flows. Conservative bankers were now obsolete, with the Banca Nazionale reduced to a mere executor of government policies, a development that undercut its legitimacy and the legitimacy of conservative banking as a whole.

Banking Crises and the Origins of the Banca d'Italia

In 1892, wildcat banking was crippled by a political scandal—namely, the discovery of substantial amounts of money illegally put into circulation, currency not backed by adequate reserves (Negri 1989). In 1887, the Banca Romana had put pressure on the government to limit the convertibility of its bank notes; the government extended the same principle to all banks of issue, thus fully deregulating circulation. A routine, government-led inspection of the banking system registered multiple irregularities, but Prime Minister Giolitti failed to make the results public, with the only consequence being the closing of two southern banks. In 1892, however, the Parliament received a copy of the inspection results and the scandal exploded: the Banca Romana had engaged in illegal activities ranging from preferential treatment of politicians to the disguising of loans and cash shortages. All other banks of issue had large amounts of nonperforming loans and had seriously exceeded limits to currency creation. This was wildcat banking at its worst because it occurred at the very center of the system, patently making a mockery of the political elites' professed commitment to a higher public good (Manacorda 1993).

Even though wildcat banking had not undermined the entire financial status quo, the Banca Nazionale found itself lacking the "prestige," in Confalonieri's words (1974), to mobilize other conservative bankers, who possessed the resources necessary to stop the entire system from collapsing. Conservative political elites blamed the existence of multiple banks of issue for the crisis of governability of the monetary system, and in particular the competition between the Banca Nazionale and the other banks of issue, especially the Banco di Napoli, the second largest.[3] But the more "decisive problem" remained the "balance of power between the authority of the government and the banks of issues—that is, the government and the Banca Nazionale" (Confalonieri 1974: 186). At the heart of the problem were several issues.

First, there was the fundamental tension between note-issue—that is, the management of money—and credit. Note-issue required that the Banca Nazionale be willing to follow the directives of the Treasury without concerning itself with profitability. Should the Treasury dictate that the BN needed to increase circulation, the bank had to follow suit, according to this logic. Yet the second, credit function *presupposed* profitability. For the bank to create new loans, it had to have the reserves to back them; and without a return on the loans, the bank faced a loss. This requirement was on many occasions in direct contrast with the "public" mission of the BN. "This was the drama, or at least the contradiction, of the BN: it could not be an efficient, ordinary bank, yet it could not or did not want to be a bankers' bank" (ibid.: 135).[4]

A second, and more important problem, was the uneasy relationship between the Banca Nazionale and other private, commercial banks. This was partly the result of technical reasons—namely, the fact that the BN tended to attract second-rate commercial paper that had been refused by other institutions. The BN specialized in three-name rather than two-name paper, as we saw in the previous chapter, which, given the competitive nature of interbank relationships at the time, meant that weaker banks would use the Banca Nazionale to discount their less reputable notes, while stronger banks avoided establishing relations with the BN altogether so as not to compromise the privacy of their clients (Gigliobianco 1990).

But on top of such logistical problems lay a second, related, perhaps even more important issue, involving the authority and autonomy of the Banca Nazionale. By law, the BN had only formal control over circulation, as the law specified absolute limits on the quantity of money it could print, but did not give the BN any guidelines on how the money supply should be managed over time. This problem could have been circumvented, had the BN developed the kinds of banking traditions through which gaps in the law could be turned into sources of advantage. But in a political context defined by the government's explicit commitment to financial expansion, such conservative practices were not possible; the government relied on the BN to execute and facilitate its monetary policies. This made the relationship between the BN and other bankers difficult to navigate. Private bankers feared the BN's formal submission to the policy directives of the Treasury. They would use the Banca Nazionale only, if at all, for their discounting operations, but would not deposit their reserves with it, unsure about the BN's ability to carry out its credit policy independently of political power. The "collection of the funds of other banks is considered with great caution, sometimes with suspicion: it is an exceptional activity, which frequently originates with the initiative of other banks, a business whose desirability must be assessed each time, and which is often used as a way to increase the circulation of one's notes" (Confalonieri 1974: 132–33).

Conservative banking was weak, and this was reflected in the ways the Italian government intervened in the financial system once the crisis broke out. A parliamentary committee was appointed to investigate the causes of the crisis further, and its proceedings prompted the passing of a new law, enacted in 1893, that decreed the dissolution of the Banca Romana and the merger of the Banca Nazionale with the two Tuscan banks, so as to form the Banca d'Italia (Manacorda 1993). The crisis made visible the limitations faced by the current system of organizing credit, and opened the way to solutions that stressed the need for austerity and tighter control over credit. The newly born Banca d'Italia was forced to assume the debt of the Banca Romana (Caracciolo 1973; Manacorda 1993). Stringent conditions were set on the circulation and issue of notes, in order to regain a semblance of control. The law was nonetheless met with a negative international reaction, which was reflected in the depreciation of the lira as well as the fall in price of the Rendita (the government securities traded in Paris). Given the price differential between the quotation of the Rendita in Italy and France, arbitrage quickly drained Italy of capital and caused the failure of major commercial banks, which were subject to an unsustainable run on deposits. The only choice left to the government was to exit the gold standard (De Cecco 1990).

Thus Italy came full circle. We have seen how inconvertibility served as a tool for liberal-conservative, rightwing governments, in power throughout the 1860s, to establish a conservative core in banking, a core of bankers that included the Banca Nazionale, and that was oriented primarily to the financing of the national arena. Yet the central government had been reluctant to invest local administrations with the authority to control local level finances. It had also failed to encourage the formation of local, conservative networks of bankers. In fact, the government had explicitly relied on the expansion of its own balance sheet as a way to pacify social constituencies that had been excluded from the prior balance of power, and that, once the project of fiscal decentralization had failed, now looked to the central state for financial backing.

The financial expansion that had accompanied this project of political centralization set the conditions for wildcat banking, which emerged on the periphery of the system (in the form of real estate speculation), to then spread to the core. The return of Italy to the gold standard regime orchestrated by the Left government in 1882—a policy that should have led to deflation and contraction—further favored the *expansion* of the banking system because it occurred in a context of weak control over the use of financial resources at the local level. In this way the government's openness to political forces that were opposed to banking conservatism turned into an implicit support for wildcat operations, based on mutual favors and eventually outright corruption.

Crisis and Shifting Identities

As Italian political institutions became more open to demands for credit expansion, the regulation of credit acquired a national and systemic orientation. The Banca Nazionale was the first institution to experience this shift. In the wake of the 1893 crisis, its name was changed to Banca d'Italia. The change was not merely cosmetic: the new Bank of Italy found itself burdened with the illiquid assets of the banks it had bailed out (the Banca Romana in particular), which gave it new responsibilities but also created a problem for its control over the money supply. The BI was no longer able to back its notes with the legally mandated ratio of reserves, now that its assets were needed for other operations. The government attempted to remedy this situation through ad hoc legislation, granting the BI temporary exemptions from note-issue limits. The first decade thus became a "period of probation" for the BI, characterized by the need on its part and the Treasury to establish a collaborative relationship, but also by mutual suspicions and recriminations (Bonelli 1991). It did not help that the BI won the right to discount two-name paper—an activity that could potentially put it in competition with the very private banks the Treasury wanted the BI to supervise (Gigliobianco 1990).

Two important changes in the governance structure of the BI eased it out of this probationary period. First, the shareholders of the BI were gradually silenced. A policy of limited dividends and recapitalization signaled how the priorities of the bank had shifted from a concern with profitability for the sake of its shareholders, to financial solidity for the sake of the financial system as a whole. As Marchiori, the first director of the Bank of Italy, was to remark, in spite of the internal political opposition of certain shareholders to the pact with the government that burdened the new Bank of Italy with the illiquid debt of a large part of the banking system, profitability was to take a back seat.

I am grateful even to those who . . . expressed a desire that the Bank should be given more advantages, and I trust that that desire, which is also mine, will be realized in the distant future. First, however, it is necessary to regulate the state of affairs that resulted from the vicissitudes of important institutions to which the Bank granted large credits; . . . it is necessary to devise ways that companies in debt will be able to fulfill their obligations. (Marchiori, June 8, 1896)

Second, and relatedly, power shifted from the "Supreme Council," the board of directors and prominent shareholders that had been the most authoritative decision-making body of the Banca Nazionale, to the General Directorate of the bank, and in particular the figure of the Central Bank governor (or director, in the vocabulary of the day). Both changes centralized power and made the task of turning the Bank of Italy into a publicly oriented institution possible (Ciocca and Toniolo 1999; Confalonieri 1974; Manacorda 1993; Bonelli 1991, 1971a). Both changes also signaled a shift in the ways that the Bank of Italy conceptualized its relationship to the financial system. The BI wanted no longer to compete with its private counterparts; it wanted to institute a regime of collaboration with them.

These changes made possible a new relationship between the Bank of Italy and the state—a relationship of mutual dependence but also, increasingly, one characterized by autonomy. It was a relationship of mutual dependence because the bank was financially weak in the wake of the crisis, and because the government, in exchange for its financial support, had given it the task of restructuring the financial system. As a result, the defining characteristic of the Bank of Italy remained its privileged relationship with the state. As its first director claimed, the "fate" of the BI "was linked to that of the State" (Marchiori, June 8, 1896). This link, in turn, reflected a common orientation toward the systemic needs of Italian finance. As Bonaldo Stringher would later put it to the Supreme Council of the bank:

There can be no disagreements between the Bank and the State. There must be a common intent to improve the state of national activities and restore their fate. Communality of intents, however, does not mean at all that we give up our autonomy to manage credit, but that we conform to the dispositions of the laws and the Banking Act. We must observe them both scrupulously and rigorously in order to keep our head up, and resist with energy all coercion, reassured to have thus gained the support of all those of a righteous mind. (Stringher, December 3, 1900)

The bank, that is, increasingly saw itself a safe-keeper of the credit system, invested with ensuring its stability, and at the same time guiding its development in appropriate directions. That the law, rather than the demands of its shareholders, or the government for that matter, specified what policies the bank should pursue, was an opportunity for the bank to gain political legitimacy. The relationship between the state and the Banca d'Italia could thereby become a precondition of autonomy.

Now that the governance structure of the bank insulated the decisions of its director from the pressures and demands of the shareholders, the bank could claim that it expressed a more general financial interest, articulated by *disinterested* officials, with which the government should not interfere. Stringer put it as follows on his inaugural speech to the Bank of Italy's shareholders' meeting on March 25, 1901:

The Bank must be a robust instrument of the economic activity of the country. In this task it has to be supported by the moral prestige that derives from not only its own [financial] condition, but also the benevolent support of public authorities: a support that cannot be taken away so long as the Bank remains in the orbit marked by the law. The Bank should be coordinating the Italian financial body and dedicate itself to linking together the actions of the various credit institutions, bearing in mind that the excessive harshness of the competition and rivalry between them can lead to ruinous consequences.

As Stringher had it, then, that there was no space for disagreement between bank and state did not mean that the bank was to be made subservient to the state. The bank, rather, had the ability to transcend the particular interests of politicians and of its shareholders. It was now to be considered an autonomous partner in the setting of the financial policies of the nation. As a matter of fact, what the Banca d'Italia envisioned for the reformed Italian credit system was still a matter of political negotiation. But credit was to be allocated and "managed" on a new basis, Stringher seemed to suggest—a basis that would raise the approval and gain the support of "those of a righteous mind."

Even though Stringher gave no indication as to what policies would generate such a response, his reference to the righteousness of the community to which his actions now appealed indicated a shift in the identity that was to be used to regulate credit. It was a shift from narrowly conceived financial interests to the systemic needs of national credit. Stringher's language, to be sure, was not *nationalist*, but the national ambitions of the Banca d'Italia he directed were soon to be made more explicit, in a complex interplay with shifts occurring outside the financial field, and with forces within finance exploiting the opportunities provided by external events. To understand the nature of these dynamics, we must first consider important changes in the structure of commercial banking. These shifts will help us understand how the Bank of Italy formed a new, conservative culture of banking, grounded on economic nationalism, with which it attempted to gain control over finance.

Wildcats against Foreign Capital

The post-1893 period was different from the one that preceded it not only because of the emergence of the Bank of Italy. Some of the most important financial actors of the previous regime had collapsed and were replaced by new ones, most notably, the universal banks. Understanding the impact of this shift is crucial to our analysis of financial conflict.

Universal, or "mixed," banks, unlike the banks of issue, did not print banknotes; rather they invested in, underwrote, and traded the stocks of other firms, financing these activities through commercial operations, and in particular by collecting deposits.[5] Universal banks were in that way primarily involved in industrial financing, even though recent studies, such as Fohlin (1999), argue that they came too late with respect to the industrial take-off of Italy to play any fundamental role (she tells a similar story about German universal banks, one confirmed by Herrigel 2000). For our purposes, the more important part of this story is not whether universal banks abetted industrial development, but how they negotiated the politics of financial circuits—industrial securities and deposits—that had until then developed separately. It is a story that also concerns the conflict between the strategies through which the universal banks controlled these financial circuits, and the priorities of the state. It was this conflict, I will argue, that created the opportunity for wildcat bankers to mount an attack on the universal banks, while simultaneously pressuring the Bank of Italy to develop new collective identities from which universal banks were excluded.

Perhaps the best way to start is to consider in what ways the universal banks challenged not only other kinds of bankers but the state as well. Highly capitalized, the universal banks tended to attract foreign capital (this was generally the case with universal banks, as Forsyth and Verdier [2003] show in other national contexts). Thus when the Banca Commerciale Italiana (COMIT) and the Credito Italiano (CREDIT) established their headquarters in Milan in 1894, they did it thanks to an influx of German money (Confalonieri 1974). The director general of COMIT (the more powerful of the two banks), Otto Joel, was himself a former Prussian citizen.[6] This was a cause of concern in a country like Italy, where foreign capital had often mobilized against the geopolitical ambitions of the state.

Secondly, the universal banks tended to be more unstable than other kinds of banking institutions, precisely because the fate of their investments was tied to the ups and downs of developing industrial sectors (Hertner 1994). The universal banks, to reiterate, performed simultaneously commercial activities, such as the collection of deposits and investment activities, such as the buying, selling, and underwriting of securities. They also connected the periphery of the banking system to its most unstable arena, the stock exchange (Bonelli 1971a; Forsyth and Verdier 2003; Verdier 2003).

A third, equally important factor made the link between high finance and the state particularly difficult for the latter to manage: the universal banks cherished a high degree of autonomy from the state. This, to be sure, was not necessarily a cause of conflict. Francesco Crispi, the Italian prime minister who, at the turn of the twentieth century, most dramatically pushed for a centralization of state power, was generally favorable to German banking, because of his more general sympathy toward Germany (one motivated by geopolitical ambitions; see Duggan 2002). And even after Crispi's centralizing and authoritarian project of state building failed, his successor, Giovanni Giolitti, remained sympathetic to foreign capital (Romanelli 1988; Webster 1975). Neither Crispi nor Giolitti, then, found the power of universal banks particularly threatening: in fact, collaboration with the universal banks could even offer important opportunities to strengthen the power of the state. Webster (1975) thus argues that the universal banks should be considered a central component of the military-industrial complex built up by the late liberal Italian regimes.[7]

Mixed banks, for their part, were certainly not interested in alienating the government by not supporting its political (militarist or commercial) international plans. But the demands and expectations of the circuits in which they were involved sometimes put them on a collision course with state authorities. Their search for autonomy generated suspicions and animosities. A contemporary reading of this dynamic was offered by Cesare Mangili, a member of the Italian Senate, who had sat on the board of directors of the Bank of Italy but who, amid much controversy, had subsequently moved to a similar position in COMIT. In a letter to Stringher dated June 19, 1908, he formulated a long explanation of the behavior of Joel (the director of COMIT), in the context of the foundation of the Antivari Company, which was to operate a harbor in Montenegro and, according to Webster (1975: 213), to serve as a springboard for Italian expansionism. He argued that COMIT had taken up the largest share in the company because no other bank had come forward, in spite of nationalist rhetoric in support of the operation. But the shares had depreciated, creating embarrassment for Joel. He had "entered the affair in perfectly good faith, hoping to serve the national interest—and to please the government—and with the enthusiasm of the apostle sought other participants among his closest and most trusted Italian friends." Joel now "has to bear with the unpleasant sarcasm of the Austrian and German members of our board every time this is a matter of discussion."

[He is] morally, rather than materially interested in injecting some vital fluids in Antivari's sick body . . . he was inspired by high ideals, wishing perhaps to dispel the criticism against the pro-German orientation of the bank through his actions—

while our fellow countrymen in pushing Joel on that path were being motivated not by a feeling of "italianità," but by personal ambition.

What Mangili revealed was in some ways common knowledge: the universal banks responded not only to the financial needs of the Italian government but to the demands of their shareholders as well, and those shareholders included individuals who did not have sympathy for the foreign policy ambitions of the Italian Kingdom (see, esp., Confalonieri 1974). But Mangili's emphasis on the nationalist inspiration of Joel's actions only brought into relief the extent to which appeals to the national interest made the international orientation of the mixed banks seem more problematic, as they led to questions about the authenticity of the mixed banks' loyalty to the Italian nation.

Even more troubling from the perspective of political elites, COMIT and CREDIT did not hesitate to turn their dealings with the BI into opportunities for the acquisition of status and power within the banking field. For instance, responding to Stringher who, as early as October 9, 1902, expressed his disappointment toward the Credito Italiano for its failure to support the Banca d'Italia in the sale of government bonds, Joel replied in writing that the actions of his rival seemed to follow a "Shakespearean satire," in which "[t]hose who raise their voice the loudest, as usual are only trying to hide their weakness." In contrast, Joel thus depicted his own actions:

I can only renew the expression of my utmost sympathy for the calm with which you, putting all personal resentments aside, defended the general interest in such a difficult moment. I can only hope that the public applause that accompanied every action of yours, served as a counterweight to the bitterness of those days of struggle. I can safely assert that, in its sphere, the Banca Commerciale did all it could to lessen the consequences of mistakes to which it had not contributed. (Joel, October 10, 1902)

Joel's response here revealed two strategies: first, that of differentiating COMIT from its rival, the Credito Italiano, sanctioning the latter's failures and building a symbolic boundary between the two; second, that of positioning COMIT as a trustworthy and understanding ally of the Bank of Italy and its governor.[8]

Another example comes from a letter Joel wrote to Stringher, where, to a question from the Turkish government, inquiring to what extent COMIT was capable of guaranteeing Turkish government bonds, Joel "naturally . . . answered [positively because] we have an excellent and most friendly relationship with the General Directorate of the Bank of Italy." Joel then asked Stringher that their institutes appear together in this operation, and insisted that

no one else be given this role, and that it remain limited to the Bank of Italy and the *Commerciale*. I believe that the intimacy of the ties between these two institutes with those [illegible] that supervise the affairs of Turkey . . . which is not shared by anyone else in Italy, makes my wish wholly justified. (Joel, August 12, 1903)

Joel's main concern here was to use his international connections and leverage as assets that could be translated into *domestic* advantages, by creating a circuit that explicitly excluded other actors. Joel did not recognize the need for unitary action involving other bankers as well. Further, he was willing to collaborate with Stringher to the extent that he drew power and authority from the international networks in which his bank was embedded; where such external support was absent, the relationship between the two bankers remained more circumspect (Gigliobianco 1990). But this made the development of a shared, conservative banking culture at the international level very difficult to achieve.

Indeed, this problem was not unique to Italian banking: Germany, for instance, had just undergone a transition from "market to territorial conceptions of interest" about two decades earlier (Mann 1993: 298), finally to embrace fully nationalist priorities for its economic development. Operations on the Berlin stock exchange were now limited to securities deemed of national interest (a restriction lifted in 1909) (Seabrooke 2006: 90 and ff). But the more differentiated banking system of the German state made industries much less dependent on universal banks (Herrigel 2000) than they were in the shallower Italian banking system (see, however, Federico 1996). It was only natural that debates on how to structure the domestic banking system would generate further disagreements and conflicts.

Stringher and Joel had vastly different visions regarding the shape they wanted the banking system to take. Joel recognized the Bank of Italy's supremacy over certain kinds of operations, yet at the same time he prioritized the establishment of a niche for his bank that would preserve the COMIT's autonomy from the Bank of Italy. In a remarkable exchange with Stringher in which he articulated this vision, Joel argued:

I must confess that, in that banking field, I do not see any future danger. . . . The catastrophe of 1890–94 was inevitable, because throughout the previous decade there had been an accumulation of "fictitious capital" [and because] private banks . . . competed fiercely over long-term investment, thus immobilizing deposits. [They had been] aided and seduced by a political course [of the Treasury] that had completely subverted the role of the banks of issue. [In contrast, now the country is] moving and working . . . . [No longer is competition] unreasonable. Yet, my friend, it is not our intention to compete with the Bank of Italy [or to] deprive it of the business that belongs to it. (Joel, January 2, 1905)

Joel not only blamed state policies for the crisis that, at the turn of the century, had plagued the banking system; he also argued that with the advent of commercial banks finally tied to proper, productive activities, concerns with the stability of the system were no longer warranted. Competition could resume precisely because it concerned parts of the banking system in which the Bank of Italy was not involved directly. Joel continued in his strategy of advocating for harmony and unity of intents at the international level, while praising domestic competition, by adding:

Private institutions must complement the Bank of issue, given their superior elasticity and mobility: they can undertake operations that the latter would not find convenient, they can be its intermediary and serve as a buffer.

Joel asserted that private banks could develop both in major urban centers, and, especially, in smaller towns and provinces. If this territorial diffusion was going to strengthen the COMIT, it was not going to be at the expense of the Bank of Italy. Joel continued:

The bank of issue remains the real, supreme regulator of credit and—with rigidity of principles, of which you have been perhaps the first advocate in Italy—shows the way to those powerful institutions and bankers without sparing them any admonition should they exceed in their action of propaganda. We see this mechanism worked to perfection in more developed countries such as England, France and Germany.

Joel thus wanted the Bank of Italy to become the conservative center of the banking system, so as to stabilize it. However, he was not willing to participate actively in this conservative project, and saw COMIT's role as separate, even through complementary, to that of the Bank of Italy: COMIT would occupy the niches left open by the Bank of Italy.

Joel's position ran counter to the project of professional closure orchestrated by Stringher. Stringher, in fact, quickly pointed to the nature of the problem:

I am afraid that I don't entirely share your assessment. I think we are losing all sense of measure, and banking institutions are multiplying excessively, especially in areas which I know from personal experience and knowledge, have absolutely no need for them. This only intensifies the use of credit and paves the way for its future abuse. (Stringher, January 7, 1905)

Without the cooperation of all private banks to a project of conservative banking and professional closure, the action of the Bank of Italy was to be ineffectual, argued Stringher. Intensifying the use of credit, he stated, was but a recipe for future abuse. The exchange reveals that, as far as the domestic field was concerned, Stringher's concerns were met with little support, if they were not altogether faced by the "silence of his interlocutors"; this, in the words of a banking historian, gave Stringher a palpable sense of the "dysfunctions of the system and particularly the conditions of isolation in which he had to operate" (Bonelli 1991: 91).

The dynamic that reproduced this dysfunctional relationship was transparent to Stringher: the commercial banks competed with the Bank of Italy, engaging in wildcat practices when necessary. In a presentation to the Board of Directors from as early as September 18, 1905, he argued that increases in the Bank of Italy's credit (discounts and advances) tended to be matched by an equivalent increase in the operations of the commercial banks (Stringher, September 18, 1905). But the Bank of Italy concentrated on extending new advances, whereas the private banks increased their contango loans—that is, loans guaranteed by the issue of securities—which tied credit to stock market fluctuations. In this way, private banks engaged in wildcat practices domestically, using the very instruments that they were helping the Bank of Italy to regulate internationally. Second, Stringher worried about the imbalance between the magnitude of contango loans and more proper banking operations. The most problematic dimension was the banks' reliance on deposits to finance these activities. "Private deposits constitute the biggest source of contango loans," he noted. Other countries had very different financial circuits in place: "[In] France, deposits served for the largest part to finance commercial operations, and for a small part for stock market operations, whereas here the stock market absorbs almost the totality of deposits." And to add to his concerns, the deposits of the Bank of Italy were decreasing just as the current accounts of the Banca Commerciale were going up—and were fueling stock market speculation. Stringher, who was keen on paraphrasing Bagehot, thus concluded: "[A] country where little is done, works with circulation, whereas a country where much is done, works with deposits." The Bank of Italy was not only deprived of the bulk of private deposits; in addition, those deposits were being directed toward speculative activities.

Unlike the director of COMIT, who argued that more control could be achieved through informal agreements among large financial players, Stringher wanted to avoid creating the perception that a small, private oligarchy controlled the upper layers of Italian finance. But this limited his ability to check the credit practices of the universal banks. Given the history of attacks against centralized banking (as we saw in the debates prior to the 1890s), it is understandable that Stringher would be so careful in dealing with such matters. He once wrote to Joel to remove from his annual reports to the COMIT's shareholders any mention of a "trust" (or cartel) of banks waiting for instructions from the ministry. Stringher argued: "In fact, such a trust was never formed, because before it could be constituted the Ministry turned its back on the [potential] participants [to the trust]. Wouldn't you agree? Forgive me if I write so starkly, as I would to a friend" (Stringher, March 13, 1903). But in a different context he argued: "[Y]ou know that I am a proponent of *viribus unitis* [forceful unity of action], especially since the Bank of Italy can push for, but not participate in, new banking institutions" (Stringher, January 7, 1905). Stringher's solution to the problem of creating a large, powerful core of private banks, on which the Bank of Italy could then rely for the implementation of monetary policy, rested on an indirect involvement of the Bank of Italy in private banking—one that would allow Stringher to maintain some degree of autonomy and independence.

Stringher was not alone in articulating the need for cohesion among banking elites. Cesare Mangili also sensed the need for more cooperation, going as far as justifying his move to the COMIT in terms that explicitly appealed to unity:

I have a great wish which is that of removing the animosity and bitterness that exist among the various private institutions, which are the legacy of old alliances and envy among people. I would like (as soon as I will have the time) to dedicate myself to a project of peace, to form a bloc of financial forces in this country so that any agreement whatsoever that the leading Institute would wish to promote for large operations of general interest, will be easily and quickly achieved. (Mangili, March 9, 1906)

But Mangili's assumption that private bankers would submit to the general interest, as articulated by the Bank of Italy, did not take into account the tension that marked the relationship between private banks and the central bank.

Cooperation in the name of what, and under what conditions, was the question. The structure of the Italian banking networks—with the two universal banks only tenuously linked with the Bank of Italy, and myriad savings banks increasingly oriented toward the financing of the state, but only through the sale and purchase of government bonds—seemed unable to generate, out of appeal to individual interest, the kinds of shared identities that would gain the commitment of its members. The "forceful unity of action" praised by Stringher remained out of reach. The challenge facing Stringher was how to construct a collective identity out of which a shared understanding of sound banking could emerge.

A striking episode marks the beginning of Stringher's search for such a collective identity, with which to focus the attention of the banking community on issues of general interest: the bailing out of the steel concerns that Stringher successfully performed in 1911. The planning of this financial operation dated back to 1907, when industrialists interceded with Giolitti to put pressure on Stringher to accommodate their demands for easier financing. Industrialists lamented the state of abandonment the universal banks had left them in, and asked Bonaldo Stringher for a conspicuous emergency loan, to which Stringher gave a firm, negative reply, as this was an unprecedented practice (Bonelli 1971a: 140–42). The problem of industrial financing, and in particular of the logic that should govern it, were now, however, on the table.

Already during Crispi's turn-of-the-century government, and partly as a consequence of the path drawn by the previous administration of Depretis, the Italian state had engaged in policy innovation that involved the building up of its military apparatus, and in particular, the steel industry and shipbuilding concerns.[9] The fact that the universal banks came late in this game, as Fohlin (1999) demonstrates, resulted in a relationship to the military-industrial sector that remained tenuous at best, even though mixed banks generally supported industrial development (Confalonieri 1974: 262–333). COMIT, for instance, began financing the Terni Steel Trust, a company that had received large amounts of state financing, just as its president was complaining about the unscrupulous nature of the Terni managers (ibid.: 302). More generally, the careful approach of the universal banks to the problem of industrial financing clashed with the industrial priorities that the Italian state now deemed most valuable.

The universal banks, that is, were conservative in their relationship with the military-industrial sector, just when the military-industrial sector, by contrast, wanted the universal banks to change their current ways of allocating credit. What the state-sponsored steel industry demanded of their banks was a long-term commitment that downplayed the importance of profitability. But during the negotiations for the 1911 steel bailout, while COMIT and CREDIT were centrally involved in them, Stringher was repeatedly struck by the extent to which the universal banks were reluctant to follow his directives, precisely because of an unwillingness to commit to such long-term projects (Cerioni 2001: 32).

Stringher recognized how financial participation in projects of national significance could constitute the beginnings of a larger, cohesive financial bloc. In one of his addresses to the shareholder's assembly of the BI (March 27, 1905), for instance, he commented on his success in involving several banks in the financing of a general pension fund and an institute of national culture, the Dante Alighieri:

It has been of comfort to see the enthusiasm with which various institutions have responded to the invitation to take part, without aims of profit, in such an operation. But the Bank is particularly pleased to note that its call was listened to. It does not hide its deep satisfaction at having been kindly joined by the representatives of the finest of the Italian institutions that attract savings, distribute credit, encourage security in various forms, and fertilize the national capital to increase its productivity. The large union of the financial forces of the country, for aims of philanthropy, that can be admired today, may be the prelude of a new one tomorrow, with these same forces becoming even more powerfully connected to implement the kinds of projects on which the restoration of finance and the national economy depend.

Stringher also thought that the role of the Bank of Italy, in this union of financial forces, would never be one of competition, and that it would not be motivated by desires of expansion. Rather, as he had earlier put it to the shareholders on March 27, 1905: "The Bank of Italy has no ambitions of expansion, and does not like, nor desire, to cross the boundaries the law assigns to it as a bank of issue; but it does not deny and will never deny its active support to initiatives of a truly national nature, which may lead to a more vigorous movement of genuine Italian activities in the world market." His words on March 20, 1911, revealed a similar logic: "After all, the conditions in which credit is managed in Italy, given current arrangements, require the supplementary, collateral intervention of the banks of issue, an intervention that is partly regulated or at least recognized by the law, an intervention that the banks carry out as a function of their ties with the state, which can fully count on their administrative boards, organically Italian as they are."

In all these pronouncements, the increased emphasis Stringher put on the Italian nature of financial collaborations became apparent. When Prime Minister Giolitti became a champion of Italian expansion in Libya (Gentile 1990, 2003), the nationalist rhetoric of Stringher intensified. To this effect, Stringher invited Joel to exercise pressure on the German press so as to moderate its "hostile language" against the Libyan expedition.

It is impossible that at least some of the eminent people who have close ties with the Banca Commerciale Italiana will not see some convenience in expressing a moderating opinion that will weaken the attacks against a country to which they are tied by intense and not scarce friendships, which must be considered certain and loyal. Motivated by this idea and by my affection towards my country and the eminent man who governs it, I did not hesitate to write to you, in the profound belief that my word will be applauded—without any doubt, since I know that you have a high sense of friendship and gratitude towards your recently acquired homeland, of which you have full citizenship. (Stringher, October 11, 1911)

In spite of Joel's quick series of telegrams informing Stringher that his request had been given utmost consideration, Stringher wrote a somewhat more pacified letter (on October 15, 1911), wherein some clearly belligerent overtones remained nonetheless: "I am pleased to learn that you were already orienting yourself to the view I expressed in my confidential letter . . . . Believe me, your Institute must have a few rotten apples, as well as some mouths that are ready to open with no meditation and only to further their vanity."[10]

There is considerable disagreement over whether Bonaldo Stringher qualified as a nationalist (Gigliobianco 2006: 118–19). Why, then, this implicit endorsement of nationalist accusations against COMIT on the part of Stringher, which stands out in the long series of correspondence between the two men, that was marked instead by politeness and mutual appreciation? One might argue that it was the central government itself that became increasingly militarist and imperialist over this period, that the Bank of Italy was dependent on the government, and that a shift in political priorities was transmitted from the government to the Bank of Italy. There is powerful evidence to justify such a characterization of Italian foreign policy. Yet historians argue that the Bank of Italy, on top of gaining a much more central role in the organization of the Italian financial system than its predecessor Banca Nazionale ever had, also succeeded in increasing its autonomy from the central government over this period (ibid.: 119).

A view of finance as organized conflict explains this shift in the rhetoric of Stringher as a function of the financial pressures he, and the Bank of Italy more generally, were under—pressures that originated with the newly acquired autonomy of the BI, and that Stringher could not control by resorting to existing banking traditions. The problem was that mixed banks did not share the same banking traditions that Stringher was trying to establish. So the lack of a collective identity tying the Bank of Italy and the universal banks to a shared set of commitments, created a stalemate among them.

Appeals to nationalism, and in particular to loyalty to the nation, were becoming increasingly widespread. As early as 1906, Cesari Mangili asked that, as a condition for his joining COMIT, only members of Italian nationality would be admitted to the enlarged board of directors from then on (Mangili, March 9, 1906). But those claims seemed to remain extraneous to the logic of the financial field. Yet the absence of shared commitments among conservative bankers, coupled with a larger political environment receptive to nationalist claims, constituted a great source of opportunities for wildcat bankers. Wildcats are invested in subverting the criteria through which a given banking tradition is defined and reproduced, and they do so by breaking the collective commitment of incumbent elites to a common identity, and by proposing new identities that transgress old boundaries. In the Italian case, their project of transgression was facilitated by the absence of a cohesive and ideologically united set of conservative bankers.

Nationalist wildcats became the vehicles through which nationalism was imported into the financial field and turned into a source of differentiation and control. They had been honing their strategy for some time. As early as 1898, a group of capitalists had formed a self-identified "Italian" counterpart to the universal banks: the Società Bancaria Italiana. Unlike COMIT and CREDIT, the Società Bancaria Italiana did not have strong international connections (although it did have important relationships with French capitalists, as Della Loggia [1970] carefully shows), but was most of all the expression of the advanced and speculative capitalist groups of the Genoese area, who self-consciously donned an Italian mantle (Bonelli 1971a: 31). Those groups imagined themselves as rivals to the Milan-based, but allegedly foreign-owned, COMIT and CREDIT. This rivalry only intensified in 1907, when the SBI, suffering severely from the crisis, was rescued by a bailout orchestrated by the Banca d'Italia and thus became even more conscious of the necessity to build an autonomous power basis.[11]

The alliance with the steel sector, one of strategic importance to the Italian military complex, became the basis for an attack on the universal banks, now framed as antipatriotic institutions (Galli Della Loggia 1970; Falchero 1981). To be sure, this occurred in the wake of nationalist criticisms of current financial arrangements. The nationalists had long accused politicians and conservative bankers of forestalling, in the name of an ill-guided protectionism, the emergence of financiers and industrialists who were willing to finance these strategic firms more effectively, but who were unable to do so because of the political obstacles the ruling elites posed against them (Aquarone 1981; Barone 1999: 283–95). But in their indictment of protectionism, nationalists had made an exception for the steel industry, for which they wanted some form of protectionism, and in this they parted ways with the *laissez faire* wing.[12]

The nationalists, excited at the perspective of an Italian nation finally able to compete militarily with other European powers, were also increasingly successful at mobilizing new constituencies. By 1911, for instance, in conjunction with the general expansion of the state's military capacity and the state's attempt to project its power abroad, a new periodical, *L'Idea Nazionale*, led by the Nationalist Association members Enrico Corradini and Alfredo Rocco, began circulating a wildly successful metaphor of Italy as a "proletarian nation" in need of emancipating itself from the financial grip of German capital—thus depicting conservative banking institutions as servants of foreign interests.[13] As they pushed for the further expansion of the state in order to gain for Italy what they thought was its "rightful place," the nationalists thus also opened a space for other actors to mobilize.

The financial elites that had rallied around the Società Bancaria Italiana eventually brought these nationalist attacks against the universal banks (see, esp., Gaeta 1981: 67–68). The Società Bancaria Italiana, the self-appointed *banca italianissima* (the most Italian of banks) rallied elites who wanted the demise of their dominant antagonists, and who found in appeals to the interests of the nation a source for new identities within which to do so (Falchero 1981). Conservative banking, already weakened by the lack of cohesion among financial elites, came under attack from this direction too: to wildcat elites the set of practices to assess creditworthiness that sound banking propagated, was simply an obstacle that got in the way of industrial development—namely, a boundary they needed to transgress. To the industrialists connected to the military-industrial complex, similarly, conservative credit allocation meant financial rigor and austerity—restrictions on their activities they wanted to escape from. Even though the universal banks were both unable and unwilling to accommodate the new constituencies created by the state, the imposition of exclusionary categories on the process of credit creation, based on criteria other than the national interest, became increasingly indefensible.

Economic nationalism afforded a solution, so to speak, to the political stalemate that the Bank of Italy increasingly found itself in. By subordinating itself to the project of state-building, and connecting the fate of banking to the fate of the nation, the Bank of Italy could begin to carve out a new, more autonomous role for itself. Drawing the boundaries between those deserving of credit, and those who should be denied access, along nationalist lines, the BI adopted an identity that commanded strong commitment from increasingly vocal sectors of the Italian population, and that, simultaneously, could not be dismissed as extraneous to credit by actors, such as COMIT, who were less than advantaged by this process. Put differently, nationalist mobilization per se did not turn creditworthiness into a matter of serving the interests of the nation rather than the credit needs of individuals or individual firms. Without the financial expansion orchestrated by the Italian government, and the creation of an opportunity structure for nationalists to take advantage of, creditworthiness would have likely remained a contested matter to be sure, but on grounds not so explicitly carved out by nationalism. But wildcat attacks increasingly impaired projects aimed at unifying the conservative bankers themselves. And while the conflict between conservatives and wildcats was soon to become a full-fledged, "parallel" war (Mori 1977) in the interwar years, to end only with the mutual destruction of both sides and their nationalization and absorption in the corporatist structures of the fascist regime (Forsyth 1993), the Bank of Italy retained a central role in the organization of Italian finance and credit, even under fascism (Gigliobianco 2006).

Conclusions

This chapter tells the complex story of the influence of economic nationalism on the dynamics of the Italian financial field, emphasizing both processes operating on the periphery of the field—namely, the emergence of a military-industrial complex financed by wildcats—and factors operating at the very center of the field—the conflict between universal banks and the Bank of Italy. Put more precisely, the chapter traces how those processes moved from the periphery to the field to its center, partly forcing conservative actors to engage with identities that had originally been extraneous to their own political culture; and partly enabling (at least some of) them to turn those identities into the grounds for new projects of financial control.

Our analysis of the use of economic nationalist ideas, in the context of the financial field of turn-of-the-century Italy, shows how *a myth of creditworthiness* developed, grounded on the understanding that credit was to be managed by and allocated to those who claimed to represent the national interest. Creditworthy behavior came to be defined as the proper use of financial instruments in ways that were congruent with the political priorities set by the Bank of Italy. There were multiple causes for the diffusion of nationalist collective identities as sources of financial commitment. They include the increasingly important role of the state in the development of the economy; worsening geopolitical conditions for the Italian government, including a defeat of its imperialist plans, prompting it to push further for the militarization of the economy; and the emergence of nationalist movements ever more vocal in their demands that the territorial ambitions of the state be realized (Webster 1975; Lanaro 1979; Duggan 2002). And the origins of Italian nationalism, of course, remain a source of debate and contention among Italian historians. Important studies trace them to the 1878 industrial tariffs, when the "historic bloc" between northern industrialists and southern landowners was consolidated (Carocci 1956); others, further back to the post-Napoleonic period, when a plethora of proposals for national development and the creation of a liberal regime began capturing the attention of economic and political elites (Banti and Ginsborg 2007). Yet another camp singles out the intellectual movements that appeared in the wake of Italy's economic take-off as the most important catalyst (De Rosa 1984; Banti 2005; Banti and Ginsborg 2007): for instance in 1910, with the founding of the Associazione Nazionalista Italiana, or earlier in 1903 with the appearance of Enrico Corradini's monthly *Il Regno*, or even earlier, in 1898, when his *Il Foglio* began publication. But a relatively uncontroversial point of agreement is that economic nationalism provided a common theme for different nationalist movements to rally around, because an appreciation of Italy's status as a weak economic community ("the proletarian nation") came to inform the larger claims that nationalists then went on to develop into full-fledged political demands (Riall et al. 2007). Recently, Mann (2004) even emphasized how this collective understanding of Italy was central to the development of a fascist ideology in the post–World War I period.

Yet it was not simply because of pressure from outside the financial field that creditworthiness became connected to a project of national development. Neither is it because the administration of the BI was filled with nationalist activists that the bank became more nationalistic (Gigliobianco 2006). Rather, the long-term source of the BI's shift toward nationalism was that, as the central government created new financial circuits—by using public debt as a means of incorporating new constituencies into the financial system—it challenged existing arrangements, making wildcat banking more prevalent and stronger. The BI was increasingly charged with the smooth functioning of the financial system, but the financial practices of the central government were sources of instability. As it searched for new ways to govern the financial system, the BI was also faced by nationalist protests against foreign capital. In order to maintain a central position in the financial system, the BI had to negotiate the moral demands and expectations of several often competing circuits of money. Each financial exchange could potentially threaten existing arrangements, if it was understood as violating the expectations (or earmarks) of the circuit to which bankers attached it. The Bank of Italy, finally, faced the enormous challenge of creating a system of cooperation with private banks, of which the (COMIT) was the largest. And those banks created formidable problems to the creation of a common set of principles, justified by an ideology of austerity and conservatism, through which the Bank of Italy and the universal banks could develop shared, collective commitments.

The Italian case is far from unique in this use of economic nationalism as a rallying point for larger projects of state-building. As Mann (1993: 297–329) shows in his discussion of Germany, its "drift," in Mann's terms, from late-development, corporate capitalism to militarism and imperialism, was an integral part of the process of state-building. From a more micro-oriented point of view, Brubaker (2003: 170; see also Brubaker and Cooper 2000) similarly argues that, while social movements can be very persuasive in their claims to representing pre-existing groups, we hardly find such concrete, strongly connected groups waiting to be spoken for; and that, therefore, "we can attend to the dynamics of *group-making* as a social, cultural, and political project, aimed at transforming categories into groups or increasing levels of groupness." From this perspective, it is not only the case that what identities refer to cannot be taken for granted; rather, identities become instruments that groups employ strategically, sometimes even cynically, to effect social change. I have argued along these lines that while the Banca d'Italia was not at the forefront of the nationalist movement, once it could channel the power of nationalist identities into projects of financial control, it did so to break the political stalemate created by the conflict among conservative bankers, while managing the pressure from nationalist wildcats.

My focus on the interpenetration of economic nationalism and finance in nineteenth-century Italy justifies a larger claim that, because of the collective dimension of economic action and the dependence of capitalism on commitments to shared identities, politics is integral to finance, and thus the political effects of financial arrangements cannot be disentangled from the economic effects. Specifically, finance is dependent on the creation of boundaries, and it is through relational work that such boundaries are demarcated (Zelizer and Tilly 2006; Zelizer 2010). However, while conservative and wildcat bankers fight about where such boundaries should be drawn, and wildcats in particular couch their demands in terms of inclusion and expansion—at times even democracy—there are limits to this conflict, and these limits are the limits of the political system in which finance takes place. In the Italian case, wildcats made claims on the basis of economic nationalism because the structure of the polity—centralized, and increasingly focused on militarism, war industries, and geopolitics—facilitated the diffusion of nationalist identities, and because the deployment of such identities in the financial field, in turn, allowed them to transgress the boundaries around creditworthy behavior that their powerful, conservative counterparts were in the process of setting. The limit of the nationalist identity that wildcats, and the Bank of Italy, made central to the Italian credit system was precisely that it excluded those conservative bankers on whose cooperation the Bank of Italy still depended. In other words, nationalism was not an "optimal" solution to a problem of coordination, but this is simply because such a solution did not exist. The point, then, is not to praise the effectiveness of nationalism in stabilizing financial relations, but to better understand the collective basis on which credit systems rest, and in that way refine the collective approach to finance that I have been developing.

7

Conclusions

ACCORDING TO AN IMPORTANT, perhaps even dominant, view in economics, political science, and economic sociology, money is not created as much as it is moved; banks are the organizations invested with this function of intermediating between people with resources and capital, and people who are willing and able to put those resources to use. Often this problem is reduced to a technical challenge of matching sellers and buyers according to market-driven and market-informed criteria. More sophisticated accounts, especially those sensitive to the scarce nature of information, and to the challenges that uncertainty poses to credit, invoke trust as a necessary precondition of any economic exchange: devising methods by which uncertainty can be reduced or controlled is paramount, they argue. They thus point to banks as the guarantors of the quality of the information that creditors rely upon to make sound lending decisions.

This book builds a sociology of money, and so questions the individualistic foundations on which coordination-based arguments are predicated. Accordingly, it shifts the problem inherent to credit from one of ascertaining creditworthiness to one of constructing it. Put differently, the argument rejects the premise that creditworthiness is a property of debtors, and that the assessment of creditworthiness is a functional solution to the problem of uncertainty or to the problem of trust. Rather, creditworthiness is about constructing the terms upon which a certain kind of trust and a certain kind of reputation can be used in the process of credit assessment, so as to reproduce the power of financial elites. Creditworthiness derives from the collective identities that bankers enforce upon the financial field. To put it more directly, creating and managing money is a question of building social networks among powerful people. It is a political process.

While the idea that the economy should be understood as an arena of conflict, rather than one of coordination, is rooted in classical sociology, we find an influential application to finance and credit in the political sociology of Schumpeter. This sociology remains relatively ignored, especially compared with Schumpeter's more famous concepts of creative destruction and monopolistic competition (but see Swedberg 1992 for an effort to bring back Schumpeter's sociology). Partly this is because Schumpeter never made the link between money and conflict explicit.[1] In what follows, I attempt to remedy this by returning to Schumpeter, so as to elaborate on the relationship between the theory of finance as organized conflict that I propose here, and Schumpeter's approach to banking. I then summarize the U.S.-Italy comparison and highlight the relationship between the political culture of financial fields and the political culture of the larger society in which the field is embedded. I conclude by returning to the defining characteristics of the two ideal types of banking, and briefly discuss how they might help elucidate certain aspects of our current financial predicament.

Schumpeter's Theory of Banking

Schumpeter argued that bankers grant credit to other elites, depending on their ability to assess reputations, and to translate those reputations into generalized commodities. But the argument that the credit process depends on the assessment of reputations is only a first step in understanding how that assessment is carried out practically. It is even potentially misleading to pose the problem as one of informational asymmetries, for which carefully crafted solutions can be devised, because this suggests that credit assessment is merely a technical matter.

Schumpeter, who to be sure is aware of the problem that scarce information creates for credit, thinks otherwise. He argues that, as bankers meet their debtors in the money market, where loans and, more generally, credit are allocated, where "what takes place is simply the exchange of present against future purchasing power," they engage in a "price struggle" over credit, which is ultimately a struggle over who should be allowed to get credit at what price.

All plans and outlooks for the future in the economic system affect it, all conditions of the national life, all political, economic, and natural events. There is scarcely a piece of news that does not necessarily influence the decisions relative to the carrying out of new combinations or the money-market position and the opinions and intentions of the entrepreneurs. The system of future values must be adapted to every new situation. This is of course not merely effected by variations in the price of purchasing power. Frequently, personal influence acts in addition to or in place of the latter. (1911: 126)

Here Schumpeter surely emphasizes the importance of information, or "news," in determining how credit is allocated. But in this formulation, it is no longer information about the particular borrower that matters. The information that matters cannot be gained from the individual borrower either, because it is information of a more general kind, information that will affect not only his or her ability to repay in the future but also the ability of borrowers in general to meet their financial obligations. It is *political* information insofar as knowledge of it serves to create a more general framework around which specific information about individual borrowers can be assessed. And it is a *political* process that guides the acquisition of information because, as Schumpeter adds at the end of the paragraph, "personal influence" matters tremendously here. Information, in fact, may even have a role secondary to the ability of powerful actors to enforce credit decisions and to impose the terms upon which credit decisions are made. Credit, in this view, thus responds to the politics of networks, rather than to uncertainty or trust.

The networks of borrowers that Schumpeter is concerned with are entrepreneurial networks. Since he considers entrepreneurs exemplars of leadership, Schumpeter also thinks that their leadership extends to the process whereby they gain credit: entrepreneurs persuade if not altogether force bankers to reward their innovative activities. But Schumpeter adds that, for this reason, sound banking requires a certain moral standing on the part of the banker, a certain austerity of manners and customs so to speak, which serves to balance out the socially disruptive tendencies of entrepreneurial borrowers. Consistently, Schumpeter also argues that, whenever the business of banking opens up to the influence of outsiders, capitalism enters into a "catastrophic" phase.

This is where I depart from Schumpeter. I reject this either/or view, with conservative bankers carrying out proper banking operations, and wildcats emerging as deviations from normal banking practices. The distinction between "conservative" and "wildcat" banking is a continuum. Financial systems can become more or less conservative, and more or less wildcat, depending on a number of conditions that I discussed at length in this book. However, at the core of banking there is the process of creating circuits of money; banking, then, is a relatively autonomous, specialized domain, but also one in which these two strategies are always possible—a strategy aimed at the hoarding of resources and opportunities, and a counterstrategy aimed at transgressing the boundaries set by conservative elites so as to reshape the logic of finance. Bankers achieve monetary stability by employing what I have called the "conservative" strategy. They specialize in producing restricted currencies—that is, they restrict credit and money to particular social groups; they maintain tight control over financial flows; and they bring stability to the system, but also turn it into an exclusive club of creditors. But a second strategy can be mobilized against conservatives. It is a speculative one, whereby bankers invent new instruments to expand existing financial flows, creating markets on commodities as well as on financial instruments themselves; and bring instability to banking.

The Schumpeterian perspective on banking also points to the conditions under which each strategy—conservative and wildcat—becomes more or less viable, especially if one heeds another specific suggestion of Schumpeter (1918): that the budget is the center of the state, and that an analysis of the budget allows us to capture power dynamics that would otherwise remain hidden. The general point is that conservative bankers need the support of political elites invested in fiscal rigor and conservatism, in order to prevail. Fiscal largesse, by contrast, spawns "wildcats," who extend credit to new social groups. This book focuses accordingly on the forces that push the state to expand the size of its budget—forces that, as my investigation of the Italian and U.S. cases in the nineteenth century reveals, often originate from within the state itself, to the effect that subnational political bodies are able to extract revenue and raise debt independently from the finances of the central state.

Political Culture and Finance

The politics of the budget is crucial to the development of national credit systems for two reasons. For one, the authorities that get to make fiscal decisions can become sources of stability and banking conservatism, to the extent that bankers develop privileged, "closed" relationships (in the

Weberian sense) with them. For another, and conversely, fiscal authorities can also create constituencies invested in the expansion of credit and finance. As scholars of the economic history of finance recognize (especially Verdier 2003 and Seabrooke 2006), there is also a *territorial* dimension to credit, which becomes particularly important in the context of democratic regimes, where institutions on different levels of the political structure are more or less open to societal pressures.

This territorial dimension is borne out by the empirical evidence presented in this book. Both the United States and Italy started off as very decentralized political and fiscal entities, but whereas the United States maintained a decentralized structure, Italy did not. In the decentralized polity of nineteenth-century North America, bankers strived to gain the support of local political authorities to defend the kinds of boundaries around the allocation of credit, on which sound banking principles normally rely. They did this without facing much resistance in the South. But in the states of the North, where state governments were democratic, bankers simultaneously benefited from political patronage, and suffered from the democratic constraints governments put on their activities— something revealed by the taxes Northern governments imposed on them. Unlike financial and monetary media, which people considered as *private*, banks had a more ambiguous status and were often understood as public entities. But precisely because this ambiguity translated into calls for more open financial systems, banks multiplied in the North.

In the Kingdom of Italy, by contrast, the political bodies that administered local communities, while increasingly open over the course of the nineteenth century to demands for political and financial inclusion, lacked the kind of credibility, authority, and infrastructural capacity of the U.S. states. Regional elites could not even enforce the law without help from the central government. Stability and order in the territories depended on the central government, and Italian bankers accordingly sought it out to establish a conservative banking system.

One way to summarize these considerations is to single out the actors involved in the constitution of credit systems in Italy and the United States (see Table 7.1). On the "political side," on the Left, we have the central government and subnational political authorities, in both cases issuing money (the central government) and public debt (both levels). On the "financial side," on the Right, we have national (for the postbellum period) and state banks in the United States, with less regulated actors (such as, toward the end of the century, trust companies) also being pulled into

TABLE 7.1

Political and Banking Actors, U.S. and Italy

United States	
Government:	Banks:
• Federal: Bonds and greenbacks • State: Bonds to finance local development (boosterism)	• State and unchartered (esp. trust companies): collected local deposits, granted call loans, engaged in private wealth managemeent, invested in stocks and bonds (Carosso and Sylla 1991; Moen and Tallman 1992) • National (postbellum period): issued banknotes, invested in commercial lending, using stocks and bonds as secondary reserve (James 1978)

Italy	
Government:	Banks:
• Central: Bonds and various note issues (e.g., banknotes issued on behalf of the Treasury) • Local: Bonds to finance local development	• Banks of Issue ("Public"): Banknotes; loans to other banks (clearing facilities and bailouts, esp. Banca Nazionale); loans to government • Commercial banks: Industrial financing; deposits • Local banks: local loans; government bonds

the national banking system; and banks of issue, commercial banks, and local banking institutions in Italy. In the United States the main problem faced by conservative financial elites was how to gain control over banks that, without submitting to federal regulations, were nonetheless fully integrated in a national credit system: those banks did not share conservative goals and priorities. In the Italian case, by contrast, conservative bankers were striving to create those very connections between local and national circuits; local banks tended not to invest in the stock market, or when they did so, they tended to buy government securities. The money they collected tended to remain close to its point of origin.

From these differences in the ways center-periphery relationships were organized flowed different ways of assessing creditworthiness. In the United States, where fiscal power was decentralized, and thereby was premised on assumptions about sovereignty and political power as belonging to the local level, bankers came to define and assess creditworthiness in terms of personal reputations. This process took similar shapes in other economic domains, such as the railroad sector (Dobbin 1994; Dobbin and Dowd 1997; Dobbin 2004), and the corporate sector more generally (Fligstein 1990): the principles through which the polity was organized came to inform the organization of the economy as well. In the case of banking, however, bankers also gained more autonomy over time, as they shifted over the course of the nineteenth century from making local alliances with local and state governments to claiming professional autonomy in the allocation of credit; but their prestige remained intimately connected to their ability to claim how they specialized in the assessment of reputations. In Italy on the other hand, the contested nature of local-central fiscal flows made the banking system oriented toward the national arena. In spite of strong local banking networks, banking was structured by its relationship with the state, because fiscal power was centralized. Systemic concerns gained priority over the financial conditions of individual borrowers. Thus in the United States, individual creditworthiness became the centerpiece in bankers' accounts of what their business was about, serving as an organizing principle of banking; whereas in Italy, an explicitly collectivist ideology—nationalism—did instead.

In both cases, those political cultures of money were not sources of consensus and harmony. Rather, they set the stage for renewed conflicts about where boundaries should be drawn: they were *political* in the sense of encouraging agonistic practices. Reputation and national creditworthiness became the *grounds* for a more general struggle between conservative and wildcat bankers. The coordination and exploitation of the multiple circuits of money that characterized U.S. finance were, for instance, a matter of setting exclusive criteria of creditworthiness in a context in which liberalism in banking had the ideological upper hand. Conservative bankers, because they could not rely on political power, and thus did not have the kind of legitimacy in defining creditworthiness that would have found a superior articulation in a relationship with the state, therefore lacked moral authority. If they were acting out of private self-interest, why should other bankers follow their rules? Why would any banker be authorized to speak for the interests of the banking profession as a whole? Conservative bankers navigated these difficulties, especially in the 1880s and 1890s, through the construction of a political culture of reputation and moral worth. The fact that they had themselves begun their careers in banking as wildcats made the importance of constructing publicly oriented identities particularly salient. Drawing from the claims to reputational assessment of decentralized banking, local banks as much as big, national ones could be integrated within the system under a common banner of credit as the activity of judging the character of the debtor.

Wildcats were central to this process—even those who, unlike the corporate consolidators of the Gilded Age, remained contented to exploit opportunities left open by their conservative counterparts. In the Jacksonian period, wildcats contested the very meaning of reputation: they forced conservatives to heed their demands for decentralized control over credit, even as the decentralization of credit was perceived as a cause of instability. Throughout the postbellum period, wildcats skillfully exploited the regulatory gaps in banking legislation to find new ways to expand the size of the financial field, thus repeatedly challenging the conservative identities of their counterparts.

In the Italian case, the centrality of the Italian state to the business of banking *politicized* the work of bankers, in the specific sense that it involved the state and the central bank in managing the conflicts internal to the banking system. This development created incentives for certain bankers to enter into an alliance with political authorities, and for other bankers to contest the legitimacy of those alliances in the name of more general calls for national solidarity. More important, the state politicized the banking system because it created the conditions for financial expansion, and created new constituencies invested in that expansion. As the central government formed new financial circuits, conservatives had to devise new frameworks through which those circuits could be controlled. Creditworthiness as nationalism was institutionalized because, in a context of financial expansion originating with the central government, it was the framework that afforded the Bank of Italy a way to control what financial actors were doing with the new instruments thereby produced.

One conclusion I want to avoid is the suggestion that the U.S. banking system was more "functional" and "harmonious" than the Italian system. Wildcats were present in both systems. If anything, the United States was often accused by contemporary international observers as a main cause of global financial instability. In fact, one can argue that the complexity of the U.S. banking system was itself a condition for instability, independently of the agendas of specific actors. Unitary elite action at the national level was justified in terms of restoring harmony—yet its more direct concern was to stave off the attacks of rival, locally entrenched elites, which was a structural feature of the system. My point is not to show the United States as a better model: rather, it is to analyze the kinds of positions on the wildcat/conservative continuum available to bankers in each context. And while there is a long historical tradition that highlights the weaknesses and deficiencies of the Italian case, Italian historians are now less negative in their interpretation of liberal Italy's economic history. A characterization of the Italian case as a failed model would be just as inaccurate.

Theoretical Conclusions and Empirical Implications

Having discussed in what ways the analytical categories of conservative and wildcat banking shed light on the political and economic history of Italy and the United States, I am now in a position to make a more general argument about bankers and their role in the construction of creditworthiness. This book focuses on conflicts internal to the banking system, and develops a general framework within which these conflicts can be located. I argue that bankers are specialists in the production of collective identities, which they attach to financial instruments, and then police by restricting their circulation to individuals or organizations that fulfill the criteria specified in the identity.

Bankers grant credit only upon the fulfillment of certain criteria; and the kind of credit they extend—short-term credit card loans, stock and bonds, securitized mortgages, and so forth—also varies dramatically, depending on the creditworthiness of the client, but more precisely on how that creditworthiness is defined. Bankers are never in full control of creditworthiness. Because boundaries generate resistance and opposition, bankers are subjected to pressure not to conform to shared identities; not to respect existing understandings about how credit should be used; and not to enforce existing exclusions. Bankers are, in short, vulnerable to difficult collective action dilemmas.

The distinction between conservative and wildcat bankers that I propose in this book serves to distill the core aspects of financial conflict. Through their *exclusionary* logic, conservative bankers assign money in specific forms to clients they deem reputable. The boundaries drawn around creditworthy behavior ensure stable returns in the future, and the collective identity through which those boundaries are specified commits other financial providers to similar goals: the identity, in other words, constitutes their interests. But there are limits to how binding this commitment will be. Bankers are differentiated and specialized actors, orienting themselves to different degrees toward local finances or national and international kinds of activities. Hence, bankers can enter into conflict

TABLE 7.2

Conservative and Wildcat Banking, Summary

	Conservative Bankers	Wildcat Bankers
Objective: What do they want?	Predictability of financial gains: They create stable relationships with exclusive clientele. Strict screening.	Unpredictability but high volume: They expand the financial system.
Plan: How do they make money?	They give credit to borrowers they know, and to those with viable business plans (i.e., those who can guarantee a future revenue stream). They stifle competition by binding financial actors to common, collective identities.	They give credit to actors (individuals or organizations) previously excluded from credit (either altogether excluded, or excluded from particular instruments).
Strategy: How do they do it?	They restrict the possession and circulation of particular financial instruments to certain networks, while excluding others.	They create new markets and/or new financial instruments.
Threat: Who challenges them?	Wildcats: New financial providers and new investment vehicles that supersede previous criteria of creditworthiness.	Ever more marginalized actors—supersession of previous boundaries does not guarantee erection of new boundaries.
Relationship to new customers	Limited and predatory: those who fulfill creditworthiness criteria but fall back are punished.	Extensive-predatory and/or idealistic: New customers served through new methods that may or may not work.

among themselves over what creditworthiness is and implies. Members of status groups in general, and banking groups in particular, can never escape the problem that what is rational at the collective level is often irrational at the individual level. Individuals may find in exchanges of financial instruments on open markets—in which they can trade with whomever they want—a better opportunity to make money than they do in restricted circuits of exchange, where financial instruments are sold only to particular kinds of individuals. Open markets, though, threaten the collective basis upon which their power is based. Because of this tension between the collective rationality of the group, and the individual rationality of its members, the struggle between conservative and wildcat bankers is intrinsic to finance.

Wildcat bankers, through their *inclusionary* logic, exploit the limits of conservative banking. As they assign more prestigious kinds of money to less prestigious clients, they profit from the expansion of the financial field. Their relationship with the excluded may or may not be idealistic—this is a difficult point to prove. Were Italian wildcat bankers wedded to nationalism out of convenience or because of deep conviction? Were Jackson-era wildcats strategic in their appeal to a larger (abhorrent to contemporary eyes) slave-owner community, or were they exploiting it as a symbolic opportunity? Sociologically, the important point remains that the structure of exclusion set up by conservative bankers generates the ideologies with which that structure can be contested. Yet as they succeed, wildcats themselves fall under pressure to create new collective identities with which to stabilize the financial field and thus reap the long-term benefits of their challenge. Hence, the dynamism of finance.

The authority that bankers wield, as they allocate credit, can be contested not only from within the financial field but also from the within the state. The state may need to respond to fiscal pressure by methods that are incongruous with those practiced by bankers.[2] This has been the major focus of the historical comparison that underlies the argument of this book. A second source, also outside of the financial field, tends to be local, as with communities that contest how bankers assign credit: this has been the main focus of the new, relational sociology of money I survey in the introduction. To capture this variability in the practices through which money is regulated by creditworthiness, an important theoretical shift is needed.[3] Just as the political sociology of the state has moved beyond rigid characterizations of states and society to a more historically nuanced and locally focused understanding of the interaction between the two (Gorski 2003; Loveman 2005), the sociology of money should move beyond insulated typologies of the forms of monetary authority toward a similarly nuanced frame of analysis, attentive to variation. Under a perspective that focuses on how monetary institutions are built from the ground up, as well as from the top down, the unmistakable differentiation of money and its simultaneous homogeneity deriving from money-of-account cease to seem paradoxical. They both become tensions managed through institutional work. And this shift in perspective makes it imperative to conduct focused historical comparisons to capture variation in sound banking institutions, and the nature of the conditions underlying the dominance of any given source of authority.[4]

During state formation, state actors were the main challengers to monetary stability because their need to extract taxes had to be negotiated with privatized networks of capitalists—a path to state-formation that Tilly (1992) defines as "capitalized coercion"—and because capitalists often resisted state demands. This trajectory (for good reasons, since it was the trajectory that was most successful) has been incorporated in the ways we think about money, and in our very theories about money—as if it were a blueprint that all subsequent instances of monetary conflicts must follow. It is as if, in other words, all instances of monetary conflict and stability were ultimately reducible to the state's interference with private exchanges.

This is too narrow a perspective, for two reasons. First, as I have argued in this book, states contributed to the constitution of markets (and continue doing so) by providing the categories through which creditworthiness could be assessed. They have not been entangled in a zero-sum relationship vis-à-vis the market, but in a mutually constitutive one, under certain conditions, and a more antagonistic one, under others. Second, and of course relatedly, the financial expansion of states often served to, if not rectify, at least challenge and transgress some of the inequalities produced by markets (a point that Max Weber understood very well). As a result, the institutionalization of money—a process managed by the state—made possible new kinds of alliances between local actors and bankers, the nature of which we have yet to understand fully. As Hicks (1969) puts it, with the emergence of deposit banks, institutions spread out over the territory and responsible for the collection and centralization of local resources, banking went from a matter of financing the sovereign to one of building nationally inclusive financial systems. State-penetration, as a result, while certainly serving as a crucial trigger to financial innovation, can only be understood as one among the many processes that linked territories and center. The diffusion of deposit banks, and more generally the creation of new currencies specifically targeting local clients, also created an infrastructure through which new connections between locales and financial centers arose independently of the fiscal policy of the state. That is to say, the history of banking is in some ways reflected in the history of the state, but it is not reducible to it.

Theorists of the commensurable, equivalent properties of money, such as Marx and Simmel, lived through that banking revolution—the spread of deposit banking in the 1800s, when notorious figures like John Law, and later the Pereire brothers, captured the public imagination,[5] and it is possibly deposit banking they had in mind when they articulated their views of money. But the fact that bankers have gradually penetrated local communities—specializing in the collection of local deposits, the management of local wealth, the extension of local loans—is a long-term process that, while replacing old boundaries and restrictions on currencies, also created new ones. It is not a march toward equivalence and commensurability but a political process through which boundaries have been contested, breached, and, most important, re-created. Some local banks specialized in serving particular constituencies, taking the form of credit unions, savings cooperatives, rural banks, and the like, and giving money a physical, tangible, and moral character. But other bankers and nonbanking financial institutions specialized in financial innovations that, once implemented at the local level, served to subvert dominant criteria of creditworthiness.

In sum, the view of money as a set of differentiated and segregated currencies that I strive to develop in this book serves to point attention to the creation of more or less homogeneous "currencies" as a process that produces economic inequalities. It also serves to direct attention to the cultural and moral frameworks through which those "currencies" achieve circulation in particular networks. Money, to put it simply, is constituted by judgments about creditworthiness. And because financial conflict is ultimately a conflict about the boundaries that should be used to delineate creditworthy behavior, wildcats can resort to individualistic criteria in order to subvert the collective projects of appropriation of their conservative counterparts.

Contemporary Wildcats

What can a conceptualization of money as a political judgment on creditworthiness tell us about more recent changes in monetary processes? Zelizer (1994: 17) identified in the turn-of-the-twentieth-century United States a process of monetary homogeneity, enforced by the federal government, leading to more, not less, monetary differentiation. Money "multiplied both within households and in public settings. Even prisons debated the right kind of money for inmates, while some orphan asylums and foster care supervisors proposed a separate currency for dependent children," to give a few examples. "Therefore, the forms of monetary earmarking multiplied just as official money became more uniform and generalized" (ibid.). The so-called financialization of the world economy in the past forty or so years has produced a new iteration of such homogenizing and differentiating processes, in particular in the United States (see Krippner 2005 and 2011 for a penetrating analysis). The boundaries and distinctions created by the financial regime of the post–New Deal era, aimed at extending access to credit but only upon fulfillment of certain criteria of full employment in Fordist organizations, have been altogether superseded by a regime of access to credit on individualistic criteria, rather than organizational affiliation, aimed at expanding the reach of the financial system into niches historically marginalized by banks: the lower classes, individuals with poor credit histories, and groups altogether excluded by the structure of power (from different political perspectives, Aglietta 2000; Ferguson 2008; G. F. Davis 2009). The system of unequal access to credit that grounded the post–New Deal regime was, in other words, superseded by the invention of new, local currencies—such as securitized real estate—that created a conflict over creditworthiness, indeed a crisis over what constitutes the moral authority of money. This crisis cannot be solved within the existing financial parameters. It is a conflict that has implicated and destabilized local circuits of money in perhaps unprecedented ways.

What made this generalized attack on the exclusionary character of creditworthiness possible is a complex set of processes. There is a story of financial instruments—namely, though not exclusively, mortgage-backed securities (MBSs). MBSs were crucial to the creation of a market in mortgages. They served as vehicles of financial inclusion: they allowed individuals to finance mortgages who would not have been able to do so otherwise. Rather than making previous criteria of credit assessment irrelevant, however, MBSs had the purported power to parcel out risk, thus turning existing inequalities into profit opportunities: through MBSs, investors could now buy assets with a quantifiable level of risk attached to them (MacKenzie 2006). Further, the idea behind MBSs was not to turn them into tokens of belonging to new, and exclusive, communities of holders. MBSs were not the kinds of currencies that, by circulating in restricted circuits, would help their holders develop a common orientation to economic opportunities. MBSs, rather, remained low-prestige instruments—to be held by established financiers off the balance sheets of their banks, in "special purpose vehicles" hidden from view and, most important, public scrutiny (Tett 2009), rather than being publicly displayed as the money of a new group demanding access to credit. Unlike the more idealistic wildcats of the early twentieth century, in other words, the financial innovators that contributed to the establishment of a market in MBSs took a more pragmatic approach to these instruments; indeed, they began seriously operating in this market only once the financial architecture began to accommodate their demands for insurance (Mehrling 2010).

This was not the case at the early stages of the process of financial innovation, when financial innovators focused on mobilizing financial constituencies that were much closer to the center of the action. Take Michael Milken, the financier who precipitated the "junk bond" revolution of the 1980s. Milken was particularly interested in bonds that, from a position of high credit rating, had fallen to "below investment grade" (hence the term "fallen angels"). The subversive idea behind junk bonds was that the debt of these companies was systematically and *arbitrarily* undervalued by rating agencies: a low credit rating, which made the bonds issued by a firm "junk" rather than prime, was a matter of "discrimination," Milken argued (Abolafia 1996: 158–59). He thus saw his providing credit to such firms as a moral responsibility and a fight for justice. As he put it in a New York *Times* op-ed (that was rejected): "Unlike other crusaders from Berkeley, I have chosen Wall Street as my battleground for improving society" (ibid.: 155).

By contrast, more contemporary wildcats seem to be disconnected from their potential constituencies. What explains this decoupling? Creditworthiness, I would suggest, in its new articulation as membership in the "ownership society," and the subsequent increase in the autonomy of finance it made possible, are the two crucial factors. As Gerald Davis (2009) persuasively argues, political elites pursued the project of the "ownership society" in order to reconfigure and shape the transition from the corporate, Fordist regime of the post–World War II period to the postindustrialism of the 1970s. And one of the central ideas behind the ownership society is that individuals are responsible for their own economic (and social) destiny through their reliance on financial markets (ibid.: 4). In this view, the logic of investing replaces the logic of earning.

The ownership society is closely linked to the increasing autonomy of finance because it gives financiers new symbolic resources with which to pursue innovation. Financialization allows wildcats to couch their subversive activities not in a political culture of justice and loyalty to an excluded community, but in an idealized representation of creditworthiness as inhering to the *choices* of individual investors. But a sociology of financial conflict suggests that the struggle over what categories should be invoked in constructing creditworthiness is a structural aspect of finance, and that, therefore, increasingly expanding financial markets—unbounded by social categories—are unsustainable. Creditworthiness is, at heart, a system of exclusions, tightly linked to categories backed up by the state, and not solely at the level of ideology, but fiscally. We have seen that, in the U.S. case at the turn of the twentieth century, creditworthiness was attached to individual reputations, but more as a way to solve conflicts within a decentralized banking system, and a decentralized polity where local administrations had the power to tax, than as a method to negotiate individual relationships of credit. This suggests that the contemporary "ownership society," for all its celebration of the individual investor's ability to choose the financial strategy that suits him or her best, remains a political construction, not a natural solution to excessive government interference. Krippner (2011) argues to this effect that the present financial crisis was precipitated by the U.S. government's attempt to *avoid* making painful fiscal choices.

The outcome of this political project to detach the allocation and distribution of resources from the political process, to then displace it onto financial markets, is that finance begins resembling what Bourdieu calls an "autonomous field." Through financial innovation, now legitimate in its own terms, finance focuses the attention of the field on itself. As argued by Collins (2000: 21), the very logic of belonging to a class of financial elites shifts the focus of the field onto the financial activities these elites carry out.

[I]ndividuals who have hundreds of millions of dollars or more can do little with that money except buy and sell financial instruments; they can trade control of one segment of the financial world for control of another segment. Wealth of this scale needs to be located not in consumption but in occupational experience. In terms of microsituational experience, possession of large amounts of financial instruments means a life-routine of frequently interacting with other financiers. The main attraction of having extremely large amounts of money may be the emotional energies and symbolic membership markers of being on the phone at all hours of night and day, engaging in exciting transactions.

The use of sophisticated financial instruments becomes a way of constructing the occupational experience of control and prestige, through which membership in the financial elite is enacted and lived.[6] And the prestige of those financial interactions also derives from the cultural milieu in which they take place, a cultural milieu that makes finance more autonomous because it detaches creditworthiness from membership in social categories, and attaches it instead to an allegedly individual capacity to succeed.

In such a context, conservative bankers cease to be the financial managers of economic elites—the investor class who does not participate directly in stock market operations but whose wealth depends on capitalization. Connie Bruck (1989: 84–85) noted their increasingly passive role as early as the 1980s, when leveraged buyouts became all the rage: "[Bankers of conservative persuasion] are not players who command attention, for good or for ill, but mere onlookers, and thus their potency has been inevitably diminished. . . . [F]or years the real action—the fortunes made overnight, the dizzying deals that seem to have no limit, the risk-taking that in itself becomes a kind of addiction and a focus of media infatuation—has all been on the field itself. The current of human interest and attention has pulled that way—not towards . . . the cautious conservative scolds." With the "microexperience, the activity of wielding money in highly prestigious circuits of exchange," increasingly deriving from success in financial dealings, being on the frontier of innovative financial techniques becomes paramount. Schumpeter (1911: 93) wrote of the "will to conquer: the impulse to fight, to prove oneself superior to others, to succeed for the sake, not of the fruits of success, but of success itself," but he confined his description to entrepreneurs. If a crucial component of the class situation of financial elites, however, becomes the willingness of innovative elites to carry out risky financial operations—for the thrill of the challenge, and the potential agonistic payoff of coming out on top—the Schumpeterian world is turned upside down. It is no longer entrepreneurs who fight for dominance over the process of development. Rather, it is increasingly financial innovators who face off with other financial innovators over the kinds of instruments that capture the focus of attention of the financial community, with the success of the operation measured in terms not of its long-term economic payoff, but in terms of its ability to impress.

Calls for fiscal austerity, which have characterized public debate on finance since the 2007–8 meltdown, suggest that a conservative undercurrent still runs through financial markets—one likely composed by wildcats, ready to capitalize on their speculative gains, much as the turn-of-the-century corporate consolidators did in the United States. Decreasing flows of debt, from the point of view of would-be conservative bankers, can serve as a strategy to tighten up control over the financial system (De Cecco 1987). As Timothy Sinclair (2000) argues, "deficit discourse," the attempt to blame government policy for the crisis of governability that afflicts neoliberal capitalism, paradoxically puts the burden back upon the state to dictate who has access to what resources, and who should be excluded. But fiscal austerity comes with considerable social cost (Eichengreen 1996). So negotiating the demands for inequality-reducing policies that austerity measures tend to generate, while containing the speculative moves of wildcats, will remain a pressing political challenge.

Progressive economists increasingly think that this challenge will not be won until states resume deficit-spending in a massive way (for example, Krugman 2012). Fiscal largesse, by contrast, may stimulate economic growth. But will it also generate a new wave of wildcat banking? By the same token, how will government policies affect the prestige of financial innovators in the eyes of a larger public, once, and if, the government will take it upon itself to put limitations on credit? One of the examples discussed in this book—the Italian case—solved this contradiction with politically devastating results: by abolishing democracy. It would be beyond the scope of this book to argue whether, and in what ways, this remains a possibility. But it is also possible to imagine a future in which states—democratic states—break this dynamic, this intermittent reliance on sound banking to ensure stability, punctuated by reliance on wildcat banking to reconfigure boundaries around credit. But will this be a future without banking? And will it still be a capitalist system?

Appendix
Historical Variation in Banking Power

Throughout this book, I have criticized the historical literature on financial system formation, but that is not meant to dismiss its contribution to highlighting the importance of the state, and of its openness to societal demands in the structuring of financial systems. Rather, it is to point to the need for a different theory of the interaction between bankers and states. In this appendix, I dig a little more deeply into that literature to emphasize similarities and differences between their approach and mine.

An important challenge to the proposition that banks have a unique role to play in financial fields comes from the comparative history of banking systems, which supports the claim that financial systems vary dramatically in terms of how central the bankers are to their exchanges (Zysman 1983; Verdier 2003). This literature on banking and finance distinguishes between systems in which credit is disbursed directly by banks, and systems where financial markets (and thus "disintermediation" and more arm's length types of exchanges) are more central (Gerschenkron 1962; Sylla 1998; Zysman 1983).

Gerschenkron's classic late-development hypothesis set the gold standard of this line of inquiry, as he identified the historical source of variation in industrial structure and its attendant financial structure in late development. Countries that entered industrialization late—late-developing, or "relatively backward" countries, as he put it—had to "catch up" with their competitors, which meant that they had to adopt their production methods and techniques. But because by the eighteenth century onward industrialization entailed large capital requirements—industry, that is, was a matter of industrial giants producing in capital-intensive sectors such as steel—finding the money to finance those capital investments offered new challenges—namely, the need for the large-scale accumulation of funds, which could then be channeled into industrial financing; and the attendant need for rapid, thus carefully coordinated, financial accumulation, which could then be put at the disposal of the large firms invested with the responsibility to pull their country out of backwardness. Hence, Gerschenkron argued, this led to the emergence of "universal banks," in the business of deposit collection as commercial banks as well as the business of financing industries through long-term credit instruments, as investment banks. Gerschenkron contrasted this path, common to Germany, Russia, France, and Italy, to the British case, where industrialization had had an early start and could therefore be financed through the slow accumulation of capital through equity markets—and where, therefore, banks specialized in deposit collection or investment banking.

John Zysman (1983) was the first to argue that the dynamic behind the dominance of banks or stock markets is political, rather than technical and industrial, and depends on the capacity of the state to govern financial flows. But the political centrality of banks to financial systems has been re-established by a new wave of economic history, centered especially on the German case (Herrigel 2000; Fohlin 2007), as well as on international political economy, in particular in the work of Verdier (2003) and Seabrooke (2006). To different degrees, these analysts shift their focus from technological determinism to patterns of political and financial interaction. Daniel Verdier (2003) develops this perspective into a theory of the territorial dimensions of monetary power that transcends the dichotomy between bank- and stock-market dominance altogether. Verdier narrows state strength to the issue of fiscal centralization, an indicator of the balance that exists between different levels of state power. Historically, his argument goes, the shape of modern financial systems was affected by the political structures in place in times of technological innovation (such as the development of more liquid financial instruments, or the consolidation of the international monetary regime of the gold standard). Where states were decentralized, local banks could lobby local political elites to create internal barriers to capital mobility—choking the flow of savings from the periphery to the center. The result was a banking system that had both decentralized institutions and what Gerschenkron calls universal banks, forced to rely on sheer size and the mixing of various kinds of financial functions in order to compete with locally entrenched banks. Where states were centralized, on the contrary, large banks were not constrained by local political authorities, and thus replaced local banks in the business of deposit collection, which gave them a solid financial backbone. Some banks went on to specialize in purely commercial activities; others, in investment banking.

Recent studies of the everyday politics of money, such as Seabrooke (2006) and Langley (2008), argue more radically that financial power is located outside financial markets altogether, since the stability of money rests on the depth of the banking system, and thus on countless voluntary decisions by nonelite actors to entrust their savings to banks. These scholars identify the crucial financial cleavage not in the opposition between financial systems that are oriented toward stock markets, in contrast to those where large banks dominate; rather, they look at the conflict that emerges between peripheral, local banks, and centralizing financial structures, both "center banks" (banks that operate in large financial centers) and the financial markets in which they do business.

This new literature, in short, states that the organization of credit is always the outcome of relational processes and struggles among bankers. Not only do bankers monitor one another, mobilizing different kinds of constituencies to protect their advantages. Ultimately, their power is territorial, and it draws from the ability of banks to accumulate local resources and then act as intermediaries between those who have capital and those who need it. This is, the reader will remember, a conceptualization of banking I called mythical, because it treats banks as institutions of intermediation. But in the political economy of financial systems literature, this myth is somewhat secondary to the political dynamics the literature highlights, which, I believe, is an important theoretical step—namely, that the sworn enemy of bankers is the competitive market, and that bankers want to prevent its encroachment in the territories in which they monopolize financial and monetary exchange by broaching alliances with political authorities.

This perspective, in short, vindicates Schumpeter's classical argument that bankers have a central, directive role in the capitalist process, and that bankers and the money markets they control are the "headquarters" of capitalism. In the political economy view, the persistence of this role derives from political lobbying, from alliances with political officials, so as to institute barriers to the circulation of capital, either territorially, when political power is decentralized, or through specialization in distinctive financial activities, when the polity is centralized—that is, not from alliances with industrialists or other private actors (pace Gerschenkron). In this view, finally, because bankers themselves specialize in different functions, it is never really a question of whether bankers are more or less central to finance; the real issue is, what kinds of bankers undertake what kinds of operations, and with what consequences.[1]

There is much to be gained from this perspective. Yet the central mechanism of political lobbying works only insofar as one makes strong assumptions about the rationality of the actors involved, a move that inevitably runs into the dilemma of collective action I discussed above. Historically, for instance, the argument about the centrality of political lobbying works only if local politicians are both invested in their authority and immune to potential demands from their constituencies for centralization. Local elites, then, are simply assumed to be able to resist the ideological appeal that certain central elites are often able to mobilize in support of their centralizing ambitions. Verdier (2003: 61) thus admits that his model cannot explain the success of Napoleon III in rallying local banks to its centralizing project. So a return to Schumpeter and the additional issues he delineates besides the alliance with political power is crucial.

Schumpeter argues that it is "authority" that, in the last instance, determines how entrepreneurs get financed. It matters little to this part of the argument that entrepreneurs are private actors, as emphasized by Schumpeter, or political ones, as Weber discusses in his typology of political capitalism. The point here is that borrowers will need to persuade the "headquarters of capitalism" of the value of their propositions. They will have to express confidence and conviction in what they have to offer. Some of them will adopt a language of soundness, predictability, and rigor to do so. Others, by contrast, will emphasize the innovative potential of their financial projects. Different borrowers will thus appeal to different types of bankers, with different visions of how credit should be organized, and, as a result, with different and potentially contradictory interests. It is from an analytical understanding of these potential rivalries and contradictions that our theory must begin. The importance of the move proposed by the political economy of financial systems, then—that we should shift attention away from banker-customer relations and play up banker-state officer relations instead—is, in this light, somewhat exaggerated.

Notes

Primary Sources

The primary, nonpublished sources consulted for Chapters 4 and 6 include the following.

For Chapter 4:

Atkinson, Edward. 1894. Letter of Edward Atkinson to R. H. Edmonds, Esq (April 16). Carton 23. SH 15LP B. Vol. 51. Massachusetts Historical Society, Boston, MA.

Lamont, Thomas. 1923. The Banker and His Function To-day. 143–4 Chicago Trust Company, September 21, 1923. Thomas W. Lamont Papers. Baker Library. Harvard Business School, Cambridge MA.

Lee, Higginson, & Co. Papers, Box XII 10 B. Baker Library, Harvard Business School.

Vanderlip, Frank Arthur. Papers. Correspondence and Business Papers Chiefly Related to Money and Banking, 1890–1937. Parts A-B. Columbia University Rare Book and Manuscript Library, New York City.

For Chapter 6:

Quotations from Giuseppe Marchiori and Bonaldo Stringher:

Comunicazioni del Direttore Generale. Fondo Banca D'Italia, Sottofondo Verbali Consiglio Superiore. Archivio Storico della Banca d'Italia, Rome, Italy.

Verbali delle Adunanze Generali degli Azionisti. Archivio Storico della Banca d'Italia, Rome, Italy.

For the correspondence between Otto Joel and Bonaldo Stringher:

Carte Stringher, Pratiche, N. Corda 13, Fasc. 1 and following. Archivio Storico Banca d'Italia.

Carte Personali e Familiari dell'Amm. Del. Otto Joel (1872–1925). PJ Cartelle 2–3, Bonaldo Stringher, 1893–1903. Archivio Storico della Banca Commerciale Italiana, Milan, Italy.

Introduction

1. Power and prestige are of course extremely complex and controversial concepts, but here I am concerned with the ways they relate to each other rather than with exhaustive definitions that attempt to parse out the distinctive characteristics of each. In this endeavor, I take a cue from "closure theory," the set of analytical concepts that systematizes Weber's notion of "status-groups" (Collins 1979b, 1986; Murphy 1984; Tilly 1998; Barnes 1992). One may immediately object that, because there is enormous variation in the value of assets denominated in the same instrument, focusing on the prestige of, say, a bond relative to the prestige of a stock does not help illuminate the issue of how an individual asset is valued. But as sociologist Ezra Zuckerman has shown, classificatory distinctions determine value within classes of assets as well, as they affect the volume and volatility of trade: "[M]arkets seem to equilibrate around a common understanding—or at least a relatively narrow range of understanding—of a stock's value. This implies a socio-cognitive process by which market participants make sense of stocks . . . . [A] key mechanism [are] classificatory structures that group assets deemed comparable to one another and distinguish them from unlike assets" (Zuckerman 2004: 410). For Zuckerman (2012), however, there is an intrinsic value to assets (a benchmark below which the price of an asset becomes undervalued), whereas what I argue here is that the question is not whether the instrument reflects the "true" value of what it buys, but whether relevant actors "agree" on how prestigious it is—with the source of the agreement being not a general cognitive process of classification but the power dynamics through which the prestige of a financial instrument is generated.

2. Weber, to be sure, wrote important passages that emphasize the centrality of conflict to economic exchange. For instance, in his description of the nature of money (Weber 1978: 79): "[M]oney can never be a harmless 'voucher' or a purely nominal unit of accounting as long as it *is* money. Its valuation is always in very complex ways dependent on its scarcity or, in the case of inflation, on its overabundance." Further (92–93): "In a market economy every form of rational calculation, especially of capital accounting, is oriented to expectations of prices and their changes as they are determined by the conflicts of interests in bargaining and competition and the resolution of these conflicts." Interests and the conflicts they generate, in this formulation, are however antecedents of money, rather than outcomes of the way credit is organized.

3. This problem has preoccupied both social movement theorists (Snow, Zurcher, and Ekland-Olson 1980; Gould 1993) and political and economic sociologists (Collins 1979b; Parkin 1983; Murphy 1984; H. C. White 2002; Tilly 1998), but was in fact formulated quite early in economics itself (Olson 1965). The realization that there was no inherent, automatic mechanism that translated self-interest into action that entailed collective benefits—the realization, that is, that markets were hardly "civilizing" (Hirschman 1982)—had devastating theoretical consequences for economics: it reduced action in markets to a neo-Hobbesian game of "nasty, brutish, and short" relations (Granovetter 2002: 39), and, most important, to a game played by individual, atomized actors (Granovetter 1985). Concerns with collective action in markets, let alone organized conflict, simply disappeared, as markets were increasingly conceptualized as the polar opposite of organization

(O. E. Williamson 1975). Unsurprisingly, then, it was in economic sociology—the field most self-consciously built in opposition to neoclassical economics—that the problem of collective action began receiving the most sustained attention (Fligstein 1990, 1996, 2001a; Fligstein and McAdam 2011; Roy 1997; Perrow 2002).

4. To be sure, this is a simplification of the debates now occurring within economic sociology. The aspects of collective action that I emphasize in this book can be described as largely belonging to the neo-Weberian tradition, but I make no claim that this is the only tradition available. Moreover, the language of "collective action" has now given way to more explicitly "relational" frameworks, where the problem of action in general is not as central because these perspectives do not share the assumption that motivates analytical focus on it (that individuals are the appropriate unit of analysis). Yet we shall see that with money, a quintessentially portable token, and with some forms of negotiable credit as well, the individual/collective dimension remains a useful part of the analysis.

5. Others emphasize the importance, even within democratic systems, of systems of controls, such as federalist constitutions, over central authority (see, esp., Weingast 1995; and Stasavage 2002 for a focus on partisan politics). In this logic, just as strong institutions can be used to protect private property, by the same token, they can also be used to confiscate it. But in federal countries, where the political system is decentralized and thus authority is diffused across different political levels, the power of the central government will be balanced against and checked by the power of subnational units, and, vice versa, with the result that no single authority will be able to stifle markets.

Chapter 1

1. The analogy may seem somewhat flawed, as money is subject to inflation, whereas the metric system is not. Yet, first, it serves to point attention to money's primary aspect as a unit of value. Second, units of measurement have their politics as well, especially clear in the early modern state's attempt to survey landed property and tax it appropriately (Porter 1996).

2. Modern money-of-account emerged in a state of political fragmentation, when, in the high Middle Ages, Western Europe was stabilized by a shared normative commitment to Christianity (Ingham 1999; Michael Mann 1993). These two conditions—fragmentation and peace—allowed for the development of international merchant networks: money, even though it ultimately originated as credit between merchants and customers, became a means of payment within those networks because it no longer symbolized directly the debt that two specific parties had incurred with each other. It was depersonalized, and could be transferred and used as a means of settlement (the merchant networks would physically come together in the medieval fairs to balance their books). In short, money thus acquired its first formal property as an abstract credit-debt relation no longer attached to a specific transaction (Braudel 1977). But money had not fully evolved into a full and viable money-of-account (Ingham 2004). It took a second, decisive event, to complete its institutional development: the Glorious Revolution in England. The compromise that ended the revolution was the settlement between London's moneyed merchants and the sovereign, guaranteed by a shared system of representation and sovereignty under

the formula "King in Parliament" (North and Weingast 1989). The merchants funded the debt of the sovereign; they got in return a charter for a bank (the Bank of England) that was invested with the management of the debt and could use it as the basis for the extension of further credit (Ingham 1984). The private debt of the king thus became the public debt of the state, a transformation that has characterized all subsequent attempts to institutionalize money by modern state-makers (ibid.). Money became a "creature of the state," in Lerner's apt phrase (1947), which meant more specifically, it became the debt that private citizens have toward state authorities, which they can settle by paying taxes in the currency that the state provides to them (Bell 2001; Wray 1999).

3. A critical literature that goes by the rubric of power elite theory has made several crucial contributions to a fuller understanding of the role of banks in the capitalist process (Mills 1956; Domhoff 1967; Mintz and Schwartz 1985; Mizruchi 1982). Partly drawing from the writing on finance capital by classic Marxist authors such as Lenin and Hilferding, power elite theorists have emphasized the controlling role banks exercise over firms by virtue of their access to capital. Yet these theories have not probed the sociological determinants of money itself—and so their empirical findings on the variable strength of banking hegemony in the capitalist system have remained somewhat undertheorized (Mizruchi 2004).

4. A neoliberal theory broadly in favor of banking liberalization emerged, prior to the 2007–8 financial crisis, to praise the advantages of free financial markets and even large banking institutions. For an example of the former, in a celebratory, influential, if somewhat ill-timed argument about the centrality of free financial markets (and the desirability thereof) to capitalism, Rajan and Zingales (2004) thus assert that finance is the primary vehicle for the spreading of economic opportunities—even the reduction of poverty (money and credit are fungible, their allocation hindered only by noneconomic variables); but they add that financial markets should be liberalized so as to counteract the tendency of vested interests and incumbents to monopolize access to market advantages and opportunities ("bad" bankers should be prevented from infringing on the activities of "good" bankers). Banking should be freed from the twin "tyrannies" of "collateral" and "connections": namely, the widespread reliance of creditors on demonstrated, past ability to repay on the part of the borrower (rather than the intrinsic value of what she intends to do with the money), and their equally common reliance on personal connections as a way to guarantee repayments. For an example of neoliberal analyses in favor of large banks: writing on the eve of the 1999 deregulatory changes that liberalized U.S. banking, Calomiris (1995) argued that financial systems dominated by big, nonspecialist banks were the natural outcome of deregulated systems, given the informational advantages that accrue to large, territorially diffuse institutions; that in countries like the United States, banks remained fragmented because of political suspicion against centralized financial systems (Roe 1994), and not because of the superiority of alternative financial arrangements; and that this fragmented credit system came at the detriment of industry, as large banks would have provided credit to firms and entrepreneurs at a lower cost. "Financial investment is fundamentally a problem of coordination. Savers and investors need a low-cost means to transact" (Calomiris 1995: 260; see also the classic Diamond

1984; also DeLong 1991; Ramirez and DeLong 2001). And big banks could do what stock markets could not—namely, gather information about their clients more efficiently and, over time, adapt their offer of credit to their specific financing needs.

5. One influential instance is the burgeoning "varieties of capitalism" literature, one that, in its sophisticated attempt to map out different models of capitalism, poses mechanisms of coordination between firms and governments to be neutrally transmitted through credit policies, without paying attention to those who materially implement those credit policies themselves—the bankers. This "varieties of capitalism literature" maps systematic differences in countries' institutional practices in several realms, such as welfare provisions, labor markets, corporate governance, interfirm relations, and financial markets; it attributes such differences to the particular ways that, historically, states and markets have interacted with each other in the context of specific national economies; and finally, it rejects the case for the superiority of any one system over others, because economic arrangements cannot be separated from the institutional context in which they develop (Berger 1983; Berger and Dore 1996; Hall and Soskice 2001). In this perspective, ultimately, it is specifically the problem of *coordination* that institutions solve, and so the function that institutions serve also explains their durability. In the specific case of finance, then, according to this framework, financial markets differ to the extent that they allocate capital on the basis of profitability, as in *liberal market* economies where labor markets are flexible and so firms can easily lay off workers when the search for profits requires them to; or on the basis of market-share, as in *coordinated market* economies where firms are less free to cut costs during downturns but also hire in times of expansion, and thereby defend their current market position at the expense of short-term profitability. Moreover, there are no general prescriptions about "good" or "bad" ways of allocating credit and assessing creditworthiness: such valuations can be made only within the context of specific national economies. Yet, within national contexts, the yardstick is that of coordination. And so the assumptions that the nature of money is functional and fungible, that money serves as a neutral medium within which resources can be mobilized efficiently, and that the criteria through which money is mobilized similarly respond to institutional pressures for coordination, all remain foundational to this literature.

6. Neoclassical economists, by contrast, think of money exclusively in terms of demand and supply, and they also have elaborate theories about the effects of imbalances between the sphere of money and the sphere of commodities—imbalances they blame for causing inflation. In fact, as Schumpeter (1994: 264) perceptively realized, neoclassical theorists are "real" analysts: they "proceed from the principle that all essential phenomena of economic life are capable of being described in terms of goods and services. . . . [So] long as it functions normally, [money] does not affect the economic process, which behaves in the same way as it would in a barter system." Money is thus conceptualized as a "garb" or "veil," he continues, relevant only when it fails. Building on heterodox approaches to money both in economics and sociology, however, here I question this conceptualization of money as derivative of "real" economic activities. There are several, and often mutually incompatible, ways to make this point (Smithin 1994; B. J. Moore

1988; Wray 1999; Wray and Bell 2004). Generally speaking, heterodox theorists think of money as *endogenous to the economic process* and thus as "real" as the goods and services it finances. By endogeneity, heterodox writers roughly mean that money is *created* in the course of financing economic activities: more specifically, they argue that money is but a form of credit; and that money as credit is created by bankers in the course of granting loans to those who demand them. In more technical terms, heterodox economists propose a *balance sheet approach* to money, because this is what the act of granting loans (marking the money *due* by the borrower to the bank as an asset, and the deposit account in which the loan is granted to the borrower as a liability) empirically looks like in the books of the lending bank (Bell 2001). Endogeneity in this case, then, means introducing "the element of money on the very ground floor of our analytical structure. [. . .] Money prices, money incomes, and saving and investment decisions bearing on these money incomes . . . acquire a life and importance of their own, and it has to be recognized that essential features of the capitalist process may depend upon the 'veil' and that the 'face behind it' is incomplete without it" (Schumpeter 1994: 265). Money truly has a life and importance of its own, to paraphrase Schumpeter, because it commodifies and circulates prestige—a prestige that is analytically independent from command over physical property or consumption experiences. Empirically, this is an uncontroversial claim. So multimillionaires continue working in the late hours of the night when it is clear that the marginal revenue they can gain from additional work does not secure them any significant improvement in their consumption experiences. This should alert us to the fact that the driver of financial speculation may not be related to the sphere of consumption at all. More abstractly, one should note that the value of any assets that allegedly back a financial instrument is itself expressed in money—which is to say that there is no underlying value intrinsic to commodities that can in turn give value to monetary assets.

7. An important reflection on the complexities that characterize the drawing of public and private boundaries in finance is Preda (2009).

8. Or, to use slightly different language, the social mechanisms that connect cause to effect (Gross 2009). In this respect, then, my analytical strategy is different from that of Dodd (2006).

9. See, esp., Latour (1987) for the concept of the "black box."

Chapter 2

1. To be sure, the signal that the currency conveys may be rather weak, this being the case with national currencies, possession of which is at most a sign of connection to a national authority through, for instance, citizenship. But this is not an entirely satisfactory example: as the new scholarship on money highlights (see, for example, Cohen 2006), global financial markets and the emergence of nonstate currencies such as corporate "money" have significantly attenuated the territorial identification implied by national currencies. And even though Helleiner (2003) emphasizes how central territorial money was to the constitution of the modern nation-state, prestate forms of money (such as international bills of exchange) were in fact instruments specifically devised to exceed the territorial control of the prince (Hicks 1969; Braudel 1977). This suggests the limited

applicability of a state-centered framework to an understanding of money in general.

2. The concept of field derives of course from Bourdieu's sociology, and has recently been fully integrated into economic sociology (in which Bourdieu developed an interest only late in life) precisely to indicate the social arenas that actors see as relevant to their practices—be they organizations mimicking the formal properties of other organizations to channel their legitimacy (DiMaggio and Powell 1983); firms monitoring potential competitors in a given market so as to find a Schumpeterian niche that shields them from competition (H. C. White 2002); or cultural and intellectual producers representing a vanguard against an established tradition, which they try to subvert so as to gain the attention of the field (Bourdieu 1984; Collins 2004).

3. In a powerful framework that borrows from Durkheim's sociology of religion, Aglietta and Orléan (1984) make a theoretical distinction between "public money" (backed by a central authority) and fragmented money (issued by private actors). Their argument is that, just as cohesive social groups—namely, groups held together by strong rituals—celebrate their unity and solidarity through the worship of one common god, so cohesive banking systems celebrate their unity and solidarity by worshiping at the altar of relatively unified and mutually consistent moneys and financial instruments, and by giving "public money" ultimate recognition. The financial activities of cohesive banking systems get focused on the exchange of a limited set of instruments, with a clear understanding of how they fit within a financial hierarchy, and of which instrument, normally government debt (public money), is at the very top of it (Bell 2001; Aglietta and Orléan 1984). This analogy between the issue of financial instruments and religion is powerful because it allows us to identify a mechanism (in fact, a cultural mechanism) through which the cohesion of the banking system is reproduced over time, just as, with religion, the cohesion of human groups is reproduced. To be sure, Aglietta and Orléan do not identify the mechanism within finance. But it is only a short step to do so: the mechanism is the articulation of sound banking principles.

4. And just as looser social groups, whose rituals are weakly shared and thus weakly binding, tend to worship multiple gods, so do less cohesive banking systems, where bankers worship at a polytheistic altar. In less cohesive, wildcat banking systems, that is, financial instruments proliferate. Wildcat bankers approximate the private end of the analytical continuum devised by Aglietta and Orléan (1984).

5. This may be one reason why, for instance, hedge fund managers tend to be outsiders to financial elites (Mallaby 2010; Lewis 2010): since their lifestyle and financial approach set them apart from other financial players, the lack of previous socialization into finance may in fact allow them to develop a culture specific to the hedge fund they manage, thereby tightening the identity of the status group and helping differentiate it from that of other financial circuits. Braudel himself recognized this dynamic, as he argued that capitalism (by which he meant finance) should never be confused with markets. But unlike Schumpeter, Braudel did not make sufficiently fine-grained distinctions within the financial class. Schumpeter's typology, then, enriches and deepens Braudel's analysis.

6. As Collins (1990: 111) puts it, this may be a structural aspect of markets: Markets

for a particular item of exchange tend to give rise to superordinate markets trading upon the terms of trade themselves. Future and long-distance exchanges become commodities that can be traded in their own market. Superordinate markets may be pyramided upon one another. Money, debts, mortgages, stock ownership, rights of purchase, licensing, and other media of exchange can become objects of superordinate media traded in yet further markets. Wildcats are the actors who make such financial pyramids possible.

7. This is also consistent with the Polanyian (Polanyi 1944/2001) point that free markets are political creations that are, in the long run, unsustainable because they attack not only the privileges of elites but also the means of livelihood of the general population.

8. As Weber (1981) most notably emphasized, one of the conditions that made possible the emergence of "rationalized" capitalism in general were state bureaucracies, because they made economic activities more calculable and predictable through the attendant spread of uniform laws and uniform practices of accounting for value. State debt had similar effects because, in order to become accepted as a safe, liquid asset that financial elites would hold, it had to come with credible guarantees about whether the state would finance it in the long run. North and Weingast (1989) famously show how this process went hand in hand with the creation of democratic institutions in the British case, and Ingham (1984) adds that a further political development served to strengthen British capitalism, when international merchant elites defeated their speculative opponents by supporting the rationalization of state finances—no longer treating the English state as a source of speculative profits, but tailoring its fiscal and monetary policies to the creation of a stable international monetary system, backed by a strong sterling pound, an independent treasury, and a technically prestigious Bank of England.

9. Historically, states would issue "too much" debt when they explicitly wanted to generate additional financial operations, often to benefit a creditor elite on whom the state was dependent for its financial health. In a famous discussion, Marx (1921: 827) points out that, with government debt, bankers built financial pyramids through which they centralized resources. Because the debt was backed by the authority of the state, it was in fact safer than private investments; but because it was negotiable, it served as a seed for new financial transactions. While Marx restricts his discussion to the Bank of England, this is not peculiar to the British experience. A similar process, for instance, characterized the evolution of the modern business corporation in the United States, which went from an organization oriented toward public service, and thus chartered by state legislatures and financed through public money (a "quasi-government agency," Roy 1997: 2), to a privately held, publicly traded company. In the United States, just as in Britain, the initial injection of public money into private coffers encouraged the development of deeper and broader capital markets. In fact, in both the U.S. and British cases, the assumption that there was a private capital market to begin with, one into which the state could inject money, is quite anachronistic: it is more correct to say that public debt helped constituted private financial circuits.

Chapter 3

1. Thus Ingham (2004) argues that capitalist banks, the only institutions capable of creating credit-money, while they certainly emerged from the international mercantile networks of the Middle Ages, had to overcome the limits inherent to those networks. This entailed a political alliance with the state that set them apart from other lending organizations and institutions.

2. Max Weber, of course, picked up on this, but see Muldrew (1998) for an excellent critique.

3. The relatively low levels of geographic mobility, high levels of cultural homogeneity, and local focus of production and exchange of the early eighteenth century could support what Zucker (1986) calls "process-based trust," the kind of trust that arises in close-knit communities whose members share similar "background expectations" as to what signals mean, what stock of common knowledge each member is likely to draw from, and what kinds of interests and desires each is likely to express. See, however, Howe (2007) and John (1998) for important arguments about the complexity of social and economic transactions in early America, as well as contra arguments such as Sellers's (1994), that date a "market revolution" only in the 1830s.

4. Even the spread of such apparently neutral means of assessing reputations and establishing trust was not met with favor and consensus. One example from mercantile credit should suffice. Complaining about what he called the "Mercantile Inquisition" carried out by a specialized mercantile credit assessment agency, an editorialist (Anon 1853) characteristically wrote in the *Merchant's Magazine:*

> The ostensible purpose of the agency was to provide a place of reference, at which merchants and others could readily learn the true character and standing of all traders, manufacturers, &c. . . . who, from convenience or want of capital, might be disposed to ask for credit on merchandise. This, at the outset, looks fair enough: and, under a mutual arrangement between debtor and creditor, might be rendered mutually beneficial to all parties. On the other hand, let the originator of the system, or any of his worthy accomplices, fill a page of one of their immense folios about a man's habits, his peculiarities, his possessions, all of which go in to make up a man's business character, and thus become the basis of credit—and these gathered piecemeal from an unreliable source, by an irresponsible agent, and the matter assumes an appearance of very serious importance. It becomes a matter of life or death to the subject of the inquisitorial process, and the whole proceeding bears upon its face the most diabolical Jesuitism that has ever cursed the world.

To complicate matters, the first mercantile rating agency, Lewis Tappan & C., was funded and managed by two prominent abolitionists, Arthur and Lewis Tappan, a fact that caused much hostility in the South (Wyatt-Brown 1966). The legitimacy of new ways of assessing the creditworthiness of debtors was, in general, highly contested. Yet over time, the legitimacy of these credit reporting agencies became more and more secure.

5. Hammond shows that Alexander Hamilton, the most prominent proponent of a national credit system, was himself rather ambiguous on this point. On the one hand,

he thought that the specie deposited in a bank "much oftener changes proprietors than place," thus suggesting that specie in fact belonged to the depositor. On the other hand, he also held the much more modern view that "every loan which a bank makes is in the first instance a credit on its books in favor of the borrower and that, unless withdrawn in specie, it remains a liability of the bank till the loan is repaid" (1957: 138).

6. Horwitz goes on to argue: "The change in the conception of the corporation marks one of the fundamental transitions from the legal assumptions of the eighteenth century to those of the nineteenth. The archetypal American corporation of the eighteenth century is the municipality, a public body charged with carrying out public functions; in the nineteenth century it is the modem business corporation, organized to pursue private ends for individual gain" (Horwitz 1979: 111–12). A large debate exists on this issue, of which John (1997) is an outstanding, critical review.

7. The literature on this issue is very large. The classic works by Hammond (1957) and Redlich (1968) remain very useful, as does Temin (1969). See also Silbey (1994) and, esp., Howe (2007) for a recent synthesis that goes beyond the economic aspects of the Jacksonians.

8. Broadly speaking, Southern states and the West (California in particular) allowed the institution of branch-banking—that is, they allowed banks to open several offices—whereas Northern states did not, forcing each bank to operate only out of its headquarters, so to speak.

9. Some of the classic works in the field, as they make it clear in their very titles, attribute this to the intimate relationship between banking and politics: Bray Hammond's (1957) *Banks and Politics in America: From the Revolution to the Civil War* is a clear example. Fritz Redlich's *The Molding of American Banking: Men and Ideas* (1968), less explicit in its title, similarly focused on the leadership of bankers in facilitating the rise of modern business. Others, such as White's work on the regulation of U.S. banking (1983), Rockoff's analysis of free banking, or Timberlake's masterful legislative history of U.S. monetary policy (1993), explicitly analyze the effects of politics on the organization of the banking system. These works are extremely valuable, and indeed, they constitute the foundation on which I build my own argument. But they are all premised on the myth of creditworthiness, buttressed by the additional assumption that with economic growth or development more generally, markets spontaneously develop effective ways of assessing creditworthiness. These works do not engage with the problem of creditworthiness in its own terms. They also conceptualize banking and politics as opposite spheres with mutually incompatible dynamics.

10. For comparative purposes, note that to the $1.96 (current) per capita extracted by the federal government in 1800, corresponded 42 cents extracted by state governments. In the 1830s, the federal government would extract more tax than local administration ($1.93 vs. $1.23 p.c., with state governments lagging at 88 cents). But in the 1890s, local level extraction would surpass federal revenue: $8.83 vs. $6.42, with state governments at $2.43. Overall, throughout the nineteenth century, the overall size of government revenue increased from about 4 percent to about 7 percent of GDP. See Wallis (2000) for additional data.

11. Economic historians will likely object to this characterization, for the term "wildcat" emerges in this period in the United States to refer to quite a different typology of banker. But here I am appropriating Schumpeter's use of the term, which lends it more generality.

12. The Bank of Virginia, chartered in 1804, was the blueprint for the Southern system. As a compromise between "merchants and planters clamoring for credit and Jeffersonian Republicans opposed to any grant of corporate privilege," it was large, and the state owned one-fifth of its shares, reserving the right to appoint one-fifth of its directors. Bodenhorn, to be sure, emphasizes that the bank was chartered upon consultation with various local economic interests, thus suggesting that, even in Virginia, there was some degree of democratic consultation. Yet the motivation behind such consultations did not seem to be the promotion of democratic exchange per se: rather, the consultations were instrumental to a project that was meant ultimately to protect the institution of slavery.

13. This is not to say, of course, that slavery did not impact relations among whites in other arenas, such as for instance relations in public spaces or kinship relations (Wyatt-Brown 2007).

14. In Gordon Wood's assessment of the early republic, for instance, most "ordinary Americans . . . came out of the war committed more than ever before to the future and the pursuit of happiness. . . . America did not become a prosperous, scrambling, money-making society because a few leaders like Hamilton created a bank . . . . America developed the way it did because hundreds of thousands of ordinary people began working harder than ever before to make money and 'get ahead.' No constitution, no institution, could have created or restrained these popular energies" (1987: 639).

Chapter 4

1. As Bensel (2000) perceptively recognizes, the "unregulated market for labor and production" along with the gold standard became the two pillars (with tariff protection being the third) on which economic development came to rest in the late nineteenth century, because each of them was a strategy forced upon, but also exploited by, the governing Republican Party to maintain power in a fragmented polity. See also Sanders (1999) for the political impact of territorial and social heterogeneity on the makeup of the American state.

2. This was not a novel idea: the Bank of England had been created in 1694 precisely for the purposes of funding the debt England had issued during the Glorious Revolution. In the U.S. case, just as had happened in England some 180 years earlier, the creation of a central bank led in turn to the creation of a market for its securities, which were, indirectly, government securities; and the marketing of government debt went on to create a larger market for private securities. This served to finance the capital of new banks. So the market for securities was, indirectly, a vehicle for private credit (see, esp., Sylla 1998, 1969; and, more generally, Sylla, Richard Tilly, and Tortella 1999).

3. Lamoreaux (1994: 42) claims that these policies "implicitly accepted the banking system as a given and aimed to extend the state's regulatory authority over it. Because these policies seemed to contradict the laissez-faire trust of their campaign against state-

created banks, they have given historians a great deal of difficulty. In actuality, however, the one set of proposals was simply the flip side of the other."

4. "The specific meaning of free banking is that contained in the landmark Free Banking Law enacted by New York State in 1838. This law allowed 'any person or association of persons' to form a bank of discount, deposit, and circulation. The capital stock of the bank had to be at least $100,000, and it had to maintain a specie reserve of 12.5 percent against its note circulation. The bank's notes had to be secured by bond securities of the United States or New York State and mortgages on land in the state. The law also stated that 'no shareholder of any such association shall be liable in his individual capacity for any contract, debt or engagement of such association,' which meant that the New York free banks were in fact limited liability corporations" (Sylla 1985: 107). Schumpeter's articulation of the concept of "wildcat banking," as we saw in the introduction, generalizes from the Jacksonian experience.

5. This point reveals how Sylla's interpretation of free banking (see, for example, 1985: 104), who equates it with a move "of democratic equity, of transforming the privileges of the few into the rights of all," is based on too restrictive a notion of democracy.

6. Hammond (1957: 329) adds: "Notwithstanding their language, therefore, the Jacksonians' destruction of the Bank of the United States was in no sense a blow at capitalism or property or the 'money power.' It was a blow at an older set of capitalists by a newer, more numerous set. It was incident to the democratization of business, the diffusion of enterprise among the mass of people, and the transfer of economic primacy from an old and conservative merchant class to a newer, more aggressive, and more numerous body of businessmen and speculators of all sorts." While Hammond does not emphasize the partisan dimension of this shift, his characterization is quite evocative and, in many ways, still accurate, even though his generalization—"The Jacksonian revolution was a consequence of the Industrial revolution and of a farm-born people's realization that now anyone in America could get rich" (328)—is regrettably functionalist.

7. Hammond (1957: 572) is much quoted and criticized for this passage, which nonetheless captures an important aspect of free banking: "The law required that anyone who set up a bank comply with certain conditions; and, those conditions being met, the appropriate administrative authority had simply to record the fact and the issuance of a charter. Though the law made any one 'free' to engage in banking, the freedom was qualified to the extent that one must have the necessary money to start and must meet certain other formalities. The result was that it might be found somewhat harder than to become a brick-layer, but not much."

8. Very usefully, the full address is available in the Media Archive of the Miller Center of the University of Virginia. See http: //millercenter.org/scripps/archive/speeches/detail/3644.

9. Accompanied by a third policy—the return to specie-based currency, which Jackson facilitated by demanding payment for federal land in coin—Jacksonian banking maneuvers precipitated a global financial crisis. Peter Temin (1969) famously argued that Jacksonian policies should not be blamed for the credit bubble of the late 1830s and the subsequent 1840s depression. The orthodox story claims that, when Jackson withdrew

government deposits and put them with country banks, the latter acted as if they had an increase in reserves, hence stretched out credit. The credit bubble soon exploded, with two crises in 1837 and 1839, and a severe depression in the early 1840s. Temin, however, maintains that the initial round of inflation was caused by specie inflow from Britain, given that the Second Bank had contracted the money supply following the removal of government deposits thus raising the interest rate and making investment from abroad profitable. "The mechanism was simple: As banks attempted to protect themselves by decreasing their liabilities, credit became hard to obtain. English capital flowed in to fill the void, creating an excess supply of foreign exchange and causing its price to fall. When the price of foreign exchange fell far enough, specie was imported, enabling the banks to strengthen their position by increasing their reserves instead of decreasing their liabilities" (67). Recent research, however, disputes Temin's absolution of Jackson's policies and points to the reserve drain created by his specie-circular and his abolition of the federal charter of the SBUS in facilitating the panic (Rousseau 2002; Knodell 2006).

10. This section draws from Polillo (2011).

11. This was a major break with economic orthodoxy, since in the nineteenth century adherence to the gold standard, which required that a national currency be convertible into specie upon demand, was an objective widely shared by governments seeking foreign investment and international trade (Eichengreen 1996).

12. In this respect, even though debt issue and alliances with powerful capitalists were political strategies that more centralized countries (such as Napoleonic France) had repeatedly resorted to themselves when faced with imminent war, the United States differed because of the particular way that resources were mobilized. The decision of the Union to impose its bonds as collateral on the issue of banknotes, and to enact a comprehensive set of banking laws that went on to constitute the National Banking System, set the United States apart from other countries. Thus, in the U.S., national banking was "adopted primarily because of fiscal reasons" (E. White 1983: 11).

13. For a historical account of U.S. patronage politics, see Shefter (1994). For evidence of financial elite criticism of Treasury policies, see Bensel (1990), esp. 270–80.

14. This uneasiness on the part of bankers to rely on the government to make the monetary system more stable continued well beyond the immediate postbellum period. For instance, New York banker Frank Vanderlip would write to Senator Aldrich on January 11, 1908: "The party in power, as well as the Secretary of the Treasury, will be exposed to criticism as long as we look to Washington, as we do now, for assistance from the United States Treasury in times of monetary stringency. Furthermore, speculative interest would always be tempted to influence officials, which might lead to corrupt political as well as business methods."

15. Frank Vanderlip, in the letter to Senator Aldrich I cited above (dated January 11, 1908), used the same language to criticize the measure: "As to the matter of Government guaranteeing deposits, let me say most emphatically, that this would be most decidedly destructive to private initiative and personal responsibility; and would impair the independence and character of Bank officials. Moreover, it would be a long step toward socialistic and paternal government." As Sanders (1999: esp. 233–34) highlights, opposition to

federal insurance on deposits cannot be reduced to conflicts among bankers, as the policy was part of a larger set of reforms supported by the agrarian movement through its influence on the Democratic Party. But here I wish simply to focus on the language through which bankers opposed the measure—a language that reflected as much a concern with the potentially larger role of government that reformers advocated, as it did a concern with the internal divisions within banking that, in the eyes of conservative bankers, made reforms destabilizing.

16. For more general accounts about the cleavages and conflicts characterizing business and financial factions in the postbellum United States, see especially Wiebe 1962 and West 1977.

17. Vanderlip had several schemes in mind to serve this purpose. For instance, he proposed the institution of a trust company affiliated with City Bank. The bank would receive deposits at interest, "competing more or less with the regular savings institutions but covering a very much wider field and offering more flexible arrangements to depositors. It would further embrace the development of a small commercial account business, this being the part of the business that would be particularly along the lines of the business of the Bank of France." Vanderlip also wanted it to undertake "banking by mail," and to establish branches throughout the city while also concentrating on the bank-starved community of the East Side of New York City. The idea was to turn it "into a great people's bank, designed to develop a business somewhat similar in character to the great detailed commercial business of the Bank of France" (Vanderlip 1907, May 10). This strategy of diversification included an expansion into those local areas where saving banks and other kinds of institutions were dominant. The reference to the Bank of France was very apposite: Napoleon's Banque de France, operating in a centralized state, allied itself with peripheral, local banks in order to contain the power of money-center, private bankers at least until the late 1890s (Verdier 2003: 62). But the perceived need for change ran deeper:

> I never really felt more strongly the possibilities that lie in the City Bank for development. But we are not developing . . . . The Bank lacks the alert business men among its officers; the sort of men who look at things from a business point of view, rather than from the restricted horizon of a grown-up clerk who has never taken any part himself in any business affair. (Vanderlip 1907, March 7)

18. In fact, there was some admiration on the part of New York bankers for the conservative practices of the Midwest. Returning from a visit at Chicago National Bank, Vanderlip reported his enthusiasm at the way business was conducted there:

> I went with considerable detail into Mr. Forgan's plan for the subdivision of work. The more I see of it, the better I am impressed. . . . He has selected a man who comes between the work of the officers and the President. This man examines every loan that is made in the light of all the information which there is on file. He never meets any person connected with a loan, and in fact never has any occasion to use any of his time with the public. His entire time is given up to a cold blooded study of each transaction in the light of such information as is on file. If, for any reason, he criticizes

a loan, the officer who made it is called upon to place on file any further information which he may have, and, if that information does not demonstrate the wisdom of the loan, the matter then comes to Mr. Forgan's attention. In this way, the President is kept in touch with every transaction against which any criticism whatever can be raised . . . . Mr. Forgan says the officers are all enthusiastic about the plan, and that one of its greatest advantages is that it has done away with any possible round for jealousies, because it has clearly outlined the field of action for each man, and he is in no way interfered with by anyone else, nor allowed to interfere with anyone else's work (Vanderlip 1905, March 9).

19. Aldrich was also responsible for organizing a massive research project headed by the National Monetary Commission that instructed a group of scholars to study and report on the banking systems of several nations (Canada, Mexico, Russia, Italy, Britain, and Germany among them), as well as on several aspects of the U.S. banking system (Livingston 1986: 188–214).

20. Historian West (1977) argues, similarly, that such optimistic faith in the self-liquidating nature of commercial assets was not shared across banking reformers. A. Piatt Andrew, Paul Warburg, and Oliver Sprague put more emphasis on the creation of a discounting agency that would create a market for commercial assets, with the aim of weakening the importance of markets for other kinds of assets (such as call loans) that were considered more speculative. This was not entirely an argument against self-liquidating assets. It was an argument against decentralization (Mehrling 2002). In fact, economist Irving Fisher was the lone proponent of the centralization of banking who did not believe in the self-regulating properties of money and credit (a position that he crystallized in the quantity theory of money, and that was very much ahead of the times). Warburg, Piatt Andrew, and Sprague, on the other hand, believed in the "banking principle," the idea, that is, that money is a form of credit, and that more generally banks lend not because they have an excess of accumulated money but because they meet an already existing demand for credit, creating money as needed (and borrowing reserves later). While they certainly emphasized the importance of more centralized institutions that would "discount" private assets—that would, that is, extend loans to other banking institutions using private assets as collateral—so as to inject liquidity when needed, they also believed that certain assets were better suited for this function than others: assets, in particular, that were closely linked to production and commercial exchange. The differences, then, were not as marked as the similarities with the real bills approach.

21. In Warburg's words (in Seligman 1908: 135), "Outside of the note-issuing banks the only European banks that are regulated by law as to their investments and their way of doing business are the savings banks. For all other banks there is no government supervision, no laws as to their reserves against deposits, and no restrictions as to indorsing or establishing branch banks, etc. On the contrary, accepting, discounting, and indorsing paper form the essence of Europe's banking, which is built up on a system of old, established, very important, general banks with large capital and with a network of branch offices and agencies all over the country, and in the centers with many branch offices in a single town. On the whole, this system of making large responsible banks and their

branches the custodians of the people's money is preferable to our system of allowing a few, often irresponsible, men to get together, hire some ground-floor corner, fit it up in marble and bronze, and call it a bank, with a capital of $100,000, and often less, and a corresponding surplus paid in, not earned. Small banks constitute a danger, particularly so, if they accumulate deposits which are out of proportion to their own resources."

22. Livingston's assessment (1986: 18) of the movement to create the Federal Reserve System as an instance of upper-class formation, as the "context within which a modern ruling class came of age," is thus correct in spirit, but less precise in contents. The movement's purpose was not "to provide for the capacities and requirements of a modern, corporate-industrial investment system." Rather, it was to define the grounds upon which creditworthiness was to be defined and controlled. Creditworthiness was less a way to deal with the financial uncertainties of a changing economy than it was a strategy to gain dominance and cultural and social cohesion within the banking system.

23. Of course, a choice will be possible only insofar as appropriate institutional conditions exist for new uses of the instrument, such as, for instance, active secondary markets. But the point remains that, without some circuit of money, to use Viviana Zelizer's term, within the specific boundaries of which the instrument is forced to circulate, borrowers may use the financial instruments in their possession in rather different ways than have been envisioned by their creditors.

Chapter 5

1. The Italian government attempted to benefit from the French "financial revolution" by playing off rival financial houses against each other. To the advantage of the Italian government, the Rothschilds faced the competition of emerging financial powers, such as the Péreire and the financial group of the Crédit Industriel et Commercial. But in order to safeguard their position, the Rothschilds placed the Italian bonds on the Parisian market and kept a substantial amount of them as a way to exert political pressure on the Italian state. The Italian government ended up provoking the angry reaction of James Rothschild, who went so far as to issue an ultimatum to the Italian government: Italy must disarm, focus entirely on its internal resources, and stop raising money in foreign markets:

> [If] the Government, attracted to the possibility of an easy loan, becomes an accomplice to those who attack its own credit, if in order to gain ephemeral resources it sacrifices the future of the country, if, reneging on all its obligations, it makes the serious mistake of issuing a new international loan . . . I, as the guarantor of Italian securities in France, will discontinue any new relationship with Italy . . . in that I do not want rich rentiers accusing my House of supporting with its name and credit . . . a debt which is weak and disproportionate to the strength of the State. (James de Rothschild to Horace Landau, his representative in Italy, April 25 1866; in De Cecco 1990)

Incidentally, this conservative posture won international high finance the continued antipathy of the Italian Left.

2. Cavour, the founder of the unified Italian state, was of liberal persuasion, but he

was also fully aware of the importance of banking to state power and often initiated political machinations to augment the bank's reach. As the kingdom was undergoing territorial expansion over the Italian peninsula, Cavour favored the expansion of the bank and its entrenchment in annexed territories often immediately after military occupation. In return, the bank lent money to the government on repeated occasions, while keeping its interest rates low. Economic historians highlight this behavior as economically irrational, especially since the bank expressed a preference for government securities, which it held up to the maximum limit allowed by its statute, instead of profiting from the discounting of private credit (Di Nardi 1953). On the contrary, we should not be surprised that long-term political motives trumped short-term profit-maximizing ones. The circuit of the national debt was being used for the construction of a political alliance between powerful bankers and state-makers. Thus, as Piedmont engaged in repeated wars against Austria, the banks gradually became involved in state-building activities, in an "active and continuous process of reciprocal exchanges of favors and privileges" (Fratianni and Spinelli 1997: 55).

3. "I firmly believe that a State that wishes to achieve a high degree of material prosperity, and see all the major activities carried out with its means of production, must have a large credit facility, and the example of all the largest nations proves this," argued Cavour. He admired the English model of banking, since he believed that English development was fostered by the Bank of England. He also understood that banks needed to be built on top of strong foundations, so that they could withstand crises. Crises, he thought, could be grouped in two categories: those that have a political nature, for which he believed prudence and caution to be the most important solution; and those of economic nature, determined by and in turn causing capital flows. A strong bank of issue would alleviate the severity of both types of crisis (De Mattia 1990: 12–93).

4. The report, written up on November 28, 1868, by the Parliamentary Committee on the Corso Forzoso, stated: "In no country is it less appropriate to speak of a single bank than in Italy; for in a country like Italy, business, not concentrated at all in a single center, is spread out among the various provinces of the Kingdom with few relationships and few links between them; and capital, though not lacking for a large company, by contrast, is completely unavailable to commerce and industry; and finally intellectual, civil and economic forces, have their own orbit motion, and are not drawn by gravity to a common center, as if there were an instinctive repulsion against centralization" (Corso Forzoso 1868).

5. Already in 1856, Carlo Bombrini of the Banca Nazionale had negotiated with Domenico Balduino the bailing out of the Cassa Commerciale-Credito Mobiliare of Turin, of which Balduino became director. The Credito Mobiliare and its sister institution, the Banca Sconto e Sete, became the main investment outlets of the Genoese and Piedmontese elites most directly involved in the process of national unification (Polsi 1993). The Banca Nazionale also forged a strong alliance with Pietro Bastogi of the Societa' Italiana Strade Ferrate Meridionali (a railway company). Bombrini, Balduini, and Bastogi, the "three Bs" of Italian economic development (Mori 1992), thus moved to the core of what critics called a financial oligarchy—a financial elite closely connected with political lead-

ers and invested with the task of building the infrastructure of the new Italian state, a task from which they profited handsomely (Conti 2000). Bonelli (1978), in more neutral terms, argues that in this period, elites set the foundations for the "political capitalism" that then characterized the entire postunification liberal regime.

6. Contemporary authors agree with this assessment: Fratianni and Spinelli (1997: 181) thus point out that inconvertibility created two layers of monetary circulation, with those who could pay in gold benefiting from lower prices, and those forced to use paper money finding the purchase of commodities costlier, and as a result demanding the issue of larger quantities of money. The government, to be sure, was initially successful in decreasing the amount of currency in circulation, by decreeing a limit on paper currency issued by the Banca Nazionale in 1868; but this initial success was impaired by the government's repeated resorts to loans from the bank. More generally, the central government had carried out the kinds of financial reforms it deemed necessary to increase the liquidity of capital markets. A law allowing the creation of limited liability companies was particularly important and consequential in this regard, as it generated a first wave of speculative banking in the immediate postunification years—a phenomenon that contemporaries dubbed "bankmania." Whereas only 8 commercial banks were operating throughout Italy in 1861, there were 40 in 1870, and 153 in 1873 (Polsi 1993: 98). Banks were turning from private partnerships to firms with a governance structure more adequate for the sharing of risks. However, this was coming at a cost: banks were becoming increasingly involved in financing real estate speculation, searching for high dividends without assessing the soundness of the financed propositions. This was happening especially at the local level, where small- and medium-size institutions were filling up empty market niches (Luzzatto 1968; Polsi 1993). A contemporary commentator argued that "Italian vanity has now changed—no longer is it obsessing about the national guard, the national assembly, meetings or universal suffrage. Every little commune and suburb now only wants local institutions: especially a Credit Bank" (Errera 1874: quoted in Polsi 1993: 99).

7. Sabetti (2000) has persuasively argued that, for all their political acumen, Italian liberal elites had a remarkably simplistic view of institutions as neutral in their effects on behavior—Cavour, for instance, believed that the state did not need particularly elaborate administrative arrangements because the sheer will power of its political elites would bring out a desired, liberal outcome. But the monetary debates reveal, I think, a different set of preoccupations and concerns, specifically with the effects that different ways of organizing money would have on the development of credit and of creditworthiness over the national territory.

8. Masi (1989) points to the financial expansion of the central government as the primary factor, highlighting its positive as well as negative effects. Public debt, she argues, first, influenced the money supply and the relationship between banks of issue and the state—a point that we have discussed at length above. Second, the *yield* on public debt affected the profitability of financial intermediaries; and third, public debt policies affected money and credit more generally, spurring the diffusion of new means of payment and encouraging the creation of new savings banks, modeled on mutualistic rather than

entrepreneurial logics. More specifically, the higher the interest rate on public debt, the more were private banks able to invest profitably in them, and the more of that profit they would then lend out to private actors. Moreover, the more savers became familiar with financial instruments such as government bonds, the more would deposit banks be able to purchase them in order to leverage their investments. On the negative side, the spread of financial instruments on the wake of the expansion of public debt made riskier investments possible as well, thus potentially leading to instability and crisis (Luzzatto 1968).

9. This may be an outcome of the more general tendency of Risorgimento elites to imagine the new nation as already marked by a state of decline, a position that, argues Riall (2009: 40), set Italian nationalists apart from their European counterparts of the period.

10. Upon Italy's exit from gold, in fact, banks reduced the number of banknotes in circulation, prompting nonbanking firms to print alternative media of exchange (such as scrip money) (Polsi 1993).

11. Italian free bankers were radical in this regard: they praised the organization of banking rather than other factors for its ability to drive the U.S. economy into expansion. They even argued that, because it monetized "the Credit of the Nation," the National Banking System "sheltered the Nation from recurring monetary and financial crises" (Semenza 1879), a point that was of course patently exaggerated.

Chapter 6

1. My discussion of economic nationalism in Italy has benefited from the theoretical reorientation of recent studies, which have shown how economic nationalism is not to be associated with any particular economic policy (such as protectionism), for its emphasis is on the nation as the appropriate referent of economic policy. Economic nationalist efforts are usually directed at creating collective commitments to the national community (Levi-Faur 1997; Crane 1998; Helleiner 2002; Pickel 2003; Nakano 2004).

2. Within the Italian banking sector, savings banks were a very important category: as late as 1900 they held 41 percent of total banking assets (Polsi 2000). Around 1873, when a financial crisis hit Italy, national government securities represented 10 percent of the assets of savings banks. The rise to power of the Left triggered a spectacular rise in the size of central government stock holdings: already in 1874, the percentage had increased to 15 percent; 18 percent in 1878; and 26 percent in 1883. By 1890, government securities represented 35 percent of the total assets of savings banks. The peak was reached in 1898, when a staggering 55 percent of the total assets of savings banks were invested in government stock; that ratio remained above 35 percent for the subsequent years leading up to World War I (Cotula 1996). The causes for this shift are complex. The decades of the 1870s and 1880s witnessed a prolonged agrarian crisis (some authors date the collapse of the southern economies to this period). As international relations, especially between Italy and France, were souring, this further weakened Italian agricultural exports, thus forcing rural banks to search for new, more profitable outlets for their investments (Carocci 1956). But in the case of the CARIPLO, its increased willingness to invest in national credit instruments was also the result of the sustained effort of the Bank of Italy to establish a durable rapport with it, as we shall soon see.

3. The latter attracted deposits by charging low interest rates, which forced the Banca Nazionale to follow suit but so worsen the outflow of specie. Crucially, Carocci notes that the Banca Nazionale was no longer playing the role it did in the 1870–76 period, when the question was how to "modernize" the economy. Now certain Italian economic sectors saw the Banca Nazionale as defense against speculation. "The more serious economic and financial environments, those of Milan and the North in general, sympathized . . . with the opposition of the Banca Nazionale to the tendency of the Banco di Napoli to lower discount rates" (1956: 352).

4. This was not, of course, a problem that afflicted only the Italian case, as the tension between the private nature of banking and its public function in the service of the needs of circulation characterized all financial systems in this period (Goodhart 1988). But in the Italian context, the banks of issue, and the Banca Nazionale in particular, were often asked by political authorities also to aid speculation and wildcat banking, as the kinds of private banks whose paper was more likely to be discounted by the Banca Nazionale were banks that concentrated on speculative investments in real estate and non–interest bearing advances to the industrial sector—banks that the expansionary policies of the government itself had made possible. The government would call on the banks of issue for help whenever the financial solvency of the wildcats came under question. The liberal newspaper *l'Economista* argued to this effect that the Banca had to support the Treasury, the banking system, and itself (quoted in Confalonieri 1974).

5. If we accept the distinction made by Bonelli (1971a) between a self-financed, Manchesterian network of small industries, and the new, large industrial concerns that emerged in the late 1880s and needed specialized banks for their financing (see, esp., Cafagna 1989), universal banks can be understood as serving this latter niche. As Gerschenkron (1962: 14) famously described their German counterparts, "and with them the Austrian and Italian banks":

A German bank, as the saying went, accompanied an industrial enterprise from the cradle to the grave, from establishment to liquidation throughout all the vicissitudes of its existence. Through the device of formally short-term but in reality long-term current accounts credits and through development of the institution of the supervisory boards to the position of most powerful organs within corporate organization, the banks acquired a formidable degree of ascendancy over industrial enterprises, which extended far beyond the sphere of financial control into that of entrepreneurial and managerial decisions.

6. Born in Danzig in 1856 of a German-Jewish family, he moved to Italy at age fourteen for health reasons. He acquired Italian citizenship in 1910. By 1894 he already had an esteemed banking career in the Banca Generale, the predecessor of COMIT. His national origin remained nonetheless salient and was often the target of attacks from the nationalist press, which forced him to resign in 1915, a year before his death in Milan.

7. Also consider that the correspondence between Stringher and Joel concerned with the refinancing of outstanding Italian government bonds at lower interest rates (an operation that succeeded in 1905; see, esp., De Cecco 1990) was characterized by

repeated expressions of mutual harmony and admiration, as well as repeated calls for more cooperation. For instance, Joel to Stringher: "I always found myself in perfect harmony with you, most commendable *Commendatore*" (Joel, March 11, 1902). Joel to Stringher: "[Y]ou can be persuaded that I am doing everything I had agreed to. It is really necessary that all forces and energies remain united, because this is a difficult moment, and I don't believe it will be soon overcome" (Joel, October 20, 1902); Stringher to Joel: "I believe it would be convenient for High Finance [l'Alta Banca] to show that it can constitute a powerful consortium, and that it could move from small things to large ones, as soon as the government will be able to take advantage of it" (Stringher, July 7, 1903); Joel to Stringher: "I would like to add that I am very satisfied and happy with the perfect agreement in our views about the best way to implement one of the biggest projects ever entertained by the financial world. You will always find me by your side to follow loyally the intentions coming from the top, which have been conceived by men of great ingenuity and strong will to increase significantly the material and moral position of our Country (Joel, February 2, 1904). Stringher to Joel: "I thank you, also on behalf of the Minister, for your most effective cooperation. All that could be done, was done in order to fight the upward trend, morally dangerous to the preparation and the unfolding of the government program [unreadable]. The Treasury and the Bank of Italy, which has been its ally when it is about the problems that affect the future of our country, could not help but worry about a cash loss [orchestrated?] to damage us [by?] the international financial world. The Banca Commerciale was an excellent ally" (Stringher, February 7, 1904).

8. As is the case throughout the correspondence, Joel did not hesitate to emphasize the nature of his assets to Stringher—namely, his connections with foreign capitalists, to once again highlight the positive influence he could exercise over them. In a later letter, Joel wrote about "the reactions [he had] witnessed in Paris, where [he] had the chance to meet people of great authority and influence both in politics and finance." He reassured Stringher that the "position towards our country expressed by both public opinion and very competent people has radically changed, in fact it is now excellent in all its aspects, but proceeding too hastily might produce many prejudices" (Joel, November 11, 1902).

9. Crispi's project to forge a more unified national consciousness tragically and inevitably led to colonial expansion, but the defeat of the Italian army at Adua in 1896 put that project on hold, and led to Crispi's resignation. As a result, historians see Crispi's government as a prelude to fascism (Lanaro 1979: 212; Banti 1996: 216; Mori 1977)—both because Crispi rejected the legitimacy of political opposition, and because he funded the buildup of a military-industrial complex. It is this second dynamic that is relevant to my discussion.

10. To which finally Joel replied in dismay on the same day:

I am pervaded by a sentiment of utter sadness in learning from such an authoritative source that there are still those who dare accuse the Institute which I am honored to represent of favoring, in fact of inciting a hostile attitude towards the large and just aspirations of the country. In pointing the finger against the Institute, they try to harm the people, in fact in this case one person, and I must not let myself believe that thirty three years of intense work in Italy, with no interruptions, amount to nothing—[years spent on] trying always to further Italian interests, often in contrast with the interests of my first homeland, whose eminent men I always told that Italy had and still has economic and political necessities which it cannot forgo. (Joel, October 15, 1911)

Stringher (October 18, 1911) tried to pacify Joel:

I confide to you that not all men in your Institute have foresight and measure as well as prudence. And I hasten to add that, contrary to what you think, no serious person doubts the loyalty and righteousness of Comm. Joel, on whom we can always fully count.

11. The most important interpretations of this period, and of the role of the SBI, remain the works by Bonelli (1971a, b) on the Terni steel complex and the 1907 crisis.

12. See, esp., the "Nota Economica" in the most important nationalist newspaper, *Il Regno*, in the February 7, 1904, issue, which dealt with the problem of industrial trust in the steel sector, making a pragmatic case in their favor (while opposing, for instance, trusts in the sugar manufacturing sector); or the debate between Mario Calderoni ("Nazionalismo antiprotezionista?" *Il Regno*, January 17, 1904, and "Nazionalismo Borghese e protezionista," *Il Regno*, February 7, 1904) and P. L. Occhini and Giuseppe Prezzolini ("Risposte a Mario Calderoni," *Il Regno*, January 24 and February 14, 1904), in turn sparked by a previous debate between Vilfredo Pareto ("La Borghesia può risorgere?" *Il Regno*, January 10, 1904) and Giuseppe Prezzolini (same issue).

13. The full development and legitimation of that narrative was achieved by 1915, when Francesco Saverio Nitti published his speech to the Academy of Sciences in Naples in a monograph titled "Foreign Capital in Italy" (Falchero 1982; Galli Della Loggia 1970). See De Grand (2001) for a detailed account of the emergence of the nationalist, anti-Giolitti movement of pre–World War I Italy. See Mann (2004), De Grand (1978), and Gaeta (1981) on the importance of this movement to the development of fascism.

Chapter 7

1. In fact, Schumpeter's own writings on money do not take his sociology of banking into account. In a never-completed manuscript on money, the first two chapters of which were translated from German into English, Schumpeter makes important theoretical advances on the political nature of money. Against arguments of money as a collective good (a la Lawrence Broz), Schumpeter argues, for instance, "If we abstract from the cognitive gulf between what 'is' (or 'is valid') and what 'should be' (or 'should be valid'), and ask ourselves the question in purely practical terms, the impossibility of a 'scientific policy,' in the proper sense of the term, derives first of all from the fact that social groups orient their desires with respect to currency policy (as with respect to all policy) toward their interest—broadly or narrowly conceived—and that a choice among various currency policies is possible only on the basis of an appraising partisanship. But this is not all. Even if no group wished to act in accordance with its own interest, and if each wished to act only in accordance with some conception of 'the general welfare,' we should not be much further ahead. For this 'general welfare' looks different from each of the standpoints from

which individuals and groups survey the social world and which are indicated to these individuals and groups by their surroundings and their cultural inheritance" (1991: 511). In support of my larger thesis (which I argued is implicit in Schumpeter's characterization of sound banking) that money depends on the construction of a moral outlook that regulates its circulation, Schumpeter also argued: "Originally 'sound money' meant, to be sure, a money consisting of gold, or reliably redeemable in gold, without much emphasis being put on the fluctuations in gold itself. But that this represented only a preliminary step toward further understanding, and was in fact a crude expression of the desire for a stable money, we see from the *moral* connotations which the expression acquired. The 'sound money man' was the man who disapproved of fluctuations in the value of money and the speculative gains resulting therefrom because he regarded them as 'unreal' from a moral and business standpoint, and who meant, by 'sound' money, above all *'honest'* money" (ibid.: 517). But the rest of Schumpeter's piece is concerned more with creating boundaries between economic and sociological explanations of money than advancing a sociological theory of it based on a consideration of the social processes through which money is reproduced as a set of relationships—for which attention to banking is crucial. (See also Swedberg 2003 and Ingham 2003.)

2. Scholars of money (Ingham 2001; Zelizer 2005b; Dodd 2006, 2007), in fact, tend to argue that money originates only with one of these sources (circuits, economic communities, states), whereas the challenge is to understand under what conditions each source complements or contrasts with the others in the production of money.

3. The following paragraphs draw from Polillo (2011).

4. The economic history of industrialization, with its move from national histories of economic development to local and regional processes of industrialization, provides a useful model here. Herrigel (2000), for instance, takes up the monumental task of reanalyzing German economic development over the past two hundred years in terms of two regional systems, embodying different logics, that he terms "decentralized" and "autarkic." Unlike earlier, seminal work such as Pollard (1981), Herrigel does not take for granted the organizational problems and contingencies faced by each system. Similarly, we should not assume that the politics of monetary conflicts, and the identity of the actors involved in it, are fixed, as economic historians often do (Mann [1993: 297–329] makes just such a critique of Gerschenkron). Variation should be introduced not only through cross-national comparisons (Sylla et al. 1999) but also through diachronic analysis.

5. Marx in some ways understood the development of a diffuse credit system as a (dialectical) precondition to the development of socialism. So he argued:

> The two characteristics immanent in the credit system are, on the one hand, to develop the incentive of capitalist production, enrichment through the exploitation of the labor of others, to the purest and most colossal form of gambling and swindling, and to reduce more and more the number of the few who exploit the social wealth; on the other hand, to constitute the form of transition to a new mode of production. It is this ambiguous nature, which endows the principal spokesman of credit from Law to Isaac Pereire with the pleasant character mixture of swindler and prophet. (1909: 441)

6. Lower classes, which have a more distant and impersonal relationship to financial structures, are confined to using "currencies" that are less prestigious (at an extreme, the food stamps of welfare recipients): currencies that not only entail less control over resources but also give access to less socially desirable experiences. Collins's is, in other words, a view that pairs the circulation of "currencies" to distinctive, segregated networks with the social experience of membership in a social class.

Appendix
1. Accounts of the demise of banking hegemony in the United States from the 1980s onward are in fact accounts of the demise of one kind of banking (commercial) at the expense of another (investment banking) (Davis and Mizruchi 1999).

References

Abolafia, Mitchel Y. 1996. *Making Markets: Opportunism and Restraint on Wall Street.* Cambridge, MA: Harvard University Press.

Abolafia, Mitchel Y., and Martin Kilduff. 1988. "Enacting Market Crisis: The Social Construction of a Speculative Bubble." *Administrative Science Quarterly* 33(2): 177–93.

Acemoglu, Daron, and James A. Robinson. 2011. "Why Did the West Extend the Franchise? Democracy, Inequality, and Growth in Historical Perspective." *Quarterly Journal of Economics* 115(4): 1167–99.

Aghion, Philippe, Patrick Bolton, and Mathias Dewatripont. 2000. "Contagious Bank Failures in a Free Banking System." *European Economic Review* 44(4–6): 713–18.

Aglietta, Michel. 2000. *A Theory of Capitalist Regulation: The US Experience.* London, New York: Verso Books.

Aglietta, Michel, and Régis Breton. 2001. "Financial Systems, Corporate Control and Capital Accumulation." *Economy & Society* 30(4): 433–66.

Aglietta, Michel, and André Orléan. 1984. *La Violence de la Monnaie.* Paris: Presses Universitaires de France.

Allen, Franklin, and Douglas Gale. 2000. *Comparing Financial Systems.* Cambridge, MA: MIT Press.

Anon. 1853. "Art. IV.—TRAITS OF TRADE—LAUDABLE AND INIQUITOUS." *Merchants' Magazine and Commercial Review* 28(5): 574.

Anon. 1873. "Congressional Record, Senate, 43rd Congress, 1st Session. Appendix."

Anon. 1878a. "I Bilanci dei Comuni." *La Rassegna Settimanale* 2(15): 245–46.

Anon. 1878b. "Le Finanze Comunali." *La Rassegna Settimanale* I(12): 206–7.

Aquarone, Alberto. 1981. *L'Italia Giolittiana.* Bologna: Il Mulino.

Arnott, Richard, and Joseph E. Stiglitz. 1991. "Moral Hazard and Nonmarket Institutions: Dysfunctional Crowding out of Peer Monitoring?" *American Economic Review* 81(1): 179–90.

Arrighi, Giovanni. 1994. *The Long Twentieth Century: Money, Power and the Origins of Our Times*. London, New York: Verso.

Ashworth, John. 1996. *Slavery, Capitalism, and Politics in the Antebellum Republic*, volume 1: *Commerce and Compromise, 1820–1850*. New York: Cambridge University Press.

Atherton, Lewis E. 1946. "The Problem of Credit Rating in the Ante-Bellum South." *Journal of Southern History* 12(4): 534–56.

Bagehot, Walter. 1920. *Lombard Street: A Description of the Money Market*. New York: E. P. Dutton and Company.

Bailey, Fenton. 1991. *The Junk Bond Revolution: Michael Milken, Wall Street & the "Roaring Eighties."* London: Fourth Estate.

Balogh, Brian. 2009. *A Government Out of Sight*. New York: Cambridge University Press.

Banti, Alberto Mario. 1990. "I Proprietari Terrieri nell'Italia Centro-Settentrionale." Pp. 45–103 in *Storia dell'Agricoltura Italiana in Età Contemporanea: Uomini e Classi*, edited by Piero Bevilaqua. Venice: Marsilio Editori.

Banti, Alberto Mario. 1996. *Storia della Borghesia Italiana: L'Età Liberale*. Bari: Donzelli Editore.

Banti, Alberto Mario. 2005. *L'Onore della Nazione*. Turin: Einaudi.

Banti, Alberto Mario, and Paul Ginsborg. 2007. "Per Una Nuova Storia del Risorgimento." Pp. xiii–xli in *Storia d'Italia: Annali: Risorgimento*, volume 22. Turin: Einaudi.

Barbagallo, Francesco. 1999. "Da Crispi a Giolitti: Lo Stato, la Politica, i Conflitti Sociali." Pp. 3–133 in *Storia d'Italia: Liberalismo e Democrazia*, volume 3. Bari: Laterza.

Barnes, Barry. 1992. "Status Groups and Collective Action." *Sociology* 26(2): 259–70.

Barone, Giorgio. 1999. "La Modernizzazione Italiana: Dalla Crisi allo Sviluppo." Pp. 249–362 in *Storia d'Italia: Liberalismo e Democrazia*, volume 3. Bari: Laterza.

Bateman, Fred, and Thomas Weiss. 2002. *A Deplorable Scarcity: The Failure of Industrialization in the Slave Economy*. Chapel Hill: UNC Press Books.

Beckert, Jens. 1996. "What Is Sociological about Economic Sociology? Uncertainty and the Embeddedness of Economic Action." *Theory and Society* 25(6): 803–40.

Beckert, Jens. 2003. "Economic Sociology and Embeddedness: How Shall We Conceptualize Economic Action?" *Journal of Economic Issues* 37(3): 769–87.

Bell, Stephanie. 2001. "The Role of the State and the Hierarchy of Money." *Cambridge Journal of Economics* 25(2): 149–64.

Benmelech, Effi, and Jennifer Dlugosz. 2009. "The Credit Rating Crisis." *SSRN eLibrary*. ssrn.com/sol3/papers.cfm?abstract_id=1415208.

Bensel, Richard Franklin. 1990. *Yankee Leviathan: The Origins of Central State Authority in America, 1859–1877*. New York: Cambridge University Press.

Bensel, Richard Franklin. 2000. *The Political Economy of American Industrialization, 1877–1900*. New York: Cambridge University Press.

Berger, Suzanne. 1983. *Organizing Interests in Western Europe*. New York: Cambridge University Press.

Berger, Suzanne, and Ronald Philip Dore. 1996. *National Diversity and Global Capitalism*. Ithaca, NY: Cornell University Press.

Berman, Marshall. 1983. *All That Is Solid Melts into Air: The Experience of Modernity*. London, New York: Verso.

Bertolotto, Sebastiano. 1867. *Banchi di Sconto e Deposito e della Necessità e del Modo d'Instituirli in Italia*. Genova: Tipografia del Commercio.

Bielby, William T., and James N. Baron. 1986. "Men and Women at Work: Sex Segregation and Statistical Discrimination." *American Journal of Sociology* 91(4): 759–99.

Blanchflower, David G., Phillip B. Levine, and David J. Zimmerman. 2003. "Discrimination in the Small-Business Credit Market." *Review of Economics and Statistics* 85(4): 930–43.

Boccardo, Gerolamo. 1879. *Le Banche ed il Corso Forzato*. Rome: Tipografia del Senato.

Boccardo, Gerolamo. 1881. *Sul Riordinamento delle Banche in Italia: Studi e Proposte del Professore Gerolamo Boccardo*. Turin: Unione Tipografico-Editrice.

Bodenhorn, Howard. 2000. *A History of Banking in Antebellum America: Financial Markets and Economic Development in an Era of Nation-Building*. Cambridge, New York: Cambridge University Press.

Bodenhorn, Howard. 2003. *State Banking in Early America: A New Economic History*. New York: Oxford University Press.

Bodenhorn, Howard. 2006. "Bank Chartering and Political Corruption in Antebellum New York: Free Banking as Reform." Pp. 231–58 in *Corruption and Reform: Lessons from America's Economic History*. National Bureau of Economic Research Report. Edited by Edward Glaser and Claudia Gordin. Chicago: University of Chicago Press.

Bohannan, Paul. 1959. "The Impact of Money on an African Subsistence Economy." *Journal of Economic History* 19(4): 491–503.

Boltanski, Luc, and Laurent Thévenot. 2006. *On Justification: Economies of Worth*. Princeton: Princeton University Press.

Bonelli, Franco. 1971a. *La Crisi del 1907: Una Tappa dello Sviluppo Industriale in Italia*. Turin: Fondazione Luigi Einaudi.

Bonelli, Franco. 1971b. *Lo Sviluppo di una Grande Impresa in Italia: La Terni dal 1884 al 1962*. Turin: Einaudi.

Bonelli, Franco. 1978. "Il Capitalismo Italiano: Linee Generali d'Interpretazione." Pp. 1193–1256 in *Storia d'Italia Annali I, Dal Feudalesimo al Capitalismo*. Turin: Einaudi.

Bonelli, Franco. 1991. *La Banca d'Italia dal 1894 al 1913: Momenti della Formazione di una Banca Centrale*. Bari: Laterza.

Boot, Arnoud W. A. 2000. "Relationship Banking: What Do We Know?" *Journal of Financial Intermediation* 9(1): 7–25.

Bourdieu, Pierre. 1984. *Distinction: A Social Critique of the Judgement of Taste*. Cambridge: Harvard University Press.

Bourdieu, Pierre, and Loïc J. D. Wacquant. 1992. *An Invitation to Reflexive Sociology*. Chicago: University of Chicago Press.

Braudel, Fernand. 1977. *Afterthoughts on Material Civilization and Capitalism*. Baltimore, MD: Johns Hopkins University Press.

Braudel, Fernand. 1992. *Civilization and Capitalism, 15th–18th Century*. Berkeley, Los Angeles: University of California Press.

Brenner, R. 2003. *The Boom and the Bubble: The US in the World Economy*. London: Verso Books.

Broz, J. Lawrence. 1997. *The International Origins of the Federal Reserve System*. Ithaca, NY: Cornell University Press.

Brubaker, Rogers. 2003. "Ethnicity without Groups." *European Journal of Sociology* 43(02): 163–89.

Brubaker, Rogers, and Frederick Cooper. 2000. "Beyond 'Identity.'" *Theory and Society* 29(1): 1–47.

Bruck, Connie. 1989. "The Old Boy and the New Boys." *New Yorker*, May 8: 81–96.

Bruner, Robert F., and Sean D. Carr. 2009. *The Panic of 1907: Lessons Learned from the Market's Perfect Storm*. Hoboken, NJ: John Wiley and Sons.

Bryan, Dick, and Michael Rafferty. 2007. "Financial Derivatives and the Theory of Money." *Economy & Society* 36(1): 134–58.

Cafagna, Luciano. 1989. *Dualismo e Sviluppo nella Storia d'Italia*. Venice: Marsilio.

Calder, Lendol Glen. 1999. *Financing the American Dream: A Cultural History of Consumer Credit*. Princeton: Princeton University Press.

Calomiris, Charles W. 1995. "The Costs of Rejecting Universal Banking: American Finance in the German Mirror, 1870–1914." Pp. 257–315 in *Coordination and Information*. Chicago: University of Chicago Press.

Calomiris, Charles W., and Charles M. Kahn. 1996. "The Efficiency of Self-Regulated Payments Systems: Learning from the Suffolk System." *Journal of Money, Credit and Banking* 28(4): 766–97.

Caracciolo, Alberto. 1973. "La Storia Economica." Pp. 511–690 in *La Storia d'Italia dal Primo Settecento all'Unità*, volume 3, edited by Ruggiero Romano and Vivanti Corrado. Turin: Giulio Einaudi Editore.

Cardarelli, Sergio. 1990. "La Questione Bancaria in Italia dal 1860 al 1892." Pp. 105–34 in *Ricerche Per la Storia della Banca d'Italia*. Bari: Laterza.

Cardarelli, Sergio. 2006. "Il Tramonto del Free Banking in Italia." *Quaderni dell'Ufficio Ricerche Storiche della Banca d'Italia*, volume 14. Rome: Banca d'Italia.

Cardoza, Anthony L. 1998. *Aristocrats in Bourgeois Italy: The Piedmontese Nobility, 1861–1930*. New York: Cambridge University Press.

Carocci, Giampiero. 1956. *Agostino Depretis e la Politica Interna Italiana dal 1876 al 1887*. Turin: Einaudi.

Carocci, Giampiero. 2002. *Destra e Sinistra Nella Storia d'Italia*. Rome-Bari: Laterza.

Carosso, Vincent P. 1970. *Investment Banking in America: A History*. Cambridge: Harvard University Press.

Carosso, Vincent P. 1987. *The Morgans: Private International Bankers, 1854–1913*. Cambridge: Harvard University Press.

Carosso, Vincent P., and Richard Sylla. 1991. "U.S. Banks in International Finance." Pp. 48–71 in *International Banking 1870–1914*, edited by Rondo Cameron. New York: Oxford University Press.

Carruthers, Bruce. 1994. "When Is the State Autonomous? Culture, Organization Theory, and the Political Sociology of the State." *Sociological Theory* 12(1): 19–44.

Carruthers, Bruce. 1996. *City of Capital: Politics and Market in the English Financial Revolution.* Princeton: Princeton University Press.

Carruthers, Bruce. 2005. "The Sociology of Money and Credit." Pp. 355–78 in *Handbook of Economic Sociology,* 2nd edition, edited by Neil Smelser and Richard Swedberg. Princeton: Princeton University Press.

Carruthers, Bruce. 2011. "What Is Sociological about Banks and Banking?" Pp. 242–63 in *The Sociology of Economic Life,* edited by Mark Granovetter and Richard Swedberg. Boulder, CO: Westview Press.

Carruthers, Bruce, and Laura Ariovich. 2010. *Money and Credit: A Sociological Approach.* London, New York: Polity.

Carruthers, Bruce, and Sarah Babb. 1996. "The Color of Money and the Nature of Value: Greenbacks and Gold in Postbellum America." *American Journal of Sociology* 101(6): 1556–91.

Carruthers, Bruce, and Arthur Stinchcombe. 1999. "The Social Structure of Liquidity: Flexibility, Markets, and States." *Theory and Society* 28(3): 353–82.

Centeno, Miguel. 2002. *Blood and Debt: War and the Nation-State in Latin America.* University Park: Pennsylvania State University Press.

Cerioni, Isabella. 2001. "La Banca d'Italia e il Consorzio Siderurgico." *Quaderni dell'Ufficio Ricerche Storiche della Banca d'Italia,* volume 2. Rome: Banca d'Italia.

Chandler, Alfred D. 1977. *The Visible Hand: The Managerial Revolution in American Business.* Cambridge: Belknap Press.

Chernow, Ron. 2001. *The House of Morgan: An American Banking Dynasty and the Rise of Modern Finance.* New York: Grove Press.

Ciocca, Pierluigi, and Gianni Toniolo. 1999. *Storia Economica d'Italia.* Bari: Laterza.

Cohen, Benjamin. 2006. *The Future of Money.* Princeton: Princeton University Press.

Collins, Randall. 1979a. "Review: The Bankers. By Martin Mayer: Ballantine Books, 1976." *American Journal of Sociology* 85(1): 190–94.

Collins, Randall. 1979b. *The Credential Society: An Historical Sociology of Education and Stratification.* New York: Academic Press.

Collins, Randall. 1980. "Weber's Last Theory of Capitalism: A Systematization." *American Sociological Review* 45(6): 925–42.

Collins, Randall. 1986. *Weberian Sociological Theory.* Cambridge: Cambridge University Press.

Collins, Randall. 1990. "Market Dynamics as the Engine of Historical Change." *Sociological Theory* 8(2): 111–35.

Collins, Randall. 1995. "The Social Meaning of Money." *Society* 33(1): 72–74.

Collins, Randall. 1999. *Macrohistory: Essays in the Sociology of the Long Run.* Stanford: Stanford University Press.

Collins, Randall. 2000. "Situational Stratification: A Micro-Macro Theory of Inequality." *Sociological Theory* 18(1): 17–43.

Collins, Randall. 2004. *Interaction Ritual Chains.* Princeton: Princeton University Press.

Confalonieri, Antonio. 1974. *Banca e Industria in Italia, 1894–1906.* Milano: Banca Commerciale Italiana.

Conti, Giuseppe. 2000. "Processi di Integrazione e Reti Locali: Tipologie del Credito e della Finanza (1861–1936)." Pp. 381–436 in *Banche e Reti di Banche nell'Italia Postunitaria*, volume 2, edited by Giuseppe Conti and Salvatore La Francesca. Bologna: Il Mulino.

Conti, Giuseppe. 2007. "Il Pendolo del Debito Pubblico Italiano: Illusione Fiscale e Consenso Sociale in una Prospettiva Storica (1861–2000)." Pp. 477–93 in *Debito Pubblico e Mercati Finanziari in Italia: Secoli XIII–XX*. Milan: Franco Angeli.

Conti, Giuseppe, and Rosanna Scatamacchia. 2009. "Stato di Fiducia, Crisi Finanziarie e Crisi Politiche Nell'italia Liberale Prima del 1914," volume 87. *Discussion Papers, Dipartimento di Scienze Economiche (DSE), University of Pisa, Pisa, Italy.*

Corso Forzoso, Commissione Parlamentare d'Inchiesta. 1868/1990. "Final Report. 28 novembre 1868." In *L'Unificazione degli Istituti di Emissione*, edited by Renato De Mattia. Bari: Laterza.

Cotula, Franco. 1996. *I Bilanci delle Aziende di Credito*. Bari: Laterza.

Crane, George T. 1998. "Economic Nationalism: Bringing the Nation Back In." *Millennium—Journal of International Studies* 27(1): 55–75.

Dal Lago, Enrico, and Rick Halpern. 2002. *The American South and the Italian Mezzogiorno: Essays in Comparative History*. Basingstoke: Palgrave Macmillan.

Das, Sanjiv Ranjan. 2005. "Working Papers: 'Hedge' Funds." Pp. 1–6 in *World of Hedge Funds: Characteristics and Analysis*, edited by H. Gifford Fong. Singapore: World Scientific Publishing Company.

Davidson, Paul. 2002. *Financial Markets, Money and the Real World*. Cheltenham UK, Northampton MA: Edward Elgar Publishing.

Davis, Gerald F. 2009. *Managed by the Markets*. New York: Oxford University Press.

Davis, Gerald F., and Mark Mizruchi. 1999. "The Money Center Cannot Hold: Commercial Banks in the US System of Corporate Governance." *Administrative Science Quarterly* 44(2): 215–39.

Davis, John A. 1994. "Review: Remapping Italy's Path to the Twentieth Century." *Journal of Modern History* 66(2): 291–320.

Davis, John A. 2001. *Italy in the Nineteenth Century: 1796–1900*. New York: Oxford University Press.

Davis, Lance. 1965. "The Investment Market, 1870–1914: The Evolution of a National Market." *Journal of Economic History* 25: 360–85.

De Cecco, Marcello. 1974. *Money and Empire*. Totowa, NJ: Rowan and Littlefield.

De Cecco, Marcello. 1986. "Modes of Financial Development: American Banking Dynamics and World Financial Crises." Pp. 115–32 in *Development, Democracy, and the Art of Trespassing: Essays in Honor of Albert O. Hirschman*, edited by A. Foxley, M. McPherson, and G. O'Donnell. Notre Dame: University of Notre Dame Press.

De Cecco, Marcello. 1987. "Financial Innovation and Monetary Theory." Pp. 1–19 in *Changing Money*, edited by Marcello De Cecco. London: Blackwell.

De Cecco, Marcello. 1990. *L'Italia e il Sistema Finanziario Internazionale (1861–1914)*. Bari: Laterza.

De Cecco, Marcello. 1993. *L'Italia e il Sistema Finanziario Internazionale (1919–1936)*. Bari: Laterza.

De Cecco, Marcello, and Alberto Giovannini. 1989. *A European Central Bank?: Perspectives on Monetary Unification after Ten Years of the EMS*. Cambridge: Cambridge University Press.

De Cesare, Carlo. 1874. *Le Banche d'Emissione*. Rome: Tipografia Barbera.

De Grand, Alexander J. 1978. *The Italian Nationalist Association and the Rise of Fascism in Italy*. Lincoln: University of Nebraska Press.

De Grand, Alexander J. 2001. *The Hunchback's Tailor: Giovanni Giolitti and Liberal Italy from the Challenge of Mass Politics to the Rise of Fascism, 1882–1922*. Westport, CT: Praeger.

De Mattia, Renato, ed. 1990. *Gli Istituti di Emissione in Italia: I Tentativi di Unificazione 1843–1892*. Bari: Laterza.

De Rosa, Luigi. 1984. "Economics and Nationalism in Italy (1861–1914)." *Journal of European Economic History* 11: 537–74.

Della Torre, Giuseppe. 2008. "Collocamento del Debito Pubblico e Assetto Normativo del Sistema Creditizio in Italia (1861–1914)." In *Storia d'Italia: Annali*, volume 23. Turin: Einaudi.

DeLong, J. Bradford. 1991. "Did J. P. Morgan's Men Add Value?" Pp. 205–36 in *The Business Enterprise: Historical Perspectives on the Use of Information*, edited by Peter Temin. Chicago: University of Chicago Press.

Di Nardi, Giuseppe. 1953. *Le Banche di Emissione in Italia nel Secolo XIX*. Turin: Unione Tipografico-Editrice Torinese.

Diamond, Douglas W. 1984. "Financial Intermediation and Delegated Monitoring." *Review of Economic Studies* 51(3): 393–414.

DiMaggio, Paul, and Walter Powell. 1983. "The Iron Cage Revisited: Institutional Isomorphism and Collective Rationality in Organizational Fields." *American Sociological Review* 48(2): 147–60.

Djelic, Marie-Laure. 1998. *Exporting the American Model*. Oxford, New York: Oxford University Press.

Dobbin, Frank. 1994. *Forging Industrial Policy: The United States, France and Britain in the Railway Age*. New York: Cambridge University Press.

Dobbin, Frank. 2004. "How Institutions Create Ideas: Notions of Public and Private Efficiency from Early French and American Railroading." *L'Année de la Régulation* 8: 15–50.

Dobbin, Frank, and Timothy J. Dowd. 1997. "How Policy Shapes Competition: Railroad Foundings in Massachusetts." *Administrative Science Quarterly* 42: 501–29.

Dobbin, Frank, and Timothy Dowd. 2000. "The Market That Antitrust Built: Public Policy, Private Coercion, and Railroad Acquisitions, 1825–1922." *American Sociological Review* 65(5): 631–57.

Dodd, Nigel. 2006. "Laundering Money: On the Need for Conceptual Clarity within the Sociology of Money." *European Journal of Sociology* 46(3): 387–411.

Dodd, Nigel. 2007. "On Simmel's Pure Concept of Money: A Response to Ingham." *European Journal of Sociology* 48(2): 273–94.

Domhoff, G. William. 1967. *Who Rules America?* Englewood Cliffs, NJ: Prentice-Hall.

Duggan, Christopher. 2002. *Francesco Crispi, 1818–1901: From Nation to Nationalism*. New York: Oxford University Press.

Durkheim, Émile. 1995. *The Elementary Forms of Religious Life*. New York: Free Press.

Eichengreen, Barry. 1996. *Globalizing Capital: A History of the International Monetary System*. Princeton: Princeton University Press.

Einhorn, Robin L. 2006. *American Taxation, American Slavery*. Chicago: University of Chicago Press.

Einhorn, Robin L. 2009. "Institutional Reality in the Age of Slavery: Taxation and Democracy in the States." *Journal of Policy History* 18(1): 21–43.

Falchero, Anna Maria. 1981. "Il Gruppo Ansaldo-Banca di Italiana di Sconto e le Vicende Bancarie Italiane nel Primo Dopoguerrra." Pp. 543–71 in *La Transizione dall'Economia di Guerra all'Economia di Pace in Italia e in Germania dopo la Prima Guerra Mondiale*, edited by Peter Hertner and Giorgio Mori. Bologna: Il Mulino.

Falchero, Anna Maria. 1982. "Banchieri e Politici: Nitti e il Gruppo Ansaldo-Banco di Sconto." *Italia Contemporanea*, volumes 146–47: 67–92.

Federico, Giovanni. 1996. "Italy, 1860–1940: A Little-Known Success Story." *Economic History Review* 49(4): 764–86.

Fehrenbacher, Don Edward. 2002. *The Slaveholding Republic: An Account of the United States Government's Relations to Slavery*. New York: Oxford University Press.

Feiner, Susan. 1982. "Factors, Bankers, and Masters: Class Relations in the Antebellum South." *Journal of Economic History* 42(1): 61–67.

Fenoaltea, Stefano. 2006. *L'Economia Italiana dall'Unità alla Grande Guerra*. Rome-Bari: Laterza.

Ferguson, Niall. 1999. *The House of Rothschild: Money's Prophets, 1798–1848*. New York: Penguin Group.

Ferguson, Niall. 2001. *The Cash Nexus: Money and Power in the Modern World, 1700–2000*. New York: Basic Books.

Ferguson, Niall. 2008. *The Ascent of Money*. New York: Penguin Group.

Ferrara, Francesco. 1866. "Il Corso Forzato dei Biglietti di Banco in Italia." *Nuova Antologia* 2(June): 343–79.

Ferrara, Francesco. 1873a. "La Questione de' Banchi in Italia." *Nuova Antologia* 24(October): 351–84.

Ferrara, Francesco. 1873b. "La Questione de' Banchi in Italia." *Nuova Antologia* 25(November): 627–52.

Ferrara, Francesco. 1873c. "La Questione de' Banchi in Italia." *Nuova Antologia* 26(December): 883–913.

Fligstein, Neil. 1990. *The Transformation of Corporate Control*. Cambridge, MA: Harvard University Press.

Fligstein, Neil. 1996. "Markets as Politics: A Political-cultural Approach to Market Institutions." *American Sociological Review* 61(4): 656–73.

Fligstein, Neil. 2001a. "Social Skill and the Theory of Fields." *Sociological Theory* 19(2): 105–25.

Fligstein, Neil. 2001b. *The Architecture of Markets*. Princeton: Princeton University Press.

Fligstein, Neil, and Doug McAdam. 2011. "Toward a General Theory of Strategic Action Fields." *Sociological Theory* 29(1): 1–26.

Fligstein, Neil, and A. S. Sweet. 2002. "Constructing Polities and Markets: An Institutionalist Account of European Integration." *American Journal of Sociology* 107(5): 1206–43.

Fohlin, Caroline. 1999. "Capital Mobilisation and Utilisation in Latecomer Economies: Germany and Italy Compared." *European Review of Economic History* 3(2): 139–74.

Fohlin, Caroline. 2007. *Finance Capitalism and Germany's Rise to Industrial Power*. New York: Cambridge University Press.

Foner, Eric. 2002. *Reconstruction: America's Unfinished Revolution, 1863–1877*. New York: Harper Perennial Modern Classics.

Formisano, Ronald P. 1974. "Deferential-Participant Politics: The Early Republic's Political Culture, 1789–1840." *American Political Science Review* 68(2): 473–487.

Forsyth, Douglas J. 1993. *The Crisis of Liberal Italy: Monetary and Financial Policy, 1914–1922*. Cambridge: Cambridge University Press.

Forsyth, Douglas J., and Daniel Verdier. 2003. *The Origins of National Financial Systems: Alexander Gerschenkron Reconsidered*. London, New York: Routledge.

Foster, John Bellamy, and Robert W. McChesney. 2010. "Listen Keynesians, It's the System! Response to Palley." *Monthly Review* 61(11).

Fratianni, Michele, and Franco Spinelli. 1997. *A Monetary History of Italy*. New York: Cambridge University Press.

Friedman, Milton, and Anna J. Schwartz. 1963. *A Monetary History of the United States: 1867–1960*. Princeton: Princeton University Press.

Fung, William, and David A. Hsieh. 1999. "A Primer on Hedge Funds." *Journal of Empirical Finance* 6(3): 309–31.

Gabriel, Stuart A., and Stuart S. Rosenthal. 2005. "Homeownership in the 1980s and 1990s: Aggregate Trends and Racial Gaps." *Journal of Urban Economics* 57(1): 101–27.

Gaeta, Franco. 1981. *Il Nazionalismo Italiano*. Rome-Bari: Laterza.

Galambos, Louis. 1970. "The Emerging Organizational Synthesis in Modern American History." *Business History Review* 44(3): 279–90.

Galli Della Loggia, Ernesto. 1970. "Problemi di Sviluppo Industriale e Nuovi Equilibri Politici alla Vigilia della Prima Guerra Mondiale: La Fondazione della Banca Italiana di Sconto." *Rivista Storica Italiana* 52: 824–66.

Genovese, Eugene. 1989. *The Political Economy of Slavery: Studies in the Economy & Society of the Slave South*. Middletown, CT: Wesleyan University Press.

Gentile, Emilio. 1990. *L'Italia Giolittiana, 1899–1914*. Milan: Il Mulino.

Gentile, Emilio. 2003. *Le Origini dell'Italia Contemporanea: L'età Giolittiana*. Rome-Bari: Editori Laterza.

Gerschenkron, Alexander. 1962. *Economic Backwardness in Historical Perspective: A Book of Essays*. Cambridge: Harvard University Press.

Gigliobianco, Alfredo. 1990. "Concorrenza e Collaborazione: Considerazioni sulla Natura dei Rapporti fra 'Banca Centrale' e Sistema Bancario nell'Esperienza Italiana (1844–1918)." Pp. 295–338 in *Ricerche Per la Storia della Banca d'Italia*. Bari: Laterza.

Gigliobianco, Alfredo. 2006. *Via Nazionale: Banca d'Italia e Classe Dirigente: Cento Anni di Storia.* Bari: Laterza.

Gilbart, James William. 1837. *The History of Banking in America: With an Inquiry How Far the Banking Institutions of America Are Adapted to This Country; and a Review of the Cause of the Recent Pressure on the Money Market.* London: Longman, Rees, Orme, Brown, Green, and Longman.

Gilje, Paul A. 1996. "The Rise of Capitalism in the Early Republic." *Journal of the Early Republic* 16(2): 159–81.

Goodhart, Charles. 1969. *The New York Money Market and the Finance of Trade, 1900–1913.* Cambridge: Harvard University Press.

Goodhart, Charles. 1988. *The Evolution of Central Banks.* Cambridge, MA: MIT Press.

Goodhart, Charles. 1989. *Money, Information, and Uncertainty.* Cambridge, MA: MIT Press.

Goodhart, Charles. 2000. "Can Central Banking Survive the IT Revolution?" *International Finance* 3(2): 189–209.

Goodrich, Carter. 1950. "The Revulsion against Internal Improvements." *Journal of Economic History* 10(2): 145–69.

Goodwyn, Lawrence. 1978. *The Populist Moment: A Short History of the Agrarian Revolt in America.* New York: Oxford University Press.

Gorski, Philip S. 2003. *The Disciplinary Revolution: Calvinism and the Rise of the State in Early Modern Europe.* Chicago: University of Chicago Press.

Gould, Roger V. 1993. "Collective Action and Network Structure." *American Sociological Review* 58(2): 182–96.

Granovetter, Mark. 1985. "Economic Action and Social Structure: The Problem of Embeddedness." *American Journal of Sociology* 91(3): 481–510.

Granovetter, Mark. 2002. "A Theoretical Agenda for Economic Sociology." Pp. 35–59 in *The New Economic Sociology: Developments in an Emerging Field.* New York: Russel Sage Foundation.

Grant, James. 1992. *Money of the Mind: Borrowing and Lending in America from the Civil War to Michael Milken.* New York: Macmillan.

Green, R. K., and S. M. Wachter. 2005. "The American Mortgage in Historical and International Context." *Journal of Economic Perspectives* 19(4): 93–114.

Grimaldi, Bernardino. 1881. *Nella Discussione del Disegno di Legge sui Provvedimenti per l'Abolizione del Corso Forzoso.* Rome: Eredi Botta.

Gross, Neil. 2009. "A Pragmatist Theory of Social Mechanisms." *American Sociological Review* 74(3): 358–79.

Guillén, Mauro F. 1994. *Models of Management.* Chicago: Chicago University Press.

Guinnane, Timothy W. 2002. "Delegated Monitors, Large and Small: Germany's Banking System, 1800–1914." *Journal of Economic Literature* 40(1): 73–124.

Guseva, Alya. 2008. *Into the Red: The Birth of the Credit Card Market in Postcommunist Russia.* Stanford: Stanford University Press.

Guseva, Alya, and Akos Rona-Tas. 2001. "Uncertainty, Risk, and Trust: Russian and American Credit Card Markets Compared." *American Sociological Review* 66(5): 623–46.

Hall, Peter, and David Soskice. 2001. *Varieties of Capitalism: The Institutional Foundations of Comparative Advantage*. New York: Oxford University Press.

Hammond, Bray. 1957. *Banks and Politics in America: From the Revolution to the Civil War*. Princeton: Princeton University Press.

Harvey, David. 1991. *The Condition of Postmodernity: An Enquiry into the Origins of Cultural Change*. Reprint. Hoboken, NJ: Wiley-Blackwell.

Hasan, Iftekhar, and Gerald P. Dwyer. 1994. "Bank Runs in the Free Banking Period." *Journal of Money, Credit and Banking* 26(2): 271–88.

Haveman, H. A., and H. Rao. 1997. "Structuring a Theory of Moral Sentiments: Institutional and Organizational Coevolution in the Early Thrift Industry." *American Journal of Sociology* 102(6): 1606–51.

Heim, Carol, and Philip Mirowski. 1987. "Interest Rates and Crowding-Out during Britain's Industrial Revolution." *Journal of Economic History* 47(1): 117–39.

Helleiner, Eric. 1999. "Historicizing Territorial Currencies: Monetary Space and the Nation-state in North America." *Political Geography* 18: 309–39.

Helleiner, Eric. 2002. "Economic Nationalism as a Challenge to Economic Liberalism? Lessons from the 19th Century." *International Studies Quarterly* 46(3): 307–29.

Helleiner, Eric. 2003. *The Making of National Money: Territorial Currencies in Historical Perspective*. Ithaca, NY: Cornell University Press.

Herrigel, G. 2000. *Industrial Constructions: The Sources of German Industrial Power*. New York: Cambridge University Press.

Hertner, Peter. 1994. "Modern Banking in Italy." In *Handbook on the History of European Banks*, edited by Manfred Pohl and Sabine Freitag. Aldershot, Hants, England; Brookfield, VT: Edward Elgar.

Hicks, John. 1969. *A Theory of Economic History*. London, Oxford: Clarendon Press.

Hilkey, Judy. 1997. *Character Is Capital: Success Manuals and Manhood in Gilded Age America*. Chapel Hill: University of North Carolina Press.

Hirsch, Fred, and John H. Goldthorpe. 1979. *The Political Economy of Inflation*. Cambridge: Harvard University Press.

Hirschman, Albert O. 1977. *The Passions and the Interests: Political Arguments for Capitalism before Its Triumph*. Princeton: Princeton University Press.

Hirschman, Albert O. 1982. "Rival Interpretations of Market Society: Civilizing, Destructive, or Feeble?" *Journal of Economic Literature* 20(4): 1463–84.

Hobson, John M. 1997. *The Wealth of States*. Cambridge: Cambridge University Press.

Holt, Michael F. 2003. *The Rise and Fall of the American Whig Party: Jacksonian Politics and the Onset of the Civil War*. New York: Oxford University Press.

Horwitz, Morton J. 1979. *The Transformation of American Law, 1780–1860*. Cambridge: Harvard University Press.

Howe, Daniel Walker. 2007. *What Hath God Wrought: The Transformation of America, 1815–1848*. New York: Oxford University Press.

Hull, Walter Henry. 1907. *Practical Problems in Banking and Currency*. New York: Macmillan.

Ingham, Geoffrey. 1984. *Capitalism Divided? The City and Industry in British Social Development*. New York: Schocken Books.

Ingham, Geoffrey. 1994. "States, Market and World Money." In *Money, Power and Space*, edited by Ron Martin, Stuart Corbridge, and Nigel Thrift. Cambridge: Blackwell.

Ingham, Geoffrey. 1996. "Money Is a Social Relation." *Review of Social Economy* 54(4): 507–29.

Ingham, Geoffrey. 1998. "On the Underdevelopment of the 'Sociology of Money.'" *Acta Sociologica* 41(1): 3–18.

Ingham, Geoffrey. 1999. "Capitalism, Money and Banking: A Critique of Recent Historical Sociology." *British Journal of Sociology* 50(1): 76–96.

Ingham, Geoffrey. 2001. "Fundamentals of a Theory of Money: Untangling Fine, Lapavitsas and Zelizer." *Economy and Society* 30(3): 304–23.

Ingham, Geoffrey. 2003. "Schumpeter and Weber on the Institutions of Capitalism." *Journal of Classical Sociology* 3(3): 297–309.

Ingham, Geoffrey. 2004. *The Nature of Money*. Cambridge, UK, Malden, MA: Polity Press.

Ingham, Geoffrey. 2006. "Further Reflections on the Ontology of Money: Responses to Lapavitsas and Dodd." *Economy and Society* 35(2): 259.

Innes, A. M. 1913. "What Is Money." *Banking Law Journal* 30(January–December): 377.

Innes, A. M. 1914. "Credit Theory of Money." *Banking Law Journal* 31(January–December): 151.

James, John A. 1978. *Money and Capital Markets in Postbellum America*. Princeton: Princeton University Press.

John, Richard R. 1997. "Governmental Institutions as Agents of Change: Rethinking American Political Development in the Early Republic, 1787–1835." *Studies in American Political Development* 11(2): 347–80.

John, Richard R. 1998. *Spreading the News*. Cambridge: Harvard University Press.

Jones, R. A. 1976. "The Origin and Development of Media of Exchange." *Journal of Political Economy* 84(4): 757–75.

Josephson, Matthew. 1962. *The Robber Barons: The Great American Capitalists, 1861–1901*. Boston: Houghton Mifflin Harcourt.

Keynes, John M. 1930. *A Treatise on Money*. London: Macmillan.

Kindleberger, Charles. 1984. *A Financial History of Western Europe*. London: Allen and Unwin.

Kindleberger, C. 1996. *History of Financial Crises: Mania, Panic and Crash*. New York: John Wiley and Sons.

Knapp, Georg Friedrich. 1924. *The State Theory of Money*. London: Macmillan.

Knodell, Jane. 2006. "Rethinking the Jacksonian Economy: The Impact of the 1832 Bank Veto on Commercial Banking." *Journal of Economic History* 66(3): 541–74.

Knorr Cetina, Karin. 2004. "Capturing Markets? A Review Essay on Harrison White on Producer Markets." *Socio-Economic Review* 2(1): 137.

Knorr Cetina, Karin, and Urs Bruegger. 2002. "Global Microstructures: The Virtual Societies of Financial Markets." *American Journal of Sociology* 107(4): 905–50.

Krippner, Greta. 2005. "The Financialization of the American Economy." *Socio-Economic Review* 3(2): 173.

Krippner, Greta. 2011. *Capitalizing on Crisis: The Political Origins of the Rise of Finance.* Cambridge: Harvard University Press.

Krugman, Paul. 2012. *End This Depression Now!* New York: W. W. Norton and Company.

Kyriacou, Andreas P. 2005. "Rationality, Ethnicity and Institutions: A Survey of Issues and Results." *Journal of Economic Surveys* 19(1): 23–42.

La Porta, Rafael, Florencio Lopez-de-Silanes, Andrei Shleifer, and Robert W. Vishny. 1997. "Legal Determinants of External Finance." *Journal of Finance* 52(3): 1131–50.

Lamoreaux, Naomi. 1994. *Insider Lending: Banks, Personal Connections, and Economic Development in Industrial New England.* New York: Cambridge University Press.

Lamoreaux, Naomi, and Christopher Glaisek. 1991. "Vehicles of Privilege or Mobility? Banks in Providence, Rhode Island, during the Age of Jackson." *Business History Review* 65(3): 502–27.

Lanaro, Silvio. 1979. *Nazione e Lavoro: Saggio Sulla Cultura Borghese in Italia.* Venezia: Marsilio.

Langley, Paul. 2008. *The Everyday Life of Global Finance: Saving and Borrowing in Anglo-America.* Oxford, New York: Oxford University Press.

Latour, Bruno. 1987. Science in Action: How to Follow Scientists and Engineers through Society. Cambridge: Harvard University Press.

Laughlin, James Laurence. 1903. *Credit.* Chicago: University of Chicago Press.

Laven, David, and Lucy Riall. 2000. *Napoleon's Legacy: Problems of Government in Restoration Europe.* Oxford: Berg.

Lavoie, Marc. 2006. *Introduction to Post-Keynesian Economics.* Basingstoke, New York: Palgrave Macmillan.

Lerner, A. P. 1947. "Money as a Creature of the State." *American Economic Review* 37(2): 312–17.

Levi-Faur, D. 1997. "Economic Nationalism: From Friedrich List to Robert Reich." *Review of International Studies* 23(3): 359–70.

Lewis, Michael. 2010. *The Big Short: Inside the Doomsday Machine.* 1st edition. New York: W. W. Norton and Company.

Livingston, James. 1986. *Origins of the Federal Reserve System: Money, Class and Corporate Capitalism, 1890–1913.* Ithaca, NY: Cornell University Press.

Lovell, Elleanor. 2009. *The Warwick Commission on International Financial Reform: In Praise of Unlevel Playing Fields.* University of Warwick (warwick.ac.uk/research/warwickcommission/report).

Loveman, M. 2005. "The Modern State and the Primitive Accumulation of Symbolic Power." *American Journal of Sociology* 110(6): 1651–83.

Luzzatti, Luigi. 1883. "L'Abolizione del Corso Forzoso." *Nuova Antologia* 38(2): 735–52.

Luzzatto, Gino. 1968. *L'Economia Italiana dal 1861 al 1894.* Turin: Einaudi.

MacKenzie, Donald. 2003. "Long-Term Capital Management and the Sociology of Arbitrage." *Economy and Society* 32(3): 349.

MacKenzie, Donald. 2006. *An Engine, Not a Camera.* Cambridge, MA: MIT Press.

MacKenzie, Donald, and Yuval Millo. 2003. "Constructing a Market, Performing Theory: The Historical Sociology of a Financial Derivatives Exchange." *American Journal of Sociology* 109(1): 107–45.

Magliani, Agostino. 1878. "La Quistione Finanziaria de' Comuni." *Nuova Antologia* 10(2): 291–320.

Mahoney, James, and Dietrich Rueschemeyer. 2003. *Comparative Historical Analysis in the Social Sciences*. Cambridge, New York: Cambridge University Press.

Majewski, John D. 2000. *A House Dividing: Economic Development in Pennsylvania and Virginia before the Civil War*. New York: Cambridge University Press.

Majorana-Calatabiano, Salvatore. 1874. *Sulla Proposta di Legge per Regolare la Circolazione Cartacea. Discorso del Deputato Maiorana-Calatabiano nelle Tornate della Camera 7 e 9 Febbraio 1874*. Rome: Eredi Botta.

Majorana-Calatabiano, Salvatore. 1879. *Considerazioni e Documenti in Appoggio al Progetto di Legge sul Riordinamento degli Istituti di Emissione (Ministri Majorana e Magliani) a Proposito dei Reclami di Alcuni fra gli Istituti Medesimi*. Rome: Eredi Botta.

Mallaby, Sebastian. 2010. *More Money Than God: Hedge Funds and the Making of a New Elite*. New York: Penguin Press.

Manacorda, Gastone. 1993. *Dalla Crisi alla Crescita: Crisi Economica e Lotta Politica in Italia, 1892–1896*. Rome: Editori Riuniti.

Mann, Bruce H. 2002. *Republic of Debtors*. Cambridge: Harvard University Press.

Mann, Michael. 1993. *The Sources of Social Power,* volume 2. New York: Cambridge University Press.

Mann, Michael. 2004. *Fascists*. New York: Cambridge University Press.

Martello, Tullio. 1881. *L'Abolizione del Corso Forzoso: Magliani e Ferrara*. Venice: Tip. del Commercio di Marco Visentinu.

Martin, Isaac William, Ajay Mehrotra, and Monica Prasad. 2009. *The New Fiscal Sociology: Taxation in Comparative and Historical Perspective*. Cambridge, New York: Cambridge University Press.

Marx, Karl. 1909. *Capital,* volume 3: *The Process of Capitalist Production as a Whole*. Chicago: Charles H. Kerr and Company.

Marx, Karl. 1921. *Capital,* volume 1: *The Process of Capitalist Production*. Translated from the 3rd German edition. Chicago: Charles H. Kerr and Company.

Masi, Paola. 1989. "L'influenza del Debito Pubblico sulla Costituzione dei Sistemi Finanziari: Il Caso Italiano 1860–93." *Rivista di Storia Economica* 6(1): 60–86.

McAdam, Doug. 1999. *Political Process and the Development of Black Insurgency, 1930–1970*. Chicago: University of Chicago Press.

McCloskey, Deirdre N. 2006. *The Bourgeois Virtues: Ethics for an Age of Commerce*. Chicago: University of Chicago Press.

Mehrling, Perry. 2002. "Retrospectives: Economists and the Fed: Beginnings." *Journal of Economic Perspectives* 16(4): 207–18.

Mehrling, Perry. 2010. *The New Lombard Street: How the Fed Became the Dealer of Last Resort*. Princeton: Princeton University Press.

Meltzer, Allan H. 2004. *A History of the Federal Reserve: 1913–1951*. Chicago: University of Chicago Press.

Menger, K. 1892. "On the Origin of Money." *Economic Journal* 2(6): 239–55.

Migdal, J. S. 2001. *State in Society: Studying How States and Societies Transform and Constitute One Another*. Cambridge: Cambridge University Press.

Mihm, Stephen. 2007. *A Nation of Counterfeiters*. Cambridge: Harvard University Press.

Mills, C. Wright. 1956. *The Power Elite*. New York: Oxford University Press.

Minsky, H. P. 1986. *Stabilizing an Unstable Economy: A Twentieth Century Fund Report*. New Haven: Yale University Press.

Mintz, Beth, and Michael Schwartz. 1985. *The Power Structure of American Business*. Chicago: Chicago University Press.

Mizruchi, Mark. 1982. *The American Corporate Network*. Beverly Hills, CA: Sage.

Mizruchi, Mark. 2004. "Berle and Means Revisited: The Governance and Power of Large U.S. Corporations." *Theory and Society* 33(5): 579–617.

Moen, Jon, and Ellis W. Tallman. 1992. "The Bank Panic of 1907: The Role of Trust Companies." *Journal of Economic History* 52(3): 611–30.

Moen, Jon, and Ellis W. Tallman. 1999. "Why Didn't the United States Establish a Central Bank Until after the Panic of 1907?" *Federal Reserve Bank of Atlanta Working Paper* 99 (repec.org/p/fip/fedawp/99–16.html).

Moore, B. J. 1988. *Horizontalists and Verticalists: The Macroeconomics of Credit Money*. Cambridge: Cambridge University Press.

Moore, Barrington. 1966. *Social Origins of Dictatorship and Democracy: Lord and Peasant in the Making of the Modern World*. Boston: Beacon Press.

Morgan, J. P. 1913a. *Letter from Messrs. J. P. Morgan & Co., in Response to the Invitation of the Sub-Committee (Hon. A. P. Pujo, Chairman) of the Committee on Banking and Currency of the House of Representatives*.

Morgan, J. P. 1913b. "Testimony." Pp. 1021–88 in *Money Trust Investigation, Investigation of Financial and Monetary Conditions in the United States under House Resolutions Nos. 429 and 504, before a Subcommittee of the Committee on Banking & Currency*. Washington, DC: Government Printing Office.

Mori, Giorgio. 1977. *Il Capitalismo Industriale in Italia: Processo d'Industrializzazione e Storia d'Italia*. Rome: Editori Riuniti.

Mori, Giorgio. 1992. "L'Economia Italiana dagli Anni Ottanta alla Prima Guerra Mondiale." Pp. 1–106 in *Storia dell'Industria Elettrica in Italia: 1. Le Origini. 1882–1914*, edited by Giorgio Mori. Rome-Bari: Laterza.

Moyer, Liz. 2007. "The World's Most Exclusive Credit Cards." *Forbes*. July 3.

Muldrew, Craig. 1998. *The Economy of Obligation: The Culture of Credit and Social Relations in Early Modern England*. New York: Palgrave Macmillan.

Murphy, Raymond. 1984. "The Structure of Closure: A Critique and Development of the Theories of Weber, Collins, and Parkin." *British Journal of Sociology* 35(4): 547–67.

Myers, Margaret G. 1971. *The New York Money Market: Origins and Development*. New York: Columbia University Press and AMS Press.

Nakano, Takeshi. 2004. "Theorising Economic Nationalism." *Nations and Nationalism* 10(3): 211–29.

Negri, Guglielmo. 1989. *Giolitti e la Nascita della Banca d'Italia nel 1893*. Bari: Laterza.

Nisco, Nicola. 1879. *Il Rinnovamento del Riordinamento Bancario nell'Interesse delle Classi Produttrici*. Rome: Tipografia Bocca.

Nitzan, Jonathan. 1998. "Differential Accumulation: Towards a New Political Economy of Capital." *Review of International Political Economy* 5(2): 169–216.

Nitzan, Jonathan, and Shimshon Bichler. 2009. *Capital as Power: A Study of Order and Creorder*. London, New York: Routledge.

North, Douglass, and Barry Weingast. 1989. "Constitution and Commitment: The Evolution of Institutional Governing Public Choice in Seventeenth-Century England." *Journal of Economic History* 49(4): 803–32.

Nussbaum, Arthur. 1957. *A History of the Dollar*. New York: Columbia University Press.

O'Connor, J. 2001. *The Fiscal Crisis of the State*. New Brunswick, NJ: Transaction Publishers.

Olegario, Rowena. 2006. *A Culture of Credit*. Cambridge: Harvard University Press.

Olson, Mancur. 1965. *The Logic of Collective Action: Public Goods and the Theory of Groups*. Cambridge: Harvard University Press.

Overby, Brooke A. 1994. "Community Reinvestment Act Reconsidered." *University of Pennsylvania Law Review* 143: 1431.

Pallavicino, Camillo. 1863. "Come Si Possano Conciliare l'unità e la Pluralità delle Banche in Italia." *Rivista Contemporanea* (December): 321–26.

Pallavicino, Camillo. 1864. "Come Si Possano Conciliare l'Unità e la Pluralità delle Banche in Italia." *Rivista Contemporanea* (October): 20–26.

Palley, Thomas I. 2010. "The Limits of Minsky's Financial Instability Hypothesis as an Explanation of the Crisis." *Monthly Review* 61(11).

Pareto, Vilfredo. 1968. *The Rise and Fall of the Elites; An Application of Theoretical Sociology*. Totowa, NJ: Bedminster Press.

Pareto, Vilfredo, and Charles H. Powers. 1984. *The Transformation of Democracy*. New Brunswick, NJ: Transaction Publishers.

Parkin, Frank. 1983. *Marxism and Class Theory*. New York: Columbia University Press.

Parry, Jonathan P., and Maurice Bloch. 1989. *Money and the Morality of Exchange*. New York: Cambridge University Press.

Pasanek, Brad, and Simone Polillo. 2011. "Guest Editors' Introduction." *Journal of Cultural Economy* 4(3): 231–38.

Perrow, Charles. 2002. *Organizing America: Wealth, Power, and the Origins of Corporate Capitalism*. Princeton: Princeton University Press.

Pessen, Edward. 1980. "How Different from Each Other Were the Antebellum North and South?" *American Historical Review* 85(5): 1119–49.

Pickel, Andreas. 2003. "Explaining, and Explaining with, Economic Nationalism." *Nations and Nationalism* 9(1): 105–27.

Pierson, Paul. 1996. "The New Politics of the Welfare State." *World Politics* 48(2): 143–79.

Piluso, Giandomenico. 2001. "La 'Capitale Finanziaria' e la Rete Regionale: Il Sistema Finanziario Lombardo tra Mercato e Istituzioni." Pp. 531–612 in *Storia D'Italia: Le Re-*

gioni Dall'Unità a Oggi: La Lombardia, edited by Duccio Bigazzi and Marco Meriggi. Turin: Giulio Einaudi.

Pizzorno, Alessandro. 1981. "Interests and Parties in Pluralism." Pp. 247–84 in *Organizing Interests in Western Europe: Pluralism, Corporatism, and the Transformation of Politics*, edited by Suzanne D. Berger. New York: Cambridge University Press.

Pizzorno, Alessandro. 1986. "Some Other Kinds of Otherness: A Critique of 'Rational Choice' Theories." Pp. 355–73 in *Development, Democracy, and the Art of Trespassing.* South Bend, IN: Notre Dame University Press.

Podolny, Joel M. 1993. "A Status-Based Model of Market Competition." *American Journal of Sociology* 98(4): 829.

Poggi, G. 1993. *Money and the Modern Mind: George Simmel's Philosophy of Money.* Berkeley, Los Angeles: University of California Press.

Polanyi, Karl. 1944. *The Great Transformation: The Political and Economic Origins of Our Time.* Boston: Beacon Press.

Polillo, Simone. 2011. "Money, Moral Authority, and the Politics of Creditworthiness." *American Sociological Review* 76(3): 437–64.

Pollard, Sidney. 1981. *Peaceful Conquest: The Industrialization of Europe, 1760–1970.* New York: Oxford University Press.

Polsi, Alessandro. 1993. *Alle Origini del Capitalismo Italiano: Stato, Banche e Banchieri Dopo l'Unità.* Turin: Einaudi.

Polsi, Alessandro. 2000. "L'articolazione Territoriale del Sistema Bancario Italiano tra Scelte di Mercato e Intervento delle Autorità Monetarie (1900–1936)." Pp. 217–62 in *Banche e Reti di Banche nell'Italia Postunitaria*, volume 1, edited by Giuseppe Conti and Salvatore La Francesca. Bologna: Il Mulino.

Porter, T. M. 1996. *Trust in Numbers: The Pursuit of Objectivity in Science and Public Life.* Princeton: Princeton University Press.

Preda, Alex. 2009. *Framing Finance: The Boundaries of Markets and Modern Capitalism.* Chicago: University of Chicago Press.

Putnam, Robert. 1993. *Making Democracy Work.* Princeton: Princeton University Press.

Ragin, Charles C., and Howard Saul Becker. 1992. *What Is a Case?: Exploring the Foundations of Social Inquiry.* New York: Cambridge University Press.

Rajan, R., and L. Zingales. 2004. *Saving Capitalism from the Capitalists: Unleashing the Power of Financial Markets to Create Wealth and Spread Opportunity.* Princeton: Princeton University Press.

Rajan, Uday, Amit Seru, and Vikrant Vig. 2008. "The Failure of Models That Predict Failure: Distance, Incentives and Defaults." *SSRN eLibrary* (ssrn.com/sol3/papers.cfm?abstract_id=1296982).

Ramirez, Carlos, and J. Bradford DeLong. 2001. "Understanding America's Hesitant Steps toward Financial Capitalism: Politics, the Depression and the Separation of Commercial and Investment Banking." *Public Choice* 106: 93–116.

Redlich, Fritz. 1968. *The Molding of American Banking: Men and Ideas.* New York, London: Johnson Reprint Corporation.

Remini, Robert Vincent. 2001. *The Life of Andrew Jackson.* New York: HarperCollins.

Renda, Francesco. 1987. "La Questione Sociale e i Fasci, 1874–94." Pp. 157–88 in *Storia d'Italia: Le Regioni dall'Unità a Oggi. La Sicilia*, edited by Maurica Aymard and Giuseppe Giannizzo. Turin: Giulio Einaudi.

Riall, Lucy. 1993. "Elite Resistance to State Formation: The Case of Italy." Pp. 46–68 in *National Histories and European History*, edited by Mary Fulbrook. Boulder, CO: Westview Press.

Riall, Lucy. 1994. *The Italian Risorgimento: State, Society and National Unification*. London, New York: Routledge.

Riall, Lucy. 1998. *Sicily and the Unification of Italy: Liberal Policy and Local Power, 1859–1866*. New York: Oxford University Press.

Riall, Lucy. 2003. "Elites in Search of Authority: Political Power and Social Order in Nineteenth-century Sicily." *History Workshop Journal* 55(1): 25–46.

Riall, Lucy. 2007. *Garibaldi: Invention of a Hero*. New Haven: Yale University Press.

Riall, Lucy. 2009. *Risorgimento: The History of Italy from Napoleon to Nation-State*. Basingstoke, New York: Palgrave Macmillan.

Riall, Lucy, Axel Körner, Maurizio Isabella, Catherine Brice, and Alberto Mario Banti. 2007. "Leggere La Nuova Storia Del Risorgimento: Una Visione Dall'esterno. Una Discussione Con Alberto M. Banti." *Storica* 13(38): 91–132.

Richards, Leonard L. 2000. *The Slave Power: The Free North and Southern Domination, 1780–1860*. Baton Rouge: Louisiana State University Press.

Ritter, Gretchen. 1997. *Goldbugs and Greenbacks: The Antimonopoly Tradition and the Politics of Finance in America*. Cambridge, New York: Cambridge University Press.

Rockoff, Hugh. 1974. "The Free Banking Era: A Reexamination." *Journal of Money, Credit and Banking* (May): 141–73.

Roe, Mark. 1994. *Strong Managers, Weak Owners: The Political Roots of American Corporate Finance*. Princeton: Princeton University Press.

Rolnick, Arthur J., and Warren E. Weber. 1983. "New Evidence on the Free Banking Era." *American Economic Review* 73(5): 1080–91.

Rolnick, Arthur J., and Warren E. Weber. 1984. "The Causes of Free Bank Failures: A Detailed Examination." *Journal of Monetary Economics* 14(3): 267–91.

Romanelli, Raffaele. 1988. *Il Comando Impossibile: Stato e Società nell'Italia Liberale*. Bologna: Il Mulino.

Romanelli, Raffaele. 1991. "Political Debate, Social History, and the Italian Borghesia: Changing Perspectives in Historical Research." *Journal of Modern History* 63(4): 717–39.

Romanelli, Raffaele. 1995. "Centralismo e Autonomie." Pp. 125–86 in *Storia dello Stato Italiano*, edited by Raffaele Romanelli. Bari: Laterza.

Romeo, Rosario. 1959. *Risorgimento e Capitalismo*. Bari: Laterza.

Rossi, Alessandro. 1878. "Del Credito Popolare." *Nuova Antologia* 12(December): 708–47.

Rousseau, Peter. 2002. "Jacksonian Monetary Policy, Specie Flows, and the Panic of 1837." *Journal of Economic History* 62(2): 457–88.

Roy, William G. 1997. *Socializing Capital: The Rise of the Large Industrial Corporation in America*. Princeton: Princeton University Press.

Rugge, Fabio. 1986. "La Città che Sale: Il Problema di Governo Municipale di Inizio Secolo." Pp. 54–71 in *Istituzioni e Borghesie Locali nell'Italia Liberale*, edited by Mariapia Bigaran. Milan: Franco Angeli.

Rugh, Jacob S., and Douglas S. Massey. 2010. "Racial Segregation and the American Foreclosure Crisis." *American Sociological Review* 75(5): 629–51.

Sabetti, Filippo. 2000. *The Search for Good Government*. Montreal: McGill-Queen's University Press.

Salandra, Antonio. 1878. "Il Riordinamento delle Finanze Comunali." *Nuova Antologia* 10(July): 345–64.

Sanders, Elizabeth. 1999. *Roots of Reform: Farmers, Workers, and the American State, 1877–1917*. Chicago: University of Chicago Press.

Savage, James D. 1988. *Balanced Budgets and American Politics*. Ithaca, NY: Cornell University Press.

Scheiber, Harry N. 1975. "Federalism and the American Economic Order, 1789–1910." *Law and Society Review* 10(1): 57–118.

Scheiber, Harry N. 1981. "Regulation, Property Rights, and Definition of 'The Market': Law and the American Economy." *Journal of Economic History* 41(1): 103–9.

Schlesinger, Arthur Meier. 1953. *The Age of Jackson*. Boston: Little, Brown.

Schumpeter, Joseph. 1911. *The Theory of Economic Development*. Cambridge, MA: Harvard University Press.

Schumpeter, Joseph. 1918. "The Crisis of the Tax State." Pp. 99–140 in *The Economics and Sociology of Capitalism*, edited by Richard Swedberg. Princeton: Princeton University Press.

Schumpeter, Joseph. 1939. *Business Cycles: A Theoretical, Historical and Statistical Analysis of the Capitalist Process*. New York: McGraw-Hill.

Schumpeter, Joseph. 1962. *Capitalism, Socialism and Democracy*. New York: Harper and Row.

Schumpeter, Joseph. 1991. "Money and Currency." *Social Research* 58(3): 499–545.

Schumpeter, Joseph. 1994. *History of Economic Analysis*. New York: Oxford University Press.

Schweikart, Larry. 1987a. *Banking in the American South from the Age of Jackson to Reconstruction*. Baton Rouge: Louisiana State University Press.

Schweikart, Larry. 1987b. "Southern Banks and Economic Growth in the Antebellum Period: A Reassessment." *Journal of Southern History* 53(1): 19–36.

Seabrooke, Leonard. 2006. *The Social Sources of Financial Power: Domestic Legitimacy and International Financial Orders*. Ithaca, NY: Cornell University Press.

Seavoy, Ronald E. 1978. "The Public Service Origins of the American Business Corporation." *Business History Review* 52(1): 30–60.

Seismit-Doda, Federico. 1873. *Discorso Pronunziato dal Deputato Federico Seismit-Doda alla Camera dei Deputati Intorno al Corso Forzoso ed al Riordinamento della Circolazione Cartacea nella Tornata del 12 Febbraio 1873*. Rome: Eredi Botta.

Seligman, Edwin, et al. 1908. *The Currency Problem and the Present Financial Situation: A Series of Addresses Delivered at Columbia University, 1907–1908*. New York: Columbia University Press.

Sella, Quintino, and S. Castagnola. 1870. *Sulla Libertà delle Banche*. Rome: Eredi Botta.

Sellers, Charles. 1994. *The Market Revolution*. New York: Oxford University Press.

Semenza, Gaetano. 1873. *La Quistione delle Banche*. Milan: Agenzia Internazionale.

Semenza, Gaetano. 1879. *Le Banche e la Questione Finanziaria in Italia*. Rome: Bocca Editore.

Shapiro, Susan P. 2005. "Agency Theory." *Annual Review of Sociology* 31(1): 263–84.

Shefter, Martin. 1994. *Political Parties and the State: The American Historical Experience*. Princeton: Princeton University Press.

Sherer, William. 1913. "Testimony." Pp. 124–63 in *Money Trust Investigation, Investigation of Financial and Monetary Conditions in the United States under House Resolutions nos. 429 and 504, before a Subcommittee of the Committee on Banking & Currency*, volume 1, edited by U.S. Congress, House Committee on Banking and Currency. Washington, DC: Government Printing Office.

Shiller, Robert J. 2006. *Irrational Exuberance*. New York: Random House.

Silbey, Joel H. 1994. *The American Political Nation, 1838–1893*. Stanford: Stanford University Press.

Simmel, Georg. 1950. *The Sociology of Georg Simmel*. Edited by Kurt H. Wolff. New York: Simon and Schuster.

Simmel, Georg. 1990. *The Philosophy of Money*.2nd enl. edition. London, New York: Routledge.

Sinclair, Timothy. 2000. "Deficit Discourse: The Social Construction of Fiscal Rectitude." Pp. 185–203 in *Globalization and Its Critics: Perspectives from Political Economy*, edited by Randall D. Germain. Basingstoke: Palgrave Macmillan.

Sklar, Martin. 1987. *The Corporate Reconstruction of American Capitalism*. Cambridge: Cambridge University Press.

Skocpol, Theda. 1992. *Protecting Soldiers and Mothers: The Political Origins of Social Policy in the United States*. Cambridge, MA: Harvard University Press.

Skocpol, Theda, and Margaret Somers. 1980. "The Uses of Comparative History in Macrosocial Inquiry." *Comparative Studies in Society and History* 22(02): 174–97.

Smith, Adam. 1976. *The Wealth of Nations*. Chicago: Chicago University Press.

Smith, Vera. 1990. *The Rationale of Central Banking and the Free Banking Alternative*. Indianapolis, IN: Liberty Fund.

Smithin, John. 1994. *Controversies in Monetary Economics: Ideas, Issues, and Policy*. Aldershot, Hants: Edward Elgar.

Smithin, John. 2000. *What Is Money?* London: Routledge.

Snow, David A., Louis A. Zurcher, and Sheldon Ekland-Olson. 1980. "Social Networks and Social Movements: A Microstructural Approach to Differential Recruitment." *American Sociological Review* 45(5): 787–801.

Snowden, Kenneth. 1995. "Mortgage Securitization in the U.S.: 20th Century Developments in Historical Perspective." P. 276 in *Anglo-American Financial Systems: Institutions and Markets in the Twentieth Century*. New York: New York University Solomon Center.

Soria, Beniamino. 1880. *Le Banche di Emissione*. Rome: Tipografia Pallotta.

Stasavage, David. 2002. "Credible Commitment in Early Modern Europe: North and Weingast Revisited." *Journal of Law, Economics, and Organization* 18(1): 155–86.

Stearns, Linda Brewster, and Kenneth D. Allan. 1996. "Economic Behavior in Institutional Environments: The Corporate Merger Wave of the 1980s." *American Sociological Review* 61(4): 699–718.

Steinmo, Sven. 1989. "Political Institutions and Tax Policy in the United States, Sweden, and Britain." *World Politics* 41(4): 500–535.

Stiglitz, Joseph E. 2011. "The Contributions of the Economics of Information to Twentieth Century Economics." *Quarterly Journal of Economics* 115(4): 1441–78.

Stiglitz, Joseph E., and A. Weiss. 1981. "Credit Rationing in Markets with Imperfect Information." *American Economic Review* 71(3): 393–410.

Stringher, Bonaldo. 1879. "Le Banche e il Corso Forzoso. Sul Riordinamento degli Istituti di Emissione." *Archivio di Statistica* IV: 590–96.

Swedberg, Richard. 1992. *Schumpeter: A Biography*. Princeton: Princeton University Press.

Swedberg, Richard. 2000. *Max Weber and the Idea of Economic Sociology*. Princeton: Princeton University Press.

Swedberg, Richard. 2003. "Answer to Geoffrey Ingham." *Journal of Classical Sociology* 3(3): 311.

Swire, Peter P. 1995. "Equality of Opportunity and Investment in Creditworthiness." *University of Pennsylvania Law Review* 143(5): 1533–59.

Sylla, Richard. 1969. "Federal Policy, Market Structure and Capital Mobilization in the United States, 1863–1913." *Journal of Economic History* 29(4): 657–86.

Sylla, Richard. 1975. *The American Capital Market, 1846–1914: A Study of the Effects of Public Policy on Economic Development*. New York: Arno Press.

Sylla, Richard. 1985. "Early American Banking: The Significance of the Corporate Form." *Business and Economic History* 14: 105–25.

Sylla, Richard. 1998. "U.S. Securities Markets and the Banking System, 1790–1840." *Review—Federal Reserve Bank of St. Louis* 80(3): 83–98.

Sylla, Richard, J. B. Legler, and John Wallis. 1995. *Sources and Uses of Funds in State and Local Governments, 1790–1915 (machine-readable dataset)*. Ann Arbor, MI: Inter-university Consortium for Political and Social Research.

Sylla, Richard, Richard Tilly, and Gabriel Tortella. 1999. *The State, the Financial System, and Economic Modernization*. Cambridge, UK, New York: Cambridge University Press.

Sylla, Richard, and John Wallis. 1998. "The Anatomy of Sovereign Debt Crises: Lessons from the American State Defaults of the 1840s." *Japan and the World Economy* 10(3): 267–93.

Tarrow, Sidney. 2001. "National Integration, National Disintegration, and Contention: A Paired Comparison of Unlike Cases." Pp. 176–204 in *Dynamics of Contention*, edited by Doug McAdam, Sidney Tarrow, and Charles Tilly. Cambridge: Cambridge University Press.

Temin, Peter. 1969. *The Jacksonian Economy*. New York: W. W. Norton and Company.

Tett, Gillian. 2009. *Fool's Gold*. New York: Simon and Schuster.

Thelen, Kathleen. 2003. "How Institutions Evolve." Pp. 208–40 in *Comparative Historical Analysis in the Social Sciences*, edited by James Mahoney and Dietrich Rueschemeyer. Cambridge, New York: Cambridge University Press.

Tilly, Charles. 1985. "State Making and War Making as Organized Crime." Pp. 169–91 in *Bringing the State Back In*, edited by Peter B. Evans, Dietrich Rueschemeyer, and Theda Skocpol. New York: Cambridge University Press.

Tilly, Charles. 1992. *Coercion, Capital, and European States, AD 990–1992*. Cambridge, MA: Blackwell.

Tilly, Charles. 1998. *Durable Inequality*. Berkeley, Los Angeles: University of California Press.

Tilly, Charles. 2005. *Trust and Rule*. New York: Cambridge University Press.

Timberlake, Richard H. 1993. *Monetary Policy in the United States*. Chicago: University of Chicago Press.

Tucker, George. 1839. *The Theory of Money and Banks Investigated*. Boston: Charles Little and James Brown.

Unger, Irwin. 1964. *The Greenback Era: A Social and Political History of American Finance, 1865–1879*. Princeton: Princeton University Press.

Verdier, Daniel. 2003. *Moving Money: Banking and Finance in the Industrializing World*. New York: Cambridge University Press.

Wallis, John. 2000. "American Government Finance in the Long Run: 1790 to 1990." *Journal of Economic Perspectives* 14(1): 61–82.

Wallis, John, Richard Sylla, and J. B. Legler. 1995. "The Interaction of Taxation and Regulation in Nineteenth Century U.S. Banking." Pp. 121–35 in *The Regulated Economy*, edited by Claudia Goldin and Gary Libecap. Chicago: University of Chicago Press.

Warburg, Paul. 1930. *The Federal Reserve System: Its Origin and Growth*. New York: Macmillan.

Watson, Harry L. 2006. *Liberty and Power: The Politics of Jacksonian America*. New York: Macmillan.

Weber, Max. 1946. "The Protestant Sects and the Spirit of Capitalism." Pp. 302–22 in *From Max Weber: Essays in Sociology*, edited by Hans H. Gerth and C. Wright Mills. New York: Oxford University Press.

Weber, Max. 1978. *Economy and Society*. Berkeley, Los Angeles, London: University of California Press.

Weber, Max. 1981. *General Economic History*. New Brunswick, NJ: Transaction Publishers.

Webster, Richard. 1975. *Industrial Imperialism in Italy, 1908–1915*. Berkeley: University of California Press.

Weingast, Barry. 1995. "The Economic Role of Political Institutions: Market-Preserving Federalism and Economic Development." *Journal of Law, Economics and Organization* 7(1): 1–31.

Wessel, David. 2009. *In Fed We Trust: Ben Bernanke's War on the Great Panic*. New York: Random House.

West, Robert C. 1977. *Banking Reform and the Federal Reserve, 1863–1923*. Ithaca, NY: Cornell University Press.

Westney, D. Eleanor. 1987. *Imitation and Innovation: The Transfer of Western Organizational Patterns to Meiji Japan*. Cambridge: Harvard University Press.

White, Eugene. 1983. *The Regulation and Reform of the American Banking System*. Princeton: Princeton University Press.

White, Harrison C. 1981. "Where Do Markets Come From?" *American Journal of Sociology* 87(3): 517–47.

White, Harrison C. 1992. *Identity and Control: A Structural Theory of Social Action*. Princeton: Princeton University Press.

White, Harrison C. 2002. *Markets from Networks: Socioeconomic Models of Production*. Princeton: Princeton University Press.

White, Leonard Dupee. 1963. *The Republican Era, 1869–1901: A Study in Administrative History*. New York: Macmillan.

Wicker, Elmus. 2005. *The Great Debate on Banking Reform: Nelson Aldrich and the Origins of the Fed*. Columbus: Ohio State University Press.

Wiebe, Robert. 1962. *Businessmen and Reform: A Study of the Progressive Movement*. Cambridge, MA: Harvard University Press.

Wiebe, Robert. 1967. *The Search for Order, 1877–1920*. New York: Macmillan.

Wilentz, Sean. 2006. *The Rise of American Democracy: Jefferson to Lincoln*. New York: W. W. Norton and Company.

Wilkins, Mira. 1989. *The History of Foreign Investment in the United States to 1914*. Cambridge, MA: Harvard University Press.

Williamson, Jeffrey G. 1974. "Watersheds and Turning Points: Conjectures on the Long-Term Impact of Civil War Financing." *Journal of Economic History* 34(3): 636–61.

Williamson, Oliver E. 1975. *Markets and Hierarchies: Analysis and Antitrust Implications*. New York: Free Press.

Willis, Henry Parker. 1915. *The Federal Reserve: A Study of the Banking System of the United States*. New York: Doubleday, Page and Company.

Wood, Gordon S. 1987. "Ideology and the Origins of Liberal America." *The William and Mary Quarterly* 44(3): 628–40.

Wray, L. Randall. 1990. *Money and Credit in Capitalist Economies: The Endogenous Money Approach*. Cheltenham UK, Northampton MA: Edward Elgar Publishing.

Wray, L. Randall. 1999. *Understanding Modern Money*. Cheltenham UK, Northampton MA: Edward Elgar Publishing.

Wray, L. Randall, and Stephanie Bell. 2004. "Introduction." In *Credit and State Theories of Money: The Contributions of A. Mitchell Innes*, edited by L. Randall Wray. Cheltenham UK, Northampton MA: Edward Elgar Publishing.

Wray, L. Randall, and Mathew Forstater. 2009. *Keynes and Macroeconomics after 70 Years: Critical Assessments of the General Theory*. Cheltenham UK, Northampton MA: Edward Elgar Publishing.

Wright, Robert Eric. 2002. *The Wealth of Nations Rediscovered: Integration and Expansion in American Financial Markets, 1780–1850*. New York: Cambridge University Press.

Wyatt-Brown, Bertram. 1966. "God and Dun & Bradstreet, 1841–1851." *Business History Review* 40(4): 432–50.

Wyatt-Brown, Bertram. 2007. *Southern Honor: Ethics and Behavior in the Old South.* New York: Oxford University Press.

Zamagni, Vera. 1993. *The Economic History of Italy 1860–1990: Recovery after Decline.* New York: Oxford University Press.

Zamagni, Vera. 1998. "Il Debito Pubblico Italiano 1861–1946: Ricostruzione della Serie Storica." *Rivista di Storia Economica* 3(December): 207–42.

Zelizer, Viviana. 1994. *The Social Meaning of Money.* New York: Basic Books.

Zelizer, Viviana. 2000. "Fine Tuning the Zelizer View." *Economy and Society* 29(3): 383–89.

Zelizer, Viviana. 2001. "Sociology of Money." In *International Encyclopedia of the Social & Behavioral Sciences*, volume 15, edited by Paul B. Baltes and Neil J. Smelser. Amsterdam: Elsevier.

Zelizer, Viviana. 2005a. "Circuits within Capitalism." Pp. 289–322 in *The Economic Sociology of Capitalism*, edited by Victor Nee and Richard Swedberg. Princeton: Princeton University Press.

Zelizer, Viviana. 2005b. "Missing Monies: Comment on Nigel Dodd, 'Reinventing Monies in Europe.'" *Economy and Society* 34(4): 584.

Zelizer, Viviana. 2005c. *The Purchase of Intimacy.* Princeton: Princeton University Press.

Zelizer, Viviana. 2010. *Economic Lives: How Culture Shapes the Economy.* Princeton: Princeton University Press.

Zelizer, Viviana, and Charles Tilly. 2006. "Relations and Categories." Pp. 1–31 in *Categories in Use*, volume 47. New York: Academic Press.

Ziblatt, Daniel. 2006. *Structuring the State: The Formation of Italy and Germany and the Puzzle of Federalism.* Princeton: Princeton University Press.

Zucker, L. G. 1986. "Production of Trust: Institutional Sources of Economic Structure, 1840–1920." *Research in Organizational Behavior* 8(1): 53–111.

Zuckerman, Ezra. 2004. "Structural Incoherence and Stock Market Activity." *American Sociological Review* 69(3): 405–32.

Zuckerman, Ezra. 2012. "Market Efficiency: A Sociological Perspective." In *Oxford Handbook of the Sociology of Finance*, edited by Alex Preda and Karen Knorr Cetina. New York: Oxford University Press.

Zysman, John. 1983. *Governments, Markets, and Growth: Financial Systems in the Politics of Industrial Change.* Ithaca, NY: Cornell University Press.

Acknowledgments

This book began as a dissertation, and as is common in dissertations, the intellectual and personal debts incurred in writing it are numerous. My advisors Randall Collins and Mauro Guillén showed faith in this project from a very early stage. They offered guidance and advice when needed and, throughout the many drafts it took to bring the project to completion, never ceased encouraging me to focus on the big picture. Sarah Babb kept me on track while I was doing archival research in Boston; her constructive feedback helped me to focus the argument at a moment when I was getting lost in details. Julia Lynch helped me bring the dissertation to a close, both by taking me on as a research assistant in my final year in graduate school, and by getting me to think systematically about the nuances of comparative research. At a later stage, when the dissertation ceased being a dissertation and began its transformation into a book, Mark Granovetter and Viviana Zelizer offered crucial advice and support. And even later on, with the transformation almost completed, Gianfranco Poggi offered feedback on the theoretical frame, and Richard Swedberg and Herman Schwartz graciously read the manuscript in its entirety, allowing me to see both the contribution the book offered, and the problems that still plagued it. Finally, at the manuscript stage, my editor Margo Fleming never failed to show her enthusiastic support for the project, and generously offered editorial assistance on significant sections of the book.

A particularly formative experience, while I was a graduate student at Penn, was my participation in a workshop on fiscal sociology at Northwestern organized by Monica Prasad, Isaac Martin, and Ajay Mehrotra, where I had the chance to meet these and other outstanding scholars whose work continues to inspire me. Among them was Leonard Seabrooke, who throughout the years has shown unrelenting support and enthusiasm toward my work, and who generously agreed to be one of the reviewers of the final manuscript. Other scholars whose advice and encouragement helped me in ways they probably don't quite realize include Erika Summers-Effler,

Lyn Spillman, Robert Fishman, Omar Lizardo, and Rory McVeigh (who all generously work-shopped a very early draft of one of my chapters with me); Douglas Forsyth, who offered very useful advice on archival research in Italy; and Greta Krippner, Mark Mizruchi, and Bruce Carruthers, whose work on finance and elites is simply exemplary.

Of course, some of my bigger debts are to scholars in career stages similar to my own. Erika Summers-Effler, longtime friend and collaborator, deserves the largest share of my gratitude, for both her relentless intellectual support and her generosity. Danielle Kane, co-organizer of two historical/cultural sociology conferences at Penn, was a source of intellectual inspiration. Anush Kapadia, Sanjay Pinto, Keith Brown, Furqan Khaldun, Kurtulus Gemici, Gabi Abend, Nick Wilson, and later, at the University of Virginia, Yarimar Bonilla, Jennifer Petersen, Rachel Rinaldo, Rina Williams, Hector Amaya, and Brad Pasanek were the most steadfast of critics and partners in crime.

The sociology departments of both Penn and the University of Virginia were ideal environments for intellectual work. Along with the Institute for Humane Studies, which offered me a much-needed dissertation grant in 2006, and the NSF, which awarded me a Dissertation Improvement grant, both departments were generous with their resources, including a Provost-funded Grant for Interdisciplinary Innovation at Penn, and funding for a sabbatical year and a manuscript workshop at UVa, for which I must also thank Krishan Kumar, who in that context offered very useful feedback. Also at UVa, Jeff Olick and Stephan Fuchs were constant sources of intellectual inspiration. Special thanks must also be given to the many archivists who made my research possible—in Rome at the Bank of Italy (where Isabella Cerioni, Sergio Cardarelli, and Alfredo Gigliobianco generously shared their knowledge of Italian banking history) and the Historical Library of the Senate; in Milan at the Banca Commerciale Italiana (now Intesa Sanpaolo); in Boston and Cambridge at the Massachusetts Historical Society and the Historical Collections at Baker Library, respectively; and in New York at the Rare Book and Manuscript Library at Columbia University. Archival research is difficult, but the support and knowledge of dedicated specialists (and the incredible structures where archives are usually housed) always made me feel lucky to be doing it.

I am a private person, so public acknowledgments of personal matters don't come easily to me, but I think that makes them all the more meaningful. My parents, Roberto and Patrizia, have been unfailingly and lovingly supportive of my endeavors: I can't thank them enough for letting me go, and for always welcoming me back. My sister Giada was always there for me, never letting geographical distance turn into emotional distance, always inspiring me with her strength and conviction. Diya Kallivayalil and Divya Errabelli were the most understanding of friends one could ask for—and it takes a lot of understanding to deal with a dissertating graduate student. Thank you for your friendship. To Nitya, whom I love, I dedicate this book. Thank you for your commitment to unbridled self-expression, aesthetic vision, and humanistic inclination.

Index

Abolafia, Mitchel Y., 8
Adams, Henry, 120–21
Aldrich, Howard, 133, 134, 249n19
Andrew, A. Piatt, 133, 249n20
Arrighi, Giovanni, 36
Assets: physical, 7; self-regulating, 135–36;
 values, 236n1. *See also* Financial
 instruments

Banca Commerciale Italiana (COMIT),
 195, 196–99, 201, 202, 203, 204, 205
Banca d'Italia (BI): bailouts by, 191, 202,
 203, 206; banknote issuance, 191–92;
 discounting notes, 192; formation, 190,
 191; governance, 192; nationalism and,
 204–5, 207, 209, 210–11; private banks
 and, 192, 197–200, 201–2, 203, 209;
 relations with state, 192–94, 204–5,
 207; role in financial system, 191–94,
 198–99, 200–201, 202, 203–4, 207,
 209. *See also* Stringher, Bonaldo
Banca Nazionale (BN): alliance with
 government, 172, 185, 189, 190;
 banknote issuance, 156, 161, 162,
 170, 189, 190, 252n6; criticism of,
 165, 174; discounting notes, 157,
 189, 190; legitimacy, 188, 189, 190;
 loans, 155, 156, 161, 189; mission, 189;
 private banks and, 189, 190, 254n4;
 reputation, 162; role in financial
 system, 155–57, 159, 170, 174, 175, 188,
 251–52n5, 254n3
Banca Nazionale Toscana, 156, 157
Banca Romana, 187–88, 190, 191
Banca Tiberina, 188
Banca di Torino, 155, 188
Banca Toscana di Credito, 156
Banco di Napoli, 156, 157, 159, 189, 254n3
Banco di Sicilia, 156, 157, 159
Bankers: collective identities, 10–13, 62,
 146, 212–13, 220; conflicts among, 35,
 220–21; functions, 1–2, 9–10, 33–34,
 35, 51–52; as gatekeepers of status
 groups, 32; individual qualities, 55–56;
 mediation role, 212; monopolies on
 credit creation, 36; political resources,
 77, 233; specialization, 233–34. *See
 also* Conservative bankers; Credit;
 Financial elites; Italian banking
 system; U.S. banking system; Wildcat
 bankers
Bankers' acceptances, 136
Bank failures, 112–13, 130
Banking: cohesive systems, 241n3;